Reflections from the Lakes

Also by Robert Gambles

Man in Lakeland (1975)

Exploring the Lakeland Fringe (1989)

The Spa Resorts and Mineral Springs of Cumbria (1993)

Walks on the Borders of Lakeland (1995)*

Yorkshire Dales Place-Names (1995)

Walks Round Windermere (1997)

Echoes of Old Lakeland (2010)

Escape to the Lakes: The First Tourists (2013)*

Lake District Place-Names (2013)

The Lakeland Dales (2016)*

Words from the Wildwood: Cumbria's Ancient Place-Names (2017)

Translated and Edited

Espen Ash Lad: Folk Tales from Norway (2014)

* Lakeland Book of the Year Award winners

Reflections from the Lakes

ROBERT GAMBLES

HAYLOFT

This revised and extended edition published by Hayloft Publishing Ltd., 2019
First edition published by Bookcase, Carlisle, 2010 as *Echoes of Old Lakeland*

A CIP catalogue record for this book is available from the British Library

ISBN 978-1-910237-49-6

Designed, printed and bound in the EU

Hayloft policy is to use papers that are natural, renewable and recyclable products and
made from wood grown in sustainable forests. The logging and manufacturing processes
are expected to conform to the environmental regulations of the country of origin.

Climate neutral
Print product
ClimatePartner.com/12667-1901-1003

Hayloft Publishing Ltd,
a company registered in England number 4802586
2 Staveley Mill Yard, Staveley, Kendal, LA8 9LR (registered office)
L'Ancien Presbytère, 21460 Corsaint, France (editorial office)

Email: books@hayloft.eu
Tel: 07971 352473

www.hayloft.eu

In memory of my beloved wife Hannemor
whose love made everything possible

Contents

Introduction

Many years ago the late George Bott suggested that I should write a series of articles on some of the less well-known aspects of the historical and cultural heritage of Cumbria and the Lake District. He assured me that there was a rich store of material in the many hundreds of books, guides, studies and learned articles that have been written on the region during the past 250 years.

To make a constructive selection from such a mountain of literature would have been a daunting task but for the generous assistance of the staff of the Cumbria Library Service and I am especially grateful to Jackie Fay and Sylvia Kelly of the Kendal Public Library whose professional expertise and formidable knowledge of the sources of information proved invaluable on many occasions.

I also acknowledge the debt I owe to all those whose studies have, over the years, helped to shed light on many of the topics referred to in these chapters. I acknowledge, too, the work and skilled craftsmanship of all those who have provided the illustrations which accompany the text throughout the book. Details of the artists are given alongside each illustration. Every effort has been made to trace copyright and any omissions are regretted.

The publication of a new, revised and extended edition provided an opportunity to select a new, more appropriate, title and to include a number of hitherto unpublished essays, legends and stories.

Finally, I wish to express by grateful thanks to my publisher, Dawn Robertson, whose encouragement and enthusiasm kept the literary spring flowing whenever it threatened to run dry.

Robert Gambles, 2018

1

The Spa Resorts and Mineral Springs of Cumbria

Mankind's oldest and most enduring faith is his belief in the magic powers of those mysterious waters which flow unbidden and unceasing from the bosom of the earth. The Christian missionaries to Anglo-Saxon Britain found a country dotted with hundreds of 'magic' springs and wells, many dedicated to local gods, goddesses and water spirits, the focus of rituals and beliefs inherited from a thousand years of pagan water-cults whose origins had long been forgotten. Four centuries of Roman occupation had reinforced this Celtic tradition and, at the time of Britain's conversion to Christianity, the Church, while deploring these heathen practices, acknowledged that it could not ignore, still less eradicate, such ancient and deep-rooted faith in the natural springs or the ceremonies attached to them.

Medieval Christian Britain acquired all those 'holy wells', rededicated to Christian Saints, which were to figure so largely in the religious life of the country for the next five hundred years and in its social life for three hundred more. Repeated exhortation and condemnation discouraged the offering of sacrifices and belief in the supernatural powers of these waters. The emphasis moved to their healing powers, both medicinal and spiritual, achieved by bathing in or drinking from the water and through the strength of one's Christian faith and the intercession of the appropriate saint. If there had to be an element of magic still, it was at least magic over which the church had some control.

Many pagan customs survived and some, such as the springtime dressing of the well-heads with complex patterns of flowers and the throwing of coins into wishing wells, still flourish, while annual pilgrimages to certain holy wells have today become important symbols of a public expression of the Christian faith. For those who suffer, these offer hope of relief from pain; for those who wish merely to renew their Faith they offer the certainty of spiritual joy: is this so very different from the dreams and expectations of all those other countless generations of humanity who sought comfort from the 'magic' waters?

It was almost inevitable that superstition and shades of the supernatural should continue to surround the holy wells. The religious reformers of the Protestant Reformation condemned as Roman Catholic superstition, practices which had once been denounced as pagan. The wells were stripped of all claim to magical or miraculous properties but, as always, it proved easier to decree a change in human beliefs than actually to achieve it.

Ecclesiastical magic and religious pilgrimages might have mostly disappeared but, throughout the country, belief in the healing powers of the ancient springs remained strong and nineteenth century students of folklore discovered a lively rural tradition of frequenting local wells to drink the health-giving waters. Indeed, within a dozen years of the establishment of the Elizabethan Protestant Church there appeared the tentative beginnings of a new water cult which was to transform English social customs and to endure for the next three and a half centuries but which was, nevertheless, firmly based in the ancient belief in the special virtues of the mineral springs, some crystal clear, others cloudy with chemical deposits, some pure and tasteless, others mephitic and nauseous, some issuing hot and steaming from the earth, others ice-cold.

In 1562, Dr William Turner, Dean of Wells, physician and botanist, published his *Booke of the Natures and Properties of the Bathes of England* in which he strongly recommended a much greater use of their waters, commenting with southern condescension that 'there are manye in the North and North-West partes of England... whyche beynge diseased wyth sore diseases woulde gladlye come to the baths of Baeth if they knewe that there were anye there.' Nine years later England's first 'spa' began its life – in the north, at Harrogate – to set a fashion which by the early seventeenth century had captured much of the upper class and, after the Restoration of the Monarchy in 1660, swept the country.

The enthusiasm of the English gentry for 'taking the waters' prompted Horace Walpole to observe that 'One would think the English were ducks; they are forever waddling to the waters.' Almost any village which had a mineral spring nearby, 'holy' or not, now aspired to the status of a 'spa'. Thomas Pennant, in an appendix to his *Tour in Scotland* (1772) enquired of the clergy of every parish in northern Britain: 'Are

Gilsland Spa – detail from an engraving by Allom and Rose, 1834.

there any mineral springs, frequented for the drinking of waters; what are they; at what season of the year are they reckoned best, and what distempers are they frequented for?'

A number of these places developed into fashionable, elegant and prosperous towns; but many more enjoyed a brief moment of glory only to fall into rapid decline when the visitors – who were almost exclusively upper class, wealthy and accustomed to urban comforts – began to demand the provision of facilities and entertainments which extended well beyond the mere imbibing of the waters. Bath, Cheltenham, Harrogate and Leamington still bask in the relict splendour of their heyday as centres of royal and aristocratic patronage, architectural sophistication, fashionable amusement, marriage contracts and questionable medical treatments. But where now are the blighted dreams of spas such as Boston, Astrop, Church Stretton, Ashby-de-la-Zouch and Gilsland? These, and a hundred others, failed to attract the commercial enterprise, medical publicity and wealthy clientele which were the keys to success.

Gilsland? A tiny hamlet on the edge of the wilderness in a remote and forgotten corner of northern Cumbria. It would be preposterous to compare such a place with the cultured elegance of the more famous

English 'spaws' and yet, for over two hundred years, Gilsland Spa was a well-known and popular resort, patronised by the gentry from the Border counties and beyond, boasting many of the facilities and a little of the sophistication of the society governed by the code of Beau Nash.

The new Spa Hotel, built in grandiose style in the 1860s, offered standards of comfort and entertainment comparable to those to be found in most other resorts of the day. Guests found rooms furnished and equipped with the best of late Victorian design and invention, dining rooms, drawing rooms, ladies' rooms, card rooms, billiard rooms and a daily programme of recreation and entertainment arranged for all who wished to take part. A quadrille band played each evening; regular and formal dress balls were held in the summer season; and in the extensive and well-tended grounds were lawns for tennis, croquet and bowls, with terraced walks leading down through woods and flowering shrubberies to the spectacular gorge of the River Irthing.

Here was a riverside walk with bathhouses, bookstalls and refreshments and the fountain of malodorous medicinal water which had drawn folk to this spot for more than two thousand years. Daily carriage excursions were organised to take visitors to Naworth and Corby Castles, to Hexham Abbey and Lanercost Priory, to Carlisle and to the Roman Wall – or, for the intrepid and energetic, tours into the wild moorlands towards the Scottish Border.

Gilsland could never aspire to be another Bath, or even another Buxton, but given its geographical remoteness and its largely provincial clientele, its success as a spa resort is remarkable when other, more favoured, aspirants fell by the wayside. The waters of Gilsland received an authoritative boost in 1857 when the British and Foreign Medico-Chirugical Review pronounced that 'the pure sulphuretted waters, powerfully charged with this gas and containing little else' were most efficacious in the treatment of rheumatism, dyspepsia, hepatic infections and skin diseases, thus confirming precisely the view expressed by William Camden in the reign of Queen Elizabeth I. These were all latter day revelations, however, for the virtues of Gilsland waters were certainly known to the Romans who dedicated an altar found nearby to the local water gods.

Long after the Romans had departed their rituals must have persisted here, for they were eventually taken over by the monks of Lanercost

Priory who walked in procession on St John's Day (24 June) each year to hold a service of Christian blessing at the fountain head; a ceremony which may have had its distant origins in a pagan summer solstice festival. This medieval Christianisation of the Gilsland waters survived the Reformation without interruption.

William Camden in 1586 tells us that the spring was much frequented by both Scots and English and, a generation later in 1625, local aristocratic interest is revealed by the visit of Lady Elizabeth Howard of Naworth Castle. Almost a century later Gilsland is, for the first time, given the status of a 'spa' and its somewhat mephitic water re-endowed with its medieval virtues of curing 'itches, scabs and ulcers'.

In 1733 the local Justices received a Humble Petition from a poor labourer, Edward Bullman, of Lanercost, who had been crippled for over five years and was unable to support his family. He had been advised 'to goe to the Bathing Wells' but he could 'scarce walk upon crutches' and so he petitioned for money 'to By him a horse to Carry him to the Wells... that he may Endeavour to get his health to provide for his family.'

Unfortunately we do not know the outcome of his Petition but it does indicate a continued local faith in the powers of healing in this bounteous spring, a faith which fifty years later had clearly spread far beyond the neighbourhood of Gilsland. For there were then three guest houses to accommodate visitors to the developing spa: Orchard House, Wardraw House and the newly-built Shaws, offering simple hospitality, the last having a drawing room for the gentry, a stone-flagged parlour for 'the second class', and outhouses for 'the poorer sort'. Here, we are told, all the forms and fashions of the better and superior hotels at the well-known spas were followed and, although it was all far removed from the Royal Crescent at Bath or the new splendours of Cheltenham or Leamington, the minor gentry of the northern counties began to flock to Gilsland in search of recreation, amusement, lively company, a change of air, and to seek a cure for their real or imagined ailments. For the most part, however, it would seem that many visitors spent their time in drinking, gambling, dancing and making love. Mrs Kitty Senhouse came here in 1782 but was apparently less than enthusiastic about her course of the nauseous medicine. Her husband wrote instructing her 'to be pleased to continue where you are... to make a more complete trial of the waters.'

A few years later Robert Burns visited this celebrated spa; to be followed in 1797 by his fellow-countryman, Sir Walter Scott, whose stay soon became a memorable occasion. For it was here that the 26 year old barrister and cavalry officer, out riding one day, met a young lady 'than whom a lovelier vision could hardly have been imagined'. The gaiety of the evening balls at Shaws provided opportunities to cultivate the lady's acquaintance and within a matter of days the romance had made such rapid progress that Scott felt able to propose marriage, a momentous occasion which took place at the now famous 'popping-stone' at the end of the riverside walk on the banks of the Irthing: 'sharp work' commented a later visitor, 'for a poet who was quaffing not of the fountain of Hippocrene but of the fetid stream of Gilsland – by no means an inspiring beverage.'

Neither this nor Dr Granville's subsequent remarks would have pleased Miss Charlotte Mary Carpenter who clearly reciprocated Scott's genuine love for her: 'Prudent mammas' he advised, 'who are anxious to see their daughters speedily and well-settled in the world had better look to the Spas of England.' Scott put his visit to Gilsland to another good use in his novel *Guy Mannering* much of which is set in the vicinity

Gilsland 'popping' stone, photograph by the author.

of Gilsland. Here were the haunts of Meg Merrilies, Tib Mumps and Guy himself, with Mumps Hall nearby.

Dr August Bozzi Granville published his volumes on *The Spas of England* in 1841 and, for the most part, they present a useful account of all the principal resorts of the time with knowledgeable analyses of the mineral waters, their chemical properties and their medicinal virtues. For good measure Granville offers a lively description of the facilities provided, the quality of the entertainment and his assessment of the company likely to be found. Of Gilsland he observed that 'The lower and middle classes of society have their spas as the great of the land have theirs... Gilsland is just such a place.' A judgement which, unfortunately, sets the tone for the remainder of his distinctly disparaging verdict on Gilsland Spa, regrettably influenced by his obvious wish to promote a rival resort developed at Shotley Bridge by one of his friends. So, we are informed, Shaws is but a sorry house of accommodation where masters and servants:

> bathe in the same rooms, nay, in the very identical tanks... This is primitive... and so are the baths themselves as well as the bathing rooms, erected in the guise of low ordinary cottages, on the very margin of the river immediately opposite to the spring. Nothing could be of ruder aspect... than this establishment, and the visitor must be little squeamish, indeed, who can long continue to use such rooms and such bathing tanks.

The water, he concedes, is 'clear and limpid; indeed, the finest crystal spring could not be more so' but it smells and tastes strongly of sulphur, creates an unpleasant 'eructation of gas such as we may perceive after eating hard-boiled eggs' and it also causes headaches. Even so, some found it pleasant to drink and it was not as disagreeable as the Harrogate water. Furthermore, Granville found the scenery at Gilsland 'nothing but a vast expanse of hilly country, grey, sombre and leaden coloured.' After no more than a twelve-hour overnight stay he departed, thoroughly disgruntled, expressing no surprise that Gilsland was 'indifferently frequented and at best only by very so-so classes of people.'

These so-so people, clearly unimpressed by Granville's strictures, came to Gilsland in ever-increasing numbers and, after the opening of the railway and the building of a new Spa Hotel in the mid-nineteenth century, the resort entered on a period of popularity and prosperity which was sustained until the 1930s. Resplendent in its shining white Italianate brickwork the hotel offered accommodation and facilities 'not inferior to that of any place of resort in England'. The mineral waters had received authoritative medical plaudits; and the landscaped gardens and woodlands, the enchanting walks and terraces, the River Irthing with its spectacular gorge and quaintly named Crammel Linn waterfall, the wild moorlands beyond and, not least the associations with Meg Merrilies and Guy Mannering, gave Gilsland all the ingredients of the late Victorian dream of the romantic and picturesque.

Mrs Eliza Lynn Linton, grand-daughter of the Bishop of Carlisle, may have found the resort 'a queer, roughish, provincial and eminently one-horse place' but she clearly appreciated the comforts of the hotel and the efficacy of the waters which she confidently expected to make her 'strong and as good as new', thereby demonstrating rather more faith in the Gilsland waters than her grandfather's eighteenth century predecessor. Bishop William Nicolson, who came here in 1711 and declared the spa to be 'more famous than it deserves'. Few heeded the Bishop's pronouncement in any age for in 1926 a local guide book asserted that in the summer season spa visitors are to be numbered in thousands rather than scores with every house in the neighbourhood called upon to provide accommodation.

These were to be the final years of the spa-cult, however, and in common with almost every other spa resort Gilsland soon fell into rapid decline. The twentieth century had brought about fundamental changes in English society

Gilsland Spa the well-head, photograph by the author.

18

and in theories of medicine which, accelerated by the profound social and economic effects of two devastating wars, dealt a fatal blow to the entire fabric of the spa economy. The more famous resorts which had grown into elegant and wealthy towns were able to adapt and survive; those such as Gilsland sank into almost total neglect and oblivion.

Gilsland Spa Hotel, circa 1890, courtesy of Cumbria Library Service

Today the Gilsland Spa Hotel still attracts many discriminating visitors seeking something of the dignity and grandeur of a past age and a place of quiet seclusion from a stressful world. The gardens, lawns, tennis courts and woodland walks are still there to be enjoyed; the riverside terrace remains but now neglected and without its bath houses, bookstalls and refreshment rooms; the 'magic waters' still pour from a restored well-head; the river still swirls over its rocky bed just as Granville described it – 'brown as the best London stout, and as frothy'.

Gilsland was not the only spa resort in Cumbria; indeed, it was not even the most renowned. There were numerous other mineral springs, but few were graced with the title 'spa' and most were little-known outside their own locality, rarely becoming more than the popular watering-holes they had always been, even though their waters might boast the same properties and medical virtues as those of more famous resorts. Such were the wells at Bewcastle, Biglands, Brampton, Gilcrux, Great Salkeld, Kirkbampton, Kirkland Wyton, Melmerby, Sebergham, Chalkfoot and Stainton (Carlisle). The springs of Gilderdale Fell, near Alston, and at Rockcliffe were notable less for any curative virtues than for their unusual attribute in producing tinctures, the former 'a yellow ochre and a Spanish brown', while the latter was said to 'tint paper a beautiful gold'. Very few of these have any significant recorded history. Among those which achieved a footnote in history were the saline springs in Borrowdale and at Stanger Spa near Cockermouth.

Many of the early guides to the Lake District include a reference to the salt wells in Borrowdale but only as an historical source of salt for the monks of Furness Abbey to whom the valley once belonged. In fact, there is no record of the manufacture of salt at this spot, not even in that most meticulous and comprehensive inventory, the Report of the Commission of Dissolution in 1537. The Great Deed of Borrowdale of 1555 includes salt as one of the minerals included in the sale of land in the valley but without detailed specification. Nor, it may be added, is the climate of Borrowdale notably propitious for the process of evaporation which was the usual method of salt production. Not until the eighteenth century is there any reference to the medical properties of these springs.

In 1766 Thomas Short's *Treatise on Cold Mineral Waters* asserted that the Manesty waters would ensure 'a rough, severe purge to a strong constituency', an aperient apparently of sufficient popular appeal to encourage the building early in the nineteenth century of a bath-house, open and free to anyone whose skin or digestive system felt the need of this drastic but no doubt beneficial treatment. This has now vanished almost without trace.

Stanger Spa in the Lorton Valley likewise has only a sparsely documented history but in 1829 it was said to be much frequented in the summer season by invalids from the surrounding country. This aperient salt spring was compared to the waters at Cheltenham, with a high impregnation of marine salt and with similar commendations for the treatment of disorders of the skin and the digestive tracts. The folk of Cockermouth made a stroll to Stanger a regular Sunday afternoon outing, and a stone building was erected over the well to provide shelter and seating. The well itself was neatly lined with dressed stone, and niches were placed in the walls for the drinking vessels. Bottles of Stanger Water were for a time dispatched to many parts of the world, a tribute to local enterprise and perhaps an indication that the spa here had acquired a much wider

fame than the records suggest. Today the map states merely 'Holy Well –
Stanger Spa (dis.)' and the well and its shelter are falling into dereliction.
The saline waters which once cost sixpence a bottle flow with undimin-
ished vigour and are free to all who pass that way.

Spas were found in many strange and unexpected locations but none
more so than Gutterby Spa, the only named feature on the long, ten-mile
stretch of sand and shingle which forms the coastline of south-west
Cumbria. This, too, is a saline spring similar in composition to the waters
at Cheltenham, and when William Hutchinson wrote his *History of Cumberland* in the 1790s it was reputed to be 'a sovereign remedy for the
scurvy and the gravel'. The spa was apparently 'much frequented' when
the Park family lived at Whitbeck nearby in the seventeenth and eighteenth centuries. It is mentioned in Parson and White's *Directory* for
1829 and in William Whellan's *History and Topography of Cumberland
and Westmoreland* in 1860, but both references seem to suggest that this
was a spa resort which depended largely on the patronage of that particular family, and when this ceased Gutterby Spa could no longer survive
in such a remote and exposed situation on one of England's most unfrequented shores. Even so, as Whellan acknowledged, 'Many persons have
benefitted by the use of this water.'

Another 'holy well', with a longer recorded history, springs from the
base of Humphrey Head, the narrow peninsula projecting into Morecambe Bay at the tip of the coast of Cartmel. This remote and now forgotten 'spa', once the property and resort of the Canons of Cartmel
Priory, was much frequented in the late sixteenth century according to
Camden's *Britannia* with a diverse clientele charmingly identified by a
Victorian writer as 'the rich voluptuary, the poor mechanic and the la-
borious miner'. It seems improbable that such 'gentle' families as the
Fells of Swarthmoor Hall or the Brownes of Troutbeck who sought relief
from these waters would recognise themselves in any of these orders of
society but *Sarah Fell's Account Book* for 1674 records a visit to
Humphrey Head, where she paid the considerable sum of nine shillings
for the use of the waters, and Thomas Browne's Accounts for 14-16 July
1779, refer to a three-day visit when he drank the waters and bathed in
them.

One might be forgiven for some speculation as to the nature of the
ailments which afflicted these good gentlefolk in the light of an analysis

in Charles Leigh's *Natural History of Lancashire and Cheshire* (1700), which maintained that ague, worms and jaundice could be treated here, although the waters were most notable for their efficacy in curing diseases contracted by miners working in the Alston lead-mines – not, one would have thought, an occupational hazard likely to have troubled the Fells or the Brownes.

Until comparatively recent times the Alston miners continued to put their faith in regular visits to Humphrey Head where they drank a gallon of the water each day to purge the poison from their bodies and bathed to cleanse their skins of various cutaneous complaints. An aged dame presided over a hot cauldron of the water with more than twenty miners gathered round the door of her ramshackle hut nearby. This was all a far cry from the Assembly Rooms at Bath and their genteel patrons but when a chemical analysis in 1867 established that the waters of Humphrey Head were comparable to those of Cheltenham, Carlsbad and Baden-Baden and when heated were almost identical to the renowned spas at Wiesbaden and Kissengen, there were those who saw a splendid future for Humphrey Head, but they built castles in the air: the Cartmel dream of an elegant Pump Room and Spa Hotel was never realised.

By the end of the Victorian era a local historian was lamenting a sharp decline in the number of 'health-seeking pilgrims' and attributed this to the shock of the chemical analysis which, he alleged, 'broke the charm with which traditional piety had surrounded the fountain of Humphrey Head.' It might be nearer the truth to accept that by this time the whole spa-cult in England had passed its heyday and if ever Humphrey Head had entertained hopes of achieving greater renown it was now too late. Perhaps we are fortunate that this pleasant headland today is known for its Nature Reserve, its splendid seascapes (compared by some to the Bay of Naples), and its variety of bird-life rather than for a grandiose spa hotel, symbol of an age long past.

A similar purging spring was discovered at Witherslack in 1656 when a group of children attempted to quench their thirst on a hot day at a local water-hole. The drastic results attracted attention and it was not long before all kinds of 'miracle cures' were being reported from the well. Thomas Machell, Chaplain to Charles II, listed some of them in his *Antiquary on Horseback* published in 1692: Kathleen Barwick of Halecat cured of jaundice, Robert Weston of Sedgwick cured of worms,

John Watheman of Carnforth cured of leprosy, a woman of Gressingham was relieved of tympany. The versatility of the waters of Witherslack impressed Thomas Short who added inappetency, cachery, gravel, corpulency and dropsy to the catalogue. Indeed, Short was quite overwhelmed by the spell of Witherslack: 'Sure England has scarce another such Romantic place... all charmingly beautiful with shrubs and plants.' This 'romantic' spa enjoyed almost two centuries of local sanctity but by 1829 Parson and White's *Directory* records that it had entirely disappeared. Spa Lane is its only memorial today.

Other 'holy wells' may be found on the earlier Ordnance Maps of Cumbria, many of which acquired their holiness from their close proximity to a church of ancient foundation. A good example is the Holy Well of St Mungo at Mealrigg near the Norman church of Bromfield, a spring which, certainly in the late eighteenth century, had a local reputation. William Hutchinson, writing in the 1790s, informs us in a guarded comment that, 'There is a spaw here, supposed to possess considerable virtues, which, however, have never been clearly ascertained.' By the mid-nineteenth century the patrons of these humble waters seem to have transferred their allegiance to the more sophisticated surroundings of Gilsland.

It was just at this time that Cumbria's best-known spa was about to achieve social and medicinal eminence. There would seem to be few spots less likely to become a fashionable watering-place than the bleak, chilly, rainswept, windswept moorland heights of Shap. Yet for three-quarters of a century the gentry and the *nouveaux riches* journeyed to the Shap Wells, as they did to spa-resorts in much gentler surroundings, to participate in the rituals of 'taking the waters' and, perhaps more especially, in the accompanying social and recreational pastimes without which no gentleman's summer was complete.

Much was made in Shap's publicity brochures of the excellent grouse-shooting on the Earl of Lonsdale's moors, the proximity of Lowther Castle and its gatherings of famous and titled names, the bracing air, the nearby attractions of the Lake District, and, of course, the efficacy of the waters which, it was emphasised, were milder than those of Harrogate and similar to those at Leamington, then the newest and most fashionable resort and favoured by Royalty. And what Victorian hypochondriac or listless gentlewoman could resist the blandishments and medical promise of the 1844 handbook which proclaimed that these sulphur-laden springs were 'beneficial to every organ with chronic ail-ments' and also 'dyspepsia, liver disorders, the nervous system, glandu-lar swellings, cutaneous infections, rheumatism, scrofula, calculi, dropsy, lung problems and diseases of the skin.' All accompanied by a resounding medical testimonial designed to dispel any doubts which might remain about the virtues of a visit to Shap:

> In all my experience I have met with no medicated spring more gener-ally efficacious than the Shap Spa in raising the energies of the debili-tated stomach and inspiring the whole frame with a new animation, giving to the blanched and cadaverous cheek the glow of health, and to the turgid and spiritless eye the sparkle of life and energy.

Shap Wells could clearly cater for all who felt the need for the water-cure and with the opening of the Earl of Lonsdale's new Spa Hotel and the arrival of the railway in 1848 Shap Spa was firmly on the map of English spa resorts. The construction of a simple but elegant well-head adorned with an impressive stone base, probably filched from Renais-sance Florence, the erection of a thirty-foot high monument with bas re-liefs of the British Lion and the goddess Hygeia to commemorate the coronation of Queen Victoria, and the planting of picturesque rhododen-dron groves and formal gardens, completed the transformation of a prim-itive water-hole into an inland spa with the essential ambience and much of the opulence of resorts of greater renown.

For many guests at Shap the comforts and cuisine of the new hotel must have been a distinctly more attractive proposition than the prospect of regular immersion in, or frequent doses of, the unappetizing waters with their unpleasant sulphuretted smell, described by the local folk as 'train smoke mixed with bad eggs'. Dr Granville gave a vivid account of his visit to Shap, full of praise for the hotel but less than enthusiastic about the water which he characterised as 'transparent but not limpid' with 'several little floating bodies whitish and milk-like suspended in it', coloured rather like a 'weak solution of soap and water' and the sur-face covered with a thin scum 'through which bubbles of gas from the bottom are seen to burst from time to time.' The sulphur smell, he found, was 'very marked' and ' instantly after drinking a glass and a half [he] experienced headache and eructation of the sulphuretted gas'. He con-ceded that when heated the water lost these unappealing aspects and lay 'more comfortably on the stomach.' The medical eulogies he regarded as 'too near an approach to the region of poetical fancy', to be taken 'cum grano salis'.

The Spa Hotel at Shap Wells, courtesy of Cumbria Library Service

In contrast he found the accommodation 'very convenient, commodious and well-arranged.' He occupied:

> a double room facing the south which would not have disgraced a first-rate hotel in London; nay, for cleanliness, abundance of furniture and contrivances, as well as for the excellency of the beds, far superior to most of them. No expense seems to have been spared to make the inmates comfortable. The drawing-room, though not large, is excellent; and so are the dining and other sitting rooms'. Granville awarded a final accolade to the servants who were ' of the best description both as to looks and appearance, and as being well-behaved and attentive.

Nor did he demur from the claims of the hotel handbook which assured its guests that 'Every delicacy of the season is supplied to tempt the weak, sickly stomach of the invalid or to gratify the more capricious one of the epicurean tourist or traveller.' While the fashionable world indulged its love-affair with the spa-waters Shap could not fail to please and for Victorian and Edwardian England its seventy beds were not one too many.

Before its transfiguration in the 1840s Shap 'spa' had been a very rudimentary affair. Although known to the Romans the well has no recorded medieval history but it was sufficiently patronised in the seventeenth century to justify the construction of a bath-house and a place of accommodation for visitors. This 'bleak,

Shap Wells - the well-head, H. W Reading, 1999.

dingy, smoky old house' and an 'old peat-cote with a rusty iron pot heated over burning turf, whins and heather, and an old hogshead for a bath' created a scene of primitive rusticity which is given a certain Arcadian charm by the story of the attendant whose task it was to carry the buckets of water from the spring to the 'bath'. He was 'exceedingly attentive, so much so that, regardless of the victim's sex, he would put his head over the edge and enquire, 'Enny more het?'

The Earl of Lonsdale's grand design was to replace this bucolic idyll with all the facilities, comforts and luxury of a Victorian Spa establishment with a standard of dignity worthy of a resort on the estates of the north's premier landlord. His wealthy patronage could never give Shap the distinctive elegance which the Duke of Devonshire created in Buxton but until the tide of fashion decreed that Baden-Baden and Aix-les-Bains were preferable to Bath and Leamington (or any other English resort), the prosperity of Shap Wells was assured.

This Edwardian desertion of English spa resorts by the upper classes was compounded by the social, economic and cultural upheavals brought about by the First World War. When the reality of these changes began to dawn there was no longer a place for the spa, either as a holiday resort or as a temporary rest-centre for rich hypochondriacs or even as a hunting ground for aspiring mammas with nubile daughters. By the 1930s all that was history. Henceforward in the twentieth century although the English continued to waddle to the waters – in ever increasing numbers – it was not to the spa resorts they made their way but to the seaside. Today the Shap Wells Hotel is still 'a green and cheering oasis surrounded by mountains thickly clad with heather' and Dr Granville would not wish to modify his praise of its facilities but the Florentine well-head, the bath-houses and the monument to Queen Victoria are not quite so unblemished by the passage of time. The age they served has long since passed away but is still, perhaps, too recent in our history to merit the attention of the 'heritage industry'.

None of the mineral springs of Cumbria could ever have aspired to the social and architectural eminence of such towns as Bath, Leamington or Harrogate or even to the modest grandeur of Buxton, Malvern or Tunbridge Wells. They were cut off from the mainstream of London Society, they were remote and isolated from the major road system, they lacked a wealthy aristocratic clientele or even a substantial body of landed gentry; they were set in an environment unpromising in its economy, its geography and its climate. After a brief age of fashionable and popular patronage all have fallen into varying degrees of dereliction and oblivion. The late twentieth century may have been inveigled into purchasing millions of expensive bottles of mineral waters each year but this represents a lack of faith in the public water supply rather than a revival of a mystic faith in the natural springs. The sulphurous and saline waters of Cumbria's 'holy wells' are very much an acquired taste and not easily marketable in an age which prefers its water to be odourless, tasteless and crystal clear.

In its declining late-Victorian years the spa cult in England received a new lease of life with the development of hydropathic institutions. These were well-appointed hotels, often of substantial size, set in attractive grounds and offering a wide variety of facilities, both indoors and outside. Their purpose was the commercial exploitation of the popular enthusiasm among the wealthy and leisured upper and middle classes for the 'water-cure'. Every hydro was provided with a suite of treatment rooms and baths equipped with the latest scientific devices designed to inflict ordeal by water on the human frame. Resident doctors and nurses supervised individual courses of treatment and prepared an appropriate dietary regime for each 'patient'.

An essential requirement for such institutions was a plentiful supply of water: water to be consumed in several large tumblers before break-fast and at intervals during the day; water for Turkish baths, Russian baths, Wave baths, Sitz baths; water for massive ice-cold douches and needle sprays; water, hot and cold, for indoor and outdoor swimming pools; and, for the truly desperate, water for the electro-magnetic bath, then the very latest invention, where (as patients were quite accurately informed), 'The application of electricity through the medium of water offers a method whereby the whole nervous system may be powerfully affected.'

For those who survived these rigours – and by no means everyone did – the sheer relief experienced when the treatment came to an end must, one suspects, have guaranteed a more sprightly step and a more buoyant attitude to each new day. It was to be many years before another, more enlightened, generation came to the conclusion that the fresh air, vigorous exercise, healthy diet and change of company and environment offered by a stay at these institutions did far more for their 'patients' than most of the hydropathy to which they were subjected. The warm baths and regular swimming would undoubtedly be beneficial for many ailments: the shock treatments must have depended on individual re-sponse and experience.

The hydros injected new life into a number of spa-resorts, some of which developed into modem seaside and inland holiday centres with all the entertainments and other attractions associated with such places of recreation. But hydropathy itself was doomed with the advance of scientific medicine and with the refusal of the National Health Service to accommodate these methods of treating illness within its embrace.

The concept of the hydro originated in the hilly, inland spa towns of Ilkley and Matlock, and it was not long before entrepreneurs were look-ing to the congenial environment of the well-watered hills of the Lake District. Grandiose schemes were planned for hydros at Grasmere,

Stanger Spa ruins, photograph by the author.

Grange-over-Sands, Windermere, and Plumgarths on the outskirts of Kendal. Of these all but the first appear to have had a half-century of prosperity; Windermere, in particular, achieving a national reputation fully justifying the optimism of its 'Invitation to Investors'.

Plumgarths was a more modest establishment but could assure potential guests that 'there is an efficient supply of water, cold or warm, for Treatment carefully and scientifically adapted to each case, and a Dietary as liberal and varied as the laws of health will permit.' Every variety of hydrotherapeutic apparatus was available and 'quiet and agreeable domestic pastimes' were encouraged. Guests would be met at Kendal, Bumeside or Windermere stations; the post arrived each day at 7 a.m. and letters were despatched at 8.30 p.m.; and First Class patients could be accommodated at a charge of £2.15s.0d. (£2.75) per week inclusive of Board and Lodging, Medical Advice and all Treatments. Furthermore, as the brochure waxes lyrical, Plumgarths is in:

> one of the most picturesque and healthy parts of the kingdom, visited alternately by the fine-tempered breezes of sea and mountain, its atmosphere is peculiarly pure and invigorating; while there is the advantage of easy access to the Lakes with the additional one of being sufficiently removed from their humid exhalations.

The advertising copy for Windermere Hydro also emphasised the climatic virtues of the establishment as well as all its other attractions and facilities: 'For a winter retreat it has the advantage of many hydropathic centres – its mild mountain air has not the bitter keeness of Ilkley, whilst it has a vitality and power to invigorate lacking in many places and its rainfall is less than in other parts of the District.' Water for the many bathrooms was 'abundant and excellent' and came from the 'copious springs in the lower spurs of the High Street range.' All patients could proceed direct from their bedrooms to the baths 'in greatest privacy' along two corridors (one for gentlemen and another for ladies) and there they would find every up-to-date facility awaiting them, including, as one astonished visitor exclaimed, 'the biggest baths with the biggest brass taps and plughole bungers I have ever seen.' The whole hotel was heated 'with hot water apparatus' but each of the 67 bedrooms also had its fireplace, 'the most healthy mode of ventilation.'

After the grand Opening Dinner on 25 March 1881 the *Westmorland Gazette* praised the new Hydro fulsomely, describing in detail the large dining rooms and drawing rooms, the ladies' drawing room, the correspondence rooms, the billiard room, and the offices for the doctor and the matron. The furnishings were 'conspicuous for elegance and good taste' while the furniture apparently surprised the reporter with 'a style and elegance throughout the whole house that we had not expected to find.' The well-tended grounds had lawns for tennis, croquet and bowls; a skittle alley and a conservatory; several terraced walks 'with entire privacy for each', and a splendid promenade with views over the lake and out to the lakeland fells. Altogether, the report concluded, Windermere Hydro 'might fittingly be styled the home of hydropathy'.

This combination of luxury hotel, health resort and social and recreational centre had more in common with the elaborate Roman thermae than with the simple rusticity of the remote medicinal springs and medieval Holy Wells – or even with the concealed squalor and bizarre etiquette of Beau Nash's eighteenth century Bath. After two thousand years the social rituals of the water-cult had come full circle.

2

Many Fleas were in the Bed

The thousands of tourists who visit the Lake District each year in modern times may be reasonably certain that when they arrive at their hotel, inn or farmhouse accommodation, they will find their rooms and their beds spotlessly clean and uninhabited by other guests or any form of wildlife. Their predecessors, the early tourists of some 200 years ago, could not be so sure. Much of what they wrote of their experience in this wild and remote comer of the country concerns the spectacular scenery which enthralled and occasionally horrified them, and it is only from scattered references that we are able to form an impression of the accommodation and hospitality they encountered. It was not only the 'stupendous crags' and the 'inhospitable terror' of the mountains which came as a shock to these adventurous gentlefolk.

Criticism of the plain and plentiful food they were offered is rare, even though some of the local dishes must have proved an unusual gastronomical experience; but rustic sleeping arrangements were often more irregular and austere than could be comfortably accepted.

In 1769 the poet Thomas Gray refused to stay at the Salutation Inn in Ambleside when he found 'the best bed-chamber' to be 'dark and damp as a cellar'. Sarah Aust, the Hon. Mrs Murray, staying at the King's Arms (now the Patterdale Hotel) in 1796, was 'obliged to pass the night in a chair by the kitchen fire, there not being a bed in the house fit to put myself upon.' Perhaps learning from this she 'lodged a week very comfortably' at the Buttermere Inn 'with the help of my own sheets, blankets, pillows and counterpane.'

It was at the inn in Patterdale that William Wordsworth, Sir Walter Scott and Sir Humphry Davy found their room was already occupied by a party of ladies who sat talking until a very late hour and appeared quite unperturbed by Scott and Davy loudly calling out the hours of the night beneath the window. On his visit to the inn at Rosthwaite, Wordsworth had to 'share a bed with a Scots pedlar', an experience which shocked Robert Southey into declaring that 'he had rather not lie in bed the next

31

forty years than sleep with a Scots pedlar.' This was probably a less trau-
matic discovery, however, than that which greeted Mrs Eliza Lynn Linton, granddaughter of the Bishop of Carlisle, at the inn in Mardale where
she found 'a tipsy parson lying in bed with his gin bottle by his side.'

The 'many fleas' which inhabited John Keats' bed at the Nag's Head
at Wythburn were, no doubt, less alarming but just as unwelcome. At
least Matthew Arnold found the inn-keeper there a jovial fellow who
'shouted greetings from his easy chair' as his guests set off on their walk
to Watendlath. It is reassuring, too, to note that Joseph Budworth discovered the landlord at Patterdale to be 'a very well-informed man' and
had only praise for Robert Newton's Inn in Grasmere. Samuel Taylor
Coleridge considered the Traveller's Rest at Ulpha to be 'very nice' and
'the landlord a very intelligent' man – surely the same knowledgeable
and quick-witted publican who, when presented by a group of noisy students with a request written in Latin, immediately replied in Greek
which his guests were unable to translate.

For the most part however the innkeepers of the Lake District were
quite unprepared to cater for these 'quality' visitors from the outside
world. John Briggs was unlucky in his choice of the Kentmere Inn where
the ale was 'nauseous' and where 'the floor was bespread with tubs,
pans, chairs, tables, piggins, dishes, tins, and other equipage of a
farmer's kitchen' all of which had to be negotiated in order to get near
the fire; and William Briggs, visiting the White Lion at Bowness in 1820
found a similar kitchen filled with guests through whom 'a greasy cook,
who looked like one of her own puddings ready bagged for boiling',
threaded her way, and 'among the rustics assembled round the fire was
the landlord whose face was the index to an excellent cellar'.

Fortunately, the majority of food and drink served in most Lakeland
hostelries of the time met with general approval. Visitors took their
meals at their inn and ate whatever the host provided. This would usually
be plain country food such as might be served in almost any other part
of the land but specifically local dishes would often be included.

The menu might feature Lakeland's most famous speciality, the char
or Alpine trout, a delicacy served either fresh from the lakes or as potted
char or even as char-pie prepared in a large earthenware dish decorated
with a picture of the fish itself. Dorothy Wordsworth was much taken
with the char from Seathwaite Tarn served for supper when she and

William stayed at the Newfield Inn in the Duddon Valley, while Arthur Young enjoyed the renowned potted char of the King's Arms in Kendal, 'the best of any in the country' according to an earlier visitor, the much-travelled Celia Fiennes.

There were certain country dishes which these sophisticated adventurers may well have regarded with some apprehension but which were part of the daily diet of the local population. One was 'crowdy', described as an excellent and invigorating species of soup made by pouring over oatmeal the liquid in which beef or mutton had been boiled. Oatmeal also figured prominently in 'poddish', a type of porridge made from oatmeal or barley boiled in water or milk, and eaten with bread and butter and sweetened with honey or treacle – a dish served to William and Dorothy Wordsworth when they stayed at the Star Inn in Martindale. Poddish may have proved more palatable than a 'curious dish' described by Joseph Budworth without comment: 'Bread is cut into thin slices and placed in rows one above another in a large kettle… The butter and sugar are dissolved in a separate one, and then poured upon the bread, where it continues until it has boiled for some space, and the bread is perfectly saturated with the mixture; it is then taken out and served by way of dessert. This curious dish is called Buttered Sops.'

This was probably an acquired taste as was the dried salted meat which Cumbrians apparently preferred to fresh meat until well into the nineteenth century. What Joseph Budworth actually thought of his buttered sops is not recorded, but both he and Arthur Young obviously relished the local apple puddings, the assortment of tarts and, especially, a dessert comprising 'three cups of preserved gooseberries with a bowl of rich cream in the centre'.

Fine French wines in elegant glasses would not have graced these inn tables but fine local ales, drunk from tankards, were always to be had, each household favouring its own distinctive brew. Budworth and the Hon. Mrs Murray were in agreement that the ale brewed at Buttermere was best of all: 'If you are fond of strong ales, I must tell you Buttermere is famous for it.' Very rarely an enterprising inn-keeper would be able to provide his visitors with a noggin (a quarter of a pint) of rum or brandy. Buttermere was also awarded a five-star accolade by James Clarke for its fish – 'the best fish of any (Ullswater only excepted)' – and by Thomas Gray for its local mutton which 'nearly resembled venison'.

Few tourists ventured to these chilly northern parts in Spring but those who did would most probably have been presented with the herb-pudding known in the Lake District as Easterledge pudding. Typical ingredients for this were large quantities of bistort and young nettles, a handful of chives, the leaves of blackcurrant, dandelion and bellflower, all chopped together with an onion and seasoned with salt and black pepper. Meat, usually veal, a beaten egg and a cupful of oatmeal and barley were added, and it was all boiled in a bag or baked in a dish. This healthy concoction would have seemed less strange in 1800 than it would today when recipes using many common herbs have been largely neglected or forgotten. Easterledge pudding may still be found in Cumbria today but it would be a brave chef who served it to the tourists.

The letters, journals and recollections compiled by the early tourists, although not so indecorous as to show a preoccupation with food and drink, do refer occasionally, and usually approvingly, to the meals provided by their Lakeland hosts. Joseph Budworth, for example, staying in 1792 at Robert Newton's Inn at Grasmere (now Church Stile, the National Trust Information Centre) had 'as good and well-dressed a dinner... as man could wish,' and at ten pence a head he considered it to be such good value that he wrote down the menu: 'Roast pike, stuffed; a boiled fowl; veal cutlets and ham; beans and bacon; cabbage, pease and potatoes; anchovy sauce; parsley and butter; plain butter; butter with cheese; wheat bread and oat cake; three cups of preserved gooseberries with a bowl of rich cream in the centre.' He added that he attempted to climb Helm Crag after dinner but found it 'formidable; and not less, to speak in plain English, from having a belly-full'.

Budworth also regales us with details of the breakfast he enjoyed at the Cherry Tree Inn at Wythburn (a well-known hostelry which, like its rival half a mile away, the Nag's Head which boasted a sign painted by George Romney, was a casualty of the Thirlmere reservoir): 'They gave us breakfast fit for labouring men. We had mutton-ham, eggs, buttermilk, whey, tea, bread and butter, and they asked us if we chose to have any cheese, all for seven pence a piece.'

It is a little surprising to see Budworth's reference to potatoes and tea for the former were almost unknown in Lakeland before the middle of the eighteenth century, and even then they were found only in a few locations, while tea although by that time becoming popular in some

The Nag's Head, Wythburn, courtesy of Revd. G. Darrall.

southern counties, was still little used in the north and was even regarded as an effeminate beverage – some eccentrics preferred to smoke it like tobacco! Perhaps a few enterprising inn-keepers were quickly learning to cater for the more fashionable tastes of this new breed of visitor: although even in 1854 Harriet Martineau could complain that at the Red Lion in Grasmere 'the traveller's choice is usually between ham and eggs and eggs and ham'.

Tourists who found accommodation in farmhouse or cottage appear to have been met with generous and spontaneous hospitality. Wordsworth and De Quincey, hungry after a long day's walking, called at High Bridge End farm in the Vale of St John and were 'ushered into a comfortable parlour' and warmly entertained by their physically intimidating host whose maidservant told them that he 'would have brained us both if we had insulted him with the offer of money'. Eliza Lynn Linton received an equally hearty welcome when she called at a farm in Heltondale, near Askham, seeking refreshment: she was offered 'wheaten bread, butter, and a huge jug of milk' and told to 'spare nothing' when presented with a large cheese specially selected from the 'rannel balk'.

The first tourists came to the Lake District primarily to view the scenery and to experience the thrill of close proximity to the 'horror of vast precipices' and the 'frightful abyss'. They were also fascinated by 'curiosities' but found the entertainments on offer unsophisticated and undeniably rustic – but the Lowood Inn, near Ambleside did boast an 'elegant upper room, furnished with a piano and an organ' while the guests at the Shap Wells Spa Hotel had to make do with 'a small jingling pianoforte and a bagatelle board' and 'dances where rank has no influence in the choice of partners', thus naively ignoring the rigid social distinctions of the time. At most inns the most likely amusement on offer was the boisterous, bucolic romp known as a 'merry neet'. Wordsworth's poem *The Waggoner* gives a lively impression of the scene at The Cherry Tree at Wythburn on one such occasion:

> *Blithe souls and lightsome hearts have we*
> *Feasting at the Cherry Tree*
> *What tankards foaming from the tap*
> *What store of cakes in every lap*
> *What thumping – stumping – overhead*

Twenty miles away John Keats, staying at the Sun Inn at Ireby, gave his eye-witness account of a merry neet dance there '…they kickit and jumpit with mettle extraordinary, and whiskit and friskit, and toe'd it and go'd it, twirled it and whirled it, and stamped it and sweated it, tattooing the floor like mad. The difference between our country dances and these Scottish figures is about the same as leisurely stirring a cup of tea and beating up batter pudding.'

All this was far removed from the sedate balls of the English country house, and many of the early travellers to the mountain wilderness of the Lakes would probably be no more than amused spectators of these rustic hoe-downs but would have treasured the experience as one of the memorable 'curiosities of our lake tour' together with the fleas, the poddish and the 'nauseous ale' of Kentmere. They did, at least, savour something of the local culture as well as gaze in awe at the beauty and horror of the mountain landscape.

Charlotte Bronte, to her great regret, saw it all 'only as it can be seen from a carriage… If I could only have dropped unseen out of the carriage, and gone away by myself in amongst those grand hills and sweet dales, I should have drank in the full power of this glorious scenery.'

This was in 1850 when the flow of tourists was steadily increasing; the archives of the Ambleside Turnpike Trust reveal that in 1855 the number of coaches passing through Troutbeck Bridge was 21,480, and most of these would be during the tourist season which was then from early June to late September. Forty years before Charlotte Bronte's visit the guide-book writer, William Green, had expressed his disapproval of those tourists whose experience of all the variety of the landscape of the Lake District was limited to a passing view from the windows of a carriage, 'What enjoyment can be experienced by those who, lolling in their chariots, confine themselves to the glimpses to be obtained from their windows?'

In this, at least, some of the first tourists clearly had much in common with many of their successors.

3

Rushlights and Candles

For all but the last two hundred years of human history in northern Europe the rushlight and the tallow candle were the principal sources of artificial light in every home. Tapers and torches made from tree-roots – such as the Scottish fir-candles – were also used; and when times were hard or when supplies ran out the light from the hearth fire had to serve. It was not until 1800 that William Murdock first discovered the possibilities of lighting by coal-gas and it was to be almost eighty years after that before the invention of the gas mantle made gas light clean enough and safe enough for domestic use. The development of the kerosene or paraffin lamp during the same period was of more practical use to rural areas where gas was not available but it, too, had its hazards and at first it offered little by way of improved illumination.

In the cottages and farmhouses of Cumbria these technological responses to the industrial and urban demand for new and better means of lighting made no great impact for most of the nineteenth century: the ancient rushlight had almost gone before 1900 but the tallow candle was found in house and byre until well into the twentieth century. As late as the 1950s in many remote hamlets among the fells you would need a candle to light you to bed and on dark winter mornings you had to dress by candlelight too.

For many centuries the traditional rushlight was more commonly used in Cumbria than the tallow candle; it was cheap and easy to make and the many damp hollows provided a plentiful supply of rushes never very far from the farmhouse door. The type of rush most sought after was the Common Rush, *juncus conglomeratus*, but Gilbert White tells us that in Selborne the Soft Rush, *juncus effusus*, was preferred. In Cumbria all rushes are known as sieves (from the Old Norse world *sef*) and quite a number of place-names remind us of this – Seavy Dub, Seavy Man, Seavy Rigg, Seavy Syke, and there is even a Candlesieve Syke and a Candlestick Moss. William Dickinson in his collection of 'Cumbriana' recalls that one of the customs which used to feature in the autumn farming calendar was the task of gathering and peeling rushes:

T'young fwoks'll gang till a cannel-seave syke.
And pick a shaff shangans for leets;
Than hotter to heamm, through bog and wet dyke.
To peel them and dip them at neets.

The peeling process involved removing the rind from the stem of the rush except for one firm strip which was left to give stability to the soft pith. It also helped the rushlight to burn more evenly by providing a channel in which it could turn as it burned. After peeling, the fragile piths were allowed to dry before being dipped in hot, salt-free fat. A mixture of half sheep-fat and half bullock-fat was reckoned to be the ideal but bacon-fat was generally used as it was often more readily available, even though it was somewhat inferior because it smelled, smoked and spluttered. The completed rushlights were finally dried by placing across thin sticks and then stored in special cylindrical boxes known as rushbarks. These were originally made from the bark of the birch tree but were later made of tin.

Gilbert White tells us that in Selborne the average length of a rushlight was 28 ½ inches and that this would burn for 57 minutes with a 'good clear light'. The northern climate did not encourage such prolific growth and the usual Cumbrian rushlight seems to have been half that length and so burned for about 30 minutes. Each household, one might calculate, would, therefore, require

Sieves or rushes.

several thousand rushlights every winter.

When the time came to use the rushlights they were fitted into iron rushlight-holders, made by the local blacksmith. These varied in design but all incorporated a rushnip which held the rush firmly in position while it burned. It was important to set the rush with the rib side down so that the grease did not drip and at an angle which ensured a clean burn and optimum illumination: if the rush was too horizontal the light burned too dimly and if it was too vertical it burned too quickly and was likely to drip. An interesting collection of rushlight holders may be seen in the museum at Barrow-in-Furness.

Many rushlight holders are constructed to include both a rushnip and a candle-socket and in many households both forms of illumination were used. Candles obviously made heavier demands on the available resources of fat and were more time-consuming to make but they did burn for a much longer time and gave a better light. The Romans found them an essential item of domestic equipment in the dark winter evenings of their northern province and tripedal candlesticks have been found in several Roman town sites in England, together with the remains of candles whose flat flaxen wicks were last extinguished well over 1500 years ago. The candle-stick was, literally, a strong wooden stick or pole fitted vertically into a block of wood and perforated with a row of holes along its length. Into these a piece of iron, bent at a right-angle and wrought with a candle-socket (and often a rushlight holder) could be fitted and moved up and down to provide the most convenient light.

The dipping method of candle-making changed little over many generations although a contrivance to mould candles was invented to simplify this slow process. One example from Hawkshead could produce six candles at once: the wick was pulled through the empty mould to emerge at the pointed end and the tallow was poured in and left to cool. It seems that not many Cumbrian households indulged in this new-fangled device and dipped candles remained part of life in the Lakeland dales until the dawn of the twentieth century.

So intrinsic a feature of daily life was the candle – and, indeed, the rushlight too – that they acquired their own place in folklore and added to the richness of the language. Phrases such as 'not worth a rush', 'not fit to hold a candle to him', 'the game is not worth the candle' are part of our literature, while the rituals of lighting votive candles and

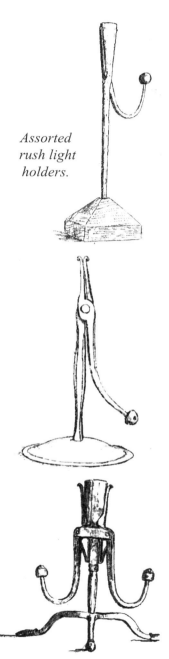

Assorted rush light holders.

excommunications by 'bell, book and candle' are well-known.

Less well-known, perhaps, is the custom of the candle-auction. This was, for several hundred years, an accepted and legally binding arrangement for determining the annual rent for a parcel of land or the current market value of a consignment of goods. The custom appears to have been well-established by the fifteenth century when John Gould of Broadway in Dorset bequeathed a meadow to the parish and gave instructions that the grazing rights should be let by inch-candle auction each New Year's Day. By the mid-seventeenth century such auctions were regarded as so trustworthy that, as John Milton informs us, the Cromwellian Council of State thought 'it meet to propose that the way of selling by inch of candle as being the most probable means to procure the true value of the goods'; and a few years later Samuel Pepys relates how he went to watch ships' cargoes being sold by the same method.

There were two procedures adopted in these auctions. In the first, a candle one inch in length was placed on a flat surface – often a broad-bladed knife – and the participants made their bids as the candle burned; the person calling the last bid before the wick fell over and the flame died won the auction. In an alternative version a pin was stuck into a candle one inch from the top and the bidding ended when the pin fell out. This latter method appears to have been that most widely adopted. Indeed, Samuel Pepys in 1662 revealed a flaw in the first method when he noted down the tip given him by a consistent winner that just before the wick falls the smoke turns downwards and that is the moment to make your final bid. No doubt others knew this too. J. M. Falkner's story *Moonfleet* has a vivid account of a candle auction.

It was obviously useful to have an independent umpire on these occasions; a task which usually fell to the vicar, an appropriate choice since in many auctions the bidding was for land owned by the church or the parish and the money raised went to assist the needy.

Grazing rights were auctioned, for Church Acre in Berkshire and Somerset, for Parish Meadows in Dorset and Lincolnshire, and for the Poor's Pasture at Hubberholme in North Yorkshire, the latter still held in January but recently moved from New Year's Day because it had become too much of a tourist attraction.

In Cumbria this ancient tradition was adopted to resolve a problem which had arisen following the enclosure and draining of the extensive mosses in the Lyth Valley in the early nineteenth century. The division of the land into enclosed fields had, of necessity, involved the creation of a number of gated access tracks with wide grass verges which could offer useful grazing but which were under no direct ownership. To avoid waste of good grazing and to forestall disputes it was decided to hold an annual candle auction in a local inn to determine which farmer should

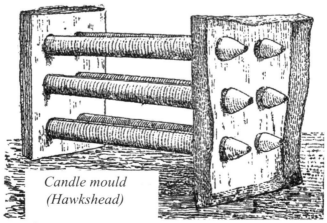

*Candle mould
(Hawkshead)*

*Ccourtesy of H. S. Cowper, Cumberland & Westmorland Antiquarian
& Archaeological Society, 1895.*

have the right to graze his beasts on these verges for that year.

It is a testimonial to the proven reliability of this simple, practical folk custom that it should be adopted to serve the needs of an entirely new farming situation. There does not appear to be any other reference to such auctions elsewhere in Cumbria but in view of the history of land-ownership and land-use in many parts of the area this is, perhaps, not surprising. Even so it is not at all improbable that somewhere in such a large and varied county there may exist a parish record or a folk memory of some similar long-forgotten custom.

4

Too Many Wild Cats in Windermere

Thomas Pennant, travelling in the Windermere area towards the end of the eighteenth century, noted, a little fearfully perhaps, that 'wild cats inhabit in too great plenty these woods and rocks'. Other writers of the time and many parish records confirm that this fearsome creature was a common sight in the woods and on the fells in almost every part of Cumbria. James Clarke in 1787 described it as 'the most fierce and daring animal we have; and they seem to be of the tyger kind, and seize their prey after the same manner.'. They ravaged young stock in the valley fields and decimated the pheasant and grouse population; they could also inflict serious injury on any human who ventured too close to their dens. Not surprisingly they had a bounty on their heads and they were shot to extinction by the middle of the nineteenth century when, it is said, the last one was killed on Great Mell Fell.

Fossil remains of wild cats and several other now extinct animals have been discovered in peat formations and in limestone caves in Cumbria. The bison and the musk ox became extinct in pre-historic times but the brown bear is thought to have survived until the eighth century. After this written records and eye-witness accounts occasionally refer to animals and birds now extinct but an often neglected source of information about contemporary wildlife is to be found in the place-names all around us. Cat Bield, Cat Cove, Cat Hole, Catstycam and many other 'cat' names confirm our eighteenth century travellers' view that this handsome but fearsome beast might be met with almost anywhere in the woodlands and on the craggy uplands of Cumbria two hundred years ago.

A study of place-names can often reveal more than archaeology about the wildlife of past ages. The farming settlers who first created these names lived very close to nature – their lives and livelihood often depended on an intimate knowledge of the plants, birds and animals in the wilderness around their tiny farmsteads. They observed everything in their natural surroundings: the edible and inedible, what was useful and what was useless, the wild creatures that were 'friendly' and those which were not. The place-names of Cumbria, most of which originated in the years of Anglian and Norse settlement between the seventh and eleventh centuries, can tell us of birds and animals which were common then but are now extinct.

The most notorious of these was the wolf which appears in Cumbrian place-names more frequently than any other animal. Over fifty names refer to the wolf, among them no fewer than six Uldales, several Ullthwaites, a number of Ulphas, Ulloeks and Ulgraves – all derived from the Old Norse word for a wolf, *ulfr*. With the introduction of large-scale sheep farming in the early medieval centuries the wolf became a serious threat to the economy of the area. Shepherds really did have to watch their flocks by night, and during the daytime they walked at the front of the flock to ward off prowling wolves while wolfhounds guarded the flanks and rear. So numerous were these predators that it was not unusual for the Crown to link grants of land with a feudal obligation to hunt them down. This was done with such vigour that by the sixteenth century the wolf was extinct in England.

Almost as great a menace to the fragile economy of medieval farming was the wild boar. This ferocious beast caused immense damage to growing crops, and, although its natural home was in the great forests, as more and more land was cleared for agriculture, it inevitably took advantage of this ready source of food. Shakespeare's contemporaries would have fully appreciated his reference to:

The wretched, bloody and usurping boar
That spoiled your summer fields and fruitful vines.

Even so, it was classified as a 'Beast of the Forest', protected by the Forest Law and so to be hunted only by the King or the elite few to whom permission was granted. The last wild boar in England was killed in the late seventeenth century, according to conflicting traditions, either by Richard Gilpin in Kentmere or by Sir Richard Musgrave on Wild Boar Fell near Kirkby Stephen. The many place-names derived from the Old Norse words *svin* (pig) or *gris* (young pig) might refer, in some locations, either to the wild boar or to the domestic pig but Goatscar in Long Sleddale and the now lost Goatbusk near Shap, are derived from the Norse *goltr*, a wild boar.

Place-names from various parts of the country suggest that the beaver survived in Britain until Saxon times. Beverley in Humberside, Bever-cotes in Gloucester and in Nottinghamshire, Beverburn in Hereford and Worcester are all derived from the Old English *beofor*, a beaver. But by the ninth century it was clearly an 'endangered species'; a beaver fur was priced at 120 pence while that of a wolf or otter was worth no more than 8 pence. There was thus a powerful incentive to hunt the beaver and it was on the verge of extinction in the north by the eleventh century. Consequently there are very few names of Norse origin referring to this once common inhabitant of the rivers of Britain. Barbon, near Kirkby Lonsdale, appears in the Domesday Book as 'Berebrune', a name which most authorities agree is derived from the Norse words *bjorr* and *brunnr* meaning 'the beaver bum'. A derivation from the Old English *bera*, a bear, while etymologically defensible, seems improbable as it is unlikely that the bear survived in this country so long after the Roman occupa-tion. Anglo-Saxon literature has many references to the wild cat, the wild boar, the wolf, the beaver and the sea-eagle but the bear strangled by Sir Artegal, a knight of King Arthur's Round Table, is an invention of late medieval romance.

Almost anywhere in the hill country of Cumbria one is likely to come across a name referring to goats or their kids: Gate Crag, Gategill, Gates-garth, Gaterigg, Gatebeck, Kidbeck, Kidshowe, Kidsty Pike, Kidmoor – all names having their origin in words from the Old English or Old Norse. The Saxon and Scandinavian settlers undoubtedly kept goats for milk and cheese but their economy was based much more on the rearing of cattle, sheep and pigs. It is, therefore, probable that some of the 'goat' place-names refer to the herds of wild goats which once roamed the dis-trict. At one time wild goats were almost as common as sheep but by 1965 only a hundred remained in Cumbria in the wild and remote moor-lands in the north-eastern corner of the county. When this area was ac-quired for extensive afforestation the goats were perceived to be an unacceptable threat to the newly-planted trees and were exterminated by shooting. Isolated small herds may still be found in the wilder parts of Wales and Scotland but in Cumbria these small, shaggy, huge-horned creatures are believed to be extinct.

Among the street-names of Cumbria's medieval towns one might come across 'Ratten Raw', a name recalling the Black Rat which arrived in this country from the Middle and Near East in the trading ships of the

Thomas Bewick's engraving of a wild cat.

tenth or eleventh century. In Britain's cooler climate it made its home in the shelter provided by the town houses and the country barns and byres, where it found a ready larder of its favourite foods. It eventually became a widespread pest and the fleas which infested it were probably responsible for the spread of the bubonic plague. The inhabitants of Ratten Raw Lane in Kendal were, no doubt, happy to change the name of their street to Captain French Lane when the black rats departed. Cats began to be kept as domestic pets in the hope of keeping the rats under control but it was not until the arrival of the larger and more aggressive brown rat in the eighteenth century that the black rat was reduced almost to extinction. It is now seen only in a few port areas and has been unknown in Cumbria for some time.

As the wolf population declined in the late Middle Ages the large grey fell fox became the most serious predator among the great flocks of sheep which were by that time the staple of Cumbria's economy, providing a livelihood for sheep farmers, shepherds, spinners, weavers, wool merchants, and others involved in the production of cloth. The small, red fox – the 'popular' Reynard – was undoubtedly as much of a danger to the flocks as it is now and was hunted with the same enthusiasm and determination, but then it was the large, grey fell fox which was the chief enemy. This was a much more formidable quarry: it was a strong beast weighing about fifteen pounds and capable of sustaining a six-hour chase over sixty miles of rugged terrain. This was the fox famously hunted by John Peel and in Cumbria usually known as the tod. It is believed to have been hunted to extinction at about the same time as Peel himself was 'run to earth' in 1854. Both the red fox and the grey are well-represented in local place-names, many of which record the dens or crags where they had their lairs: Todd Crag, Tod Hole, Tod Gill, Fox Bield, Foxerth, Fox How and many more.

Two animals, once extremely common throughout the county but probably hunted to the point of extinction by Victorian shooting enthusiasts in the nineteenth century, are the pine marten and the polecat – the sweet mart and the foul mart (polecat). Neither was ever a threat to man's activities but both were prized for their fur. They were looked upon as sporting targets; one Cumbrian marksman proudly claimed to have shot 250 polecats over a period of 25 years. It is possible that the polecat did disappear from Cumbria for a time but the pine marten may have survived in tiny numbers in remote forests. Recent attempts to reintroduce both are apparently meeting with some success – 51 sightings of the pine marten were reported in the 1990s. Mart Crag, Mart Bield, Mart Knott, Foulmart Gill, Foulmart Fold, remind us that these wild creatures were once so notable that their haunts were known by name.

A number of birds, too, which were once common in Cumbria and gave their names to many local place-names, are now either extinct or are struggling to re-establish a precarious presence. Among the latter is the goshawk, much-prized in the days of medieval falconry and mentioned in several contemporary legal documents: a lawsuit of 1256 refers to 'the eyry of goshawks in Bastonwayt' (Bassenthwaite) and Edward I appointed a forester of Inglewood to be responsible for his goshawks there. It was probably never present in significant numbers and is a very secretive bird; it is now rarely seen in Cumbria. Goshawkstone is the only specific place-name reference. Similarly, the red kite and the sea-eagle are occasional visitors but, unlike the osprey (once better known as the fish-eagle), they have not yet found congenial sites to breed. Dorothy Wordsworth in 1800 wrote of the 'kites sailing over our head' near Grasmere but by 1900 gamekeepers and trigger-happy Victorian sportsmen had decimated its numbers. Names such as Glade How and Glade Hill recall its old name, the glead, while many of the numerous Kit Crags are derived from the Old English *cyta*.

In almost every Lakeland valley the map will show names referring to the eagle. All are derived from the Old English *earn* with Old French *aigle* influence at a later date. To the many Eagle Crags we can add names such as Erne Crag, Arnison Crag and several of the numerous Heron Crags and Heron Pikes. It is not possible to say which of the eagles these names refer to. To the sheep farmers and sportsmen who shot them and to the egg collectors who robbed their nests all were regarded as legitimate targets and by the mid-nineteenth century the last eagle had been shot or had fled the district. The golden eagle and the fish eagle have both made a welcome return in recent years but the sea eagle has so far ventured only on elusive reconnaissance flights.

It seems possible that, in the foreseeable future, we shall be given a glimpse of one of the most visible of all birds. Until about 300 years ago the tall, bushy-tailed crane could be seen striding across the marshes and grassy wetlands of Cumbria but it had always led a precarious existence. Its size and slow flight made it the ideal target for training hawks and falcons; it appeared frequently in the menu at the festive tables of the nobility; its demise was almost inevitable with the invention of the sporting gun in the late seventeenth century. There was a spectacular collapse of the British bird population in the following 150 years. The crane was soon no more than a memory and part of folklore superstition. Numerous place-names derived from the Old Norse *trani* (crane) remind us that this large grey bird with its colourful head was once a common sight on the Cumbrian marshes – Tranthwaite, Trantrams, Tranmoor, Tranteme and many more.

With the possible exception of the black rat all these animals and birds were reduced to near extinction by the hand of man. The need to protect farmstock, growing crops and food stores has always been used as a practical and moral justification for the persecution of wildlife. Acts of Parliament in Tudor and Stuart times authorised parishes to raise funds to pay 'rewards' to those who brought in the heads of a large list of 'vermin', a list which included almost every form of wildlife in the countryside. The indiscriminate destruction of wildlife now had the moral and legal backing of the Law and the sporting rifle became a necessary accessory for gentlemanly respectability. It has been claimed that there was a greater change in British wildlife between 1750 and 1900 than in any other period of recorded history. Some of this may be attributed to loss of habitat as more and more land was brought into agricultural use or was lost to industrial and urban development, but there can be no avoiding the unpleasant fact that the greater part of it was the result of heedless and self-indulgent slaughter.

Attitudes have slowly changed in recent generations and there are now positive policies in place to try to prevent further catastrophic losses. National and local nature reserves, wildlife and woodland trusts, landscape conservation and restoration, environmental enhancement programmes and similar projects are helping to recreate lost habitats, while special 'targeted' schemes have developed in efforts to secure a Cumbrian future for the red squirrel, the golden eagle, the osprey and the pine marten, which has acquired special favour as the chief predator of the grey squirrel.

Seriously at risk from Man's continuing disregard of the effects of his actions on wildlife is the Cumbrian population of lapwings and golden plovers. Both these birds have suffered from breeding failure in the past 50 years as a result of the widespread use of agricultural chemicals. The number of lapwings in Cumbria has declined by about two-thirds since 1987, a collapse exacerbated by the sport of hang-gliding which has driven birds from their traditional breeding grounds. A particularly disastrous consequence of the intrusion of hang-gliders has been noted on the moors near Kirkby Stephen, described in 1998 as having, just a few years earlier, the highest breeding density of golden plovers recorded anywhere in the world: by the year 2000 only three pairs of these stunningly handsome birds remained.

Earlier generations justifiably fought predatory birds and animals in the struggle for subsistence and as the human population has rapidly expanded there has always been pressure to bring more land into cultivation or into economic use, with the inevitable loss of habitats and a diminution of wildlife. Yet sport and pleasure rather than need have also been responsible for the slaughter, harassment and even the extermination of a number of species.

5

The Three Shire Stones

In July 1997 a limestone column which had stood since 1861 beside the road a few metres from the summit of Wrynose Pass was broken – in all probability by a vehicle being inexpertly reversed. This had been a familiar landmark for over a century to farmers on their way to Broughton Market, to fell-walkers and to car-borne tourists, and throughout the twentieth century it was referred to as The Three Shires Stone or The Three Shire Stone since, historically, it marked the junction of the three counties of Cumberland, Westmorland and Lancashire – even though it was inscribed with the name Lancashire only, an inequity which in itself casts doubt on the credentials of this monument.

Engraved on the other side of the column is the legend 'W.F. 1816'. W.F. was William Field from Cartmel, a man of many talents and considerable influence whose powerful personality and varied activities earned him respect and authority: he was dubbed The Father of Cartmel. His business interests included those of ironmonger, chandler, grocer,

The Three Shires Stones, 2001, photograph courtesy of Jan Darrall.

moneylender and agent to several local estates; he was also a bank treasurer, a vestry clerk and manager of various charities; he held the official posts of High Constable and Bridge- and Road-master; and he had acquired the legal knowledge to draw up wills and contracts. He was an enthusiastic antiquarian and a proud Lancastrian. In 1816 he had the limestone monolith carved bearing his initials, the date and the name of his county. For some unknown reason the stone was then left in an alleyway near Cartmel village square, and it was not until 1860, after his death at the age of almost 90, that it was erected, presumably as he intended, in its position at the summit of Wrynose Pass, imperiously set in the centre of the triangle of three small stones which for many centuries had marked this meeting point of the three counties.

For there is no doubt that Field's monument was a presumptuous intruder in an ancient landscape. The three existing stones were described in 1854 by A. C. Gibson as 'of the size of a high-crowned hat – about five feet distant from each other – and forming a triangle.' The maps of Christopher Saxton (1576) and John Speed (1610) and their many eighteenth and nineteenth century successors all refer to (and some actually mark) the Three Shire Stones. Private journals and popular guide books also confirm that the meeting point of the three counties was marked by three typical boundary stones: Daniel Fleming of Rydal Hall in 1671 referred to the 'three Shire-stones on Wreynose'; as did others such as Thomas Machell (1692), Thomas West (1778), and Nicolson and Burns' *History and Antiquities of the counties of Westmorland and Cumberland* (1777).

A. C. Gibson in 1854 described how 'if you are tolerably lish and lengthy of limb, you may place a foot upon one stone, the other foot on another, and your hands on the third, or should the circumstances under which you visit the spot require you to do the feat more decorously, you may place both feet on one stone and distribute your hands between the other two; either way you perform it you may brag thereafter that you have been in three counties at one and the same time' – an exercise endorsed by Harriet Martineau a year later. It would seem that this was one of the 'tourist attractions' of the time for those who were brave enough to endure the rough and intimidating track up to the summit of Wrynose.

The early history of the three shire stones has yet to be discovered.

Saxton's map of 1576 is the earliest documentary reference to them but their origin may well lie in the violent disputes over these northern territories between the Kings of England and Scotland in the years following the Norman Conquest. In 1092 William II gave the lands between the Duddon and Lake Windermere to Roger of Poitou, thus adding the district which later became known as Lancashire-north-of-the-Sands to the Lancastrian estates of this powerful Norman barony.

The Three Shires Stones original drawing by T. L. Aspland, 1852,
engraving courtesy of the Armitt Library.

More than eighty years of ruthless, diplomacy and open conflict later, King Henry II wrested the lands south of Solway from the King of Scotland and created the counties of Cumberland and Westmorland, controlled in the King's name from the strongholds of Carlisle and Appleby. Much of Cumberland was 'ungoverned' territory and in the course of the next hundred years a feature of its history was a succession of boundary disputes between various landowners, prominent among whom were the religious foundations which were endowed with vast tracts of the new county. The creation of Cumberland's many Royal Forests also involved the delineation of boundaries as did the development of new farming settlements as areas of wasteland were brought into agricultural use. Amid all this marking of new boundaries it is not inconceivable that the Crown considered it prudent to place clearly recognised markers at the point where the boundaries of the two new English counties met the Lancastrian limits of the lands controlled by the powerful and volatile feudal barons who held the honour of Lancaster, a point which also marked the boundary of the Upper Eskdale estates of Furness Abbey.

No historical evidence has yet been found to determine a date for the setting in place of the three shire stones but in the four centuries which elapsed between the creation of the new counties and the drawing of Saxton's map in 1576 the many boundary settlements of the thirteenth century would seem to be a useful pointer.

It is, therefore, possible that the original three shire stones had been in position for some 600 years when in 1860 their ancient unobtrusive vigil was rudely disturbed by the erection in their midst of a six-feet tall rectangular interloper brazenly proclaiming the name of one county only. Not everyone agreed with Harriet Martineau that the 'spirited citizen' who initiated this enterprise had placed his neighbours 'under great obligations' as 'the position of the counties may not (now) be overlooked'. Certainly the athletic three-stone exercise for 'young tourists' which she then described was no longer a realistic proposition.

Several accounts of the scene written after 1861 indicate that the three original stones remained in place for many years but, according to Canon Rawnsley, a photograph taken in 1904 clearly shows that they had disappeared by that date. Later writings, maps and photographs show only the 'Lancashire' stone and references were now to 'The Three Shire Stone'.

The fate of the three original stones is unknown. Who removed them? Why were they removed? Where were they removed to? When, precisely, were they removed? Tales that they were dug up and buried elsewhere during the Second World War (presumably to thwart the plans of an invading Wehrmacht) are clearly mistaken as they had disappeared long before 1940. Perhaps more convincing answers to these questions will one day be revealed.

Meanwhile, with a deeper sense of history than was shown in 1861, the appropriate authorities at the dawn of the twenty-first century decided to replace the missing stones by three new ones engraved with the letters C, W and L and placed, as before, in a triangle, or, as the old land deeds put it, in the form of a brandreth, a reference to the Old Norse word for a tripod used to support a cooking pot or hill-top beacon. Brandreth near Great Gable and Three-footed Brandreth above Thirlmere were also the meeting point of boundaries.

Less inspired, perhaps, was the decision to repair the broken column and restore it to its arrogant site in the middle of the triangle. The repair was achieved successfully and with great skill and the new 'Three-Shire Stones', engraved L, C and W, were designed with unobstrusive sensitivity, but there are many who believe that W.F.'s monument should not have been replaced but consigned to a museum. It had, after all, enjoyed well over a century of usurped dominion over the original, more genuinely historic stones which were also much less intrusive in the wild and rugged landscape.

6

Richard Braithwaite:
First of the Lake Poets

A little more than a mile upstream from Kendal the River Kent is joined by the waters of the River Sprint. Here in the angle of this junction and set in gentle pastoral country is the grassy knoll of Burneside Heads, and on its north-eastern spur stands the medieval pele tower and seventeenth century homestead of Burneside Hall. This was the birthplace and for many years the manorial home of Richard Braithwaite, gentleman-scholar and author of more than 60 volumes of poetry, plays, prose and madrigals, and sometimes described as the first of the Lake poets.

Braithwaite was born in 1588 into the prosperous ranks of the Elizabethan gentry who, in all parts of the country, were building their manor houses and transforming medieval fortresses into well-appointed residences. The house at Burneside where Richard Braithwaite grew up was a massive fourteenth century pele tower with a Tudor-style hall recently added by the Bellingham family. The Braithwaites who lived here for seven generations built a further wing in the Jacobean style and adorned the grounds with gardens and ornamental ponds.

The description of Burneside Hall given in 1692 by Thomas Machell portrays it as an elegant estate with spacious, oak-panelled and ornately decorated rooms. The Great Chamber, 50 feet long and 25 feet wide, was comparable to the halls of the Colleges of Oxford and Cambridge 'beautifully enriched with elaborate mouldings and carvings'. And it was from here that in 1604 young Richard was sent to Oriel College, Oxford.

His choice of studies at the university reveals an early affinity with literary subjects for instead of the usual course in philosophy and logic he chose to read classical poetry and history. From Oxford he went on to Cambridge where, again, he revelled in further study of classical literature:

> What choice delights were then afforded us
> In reading Plutarch, Livié, Tacitus.

Burneside Hall, 1835, by T. Allom,
courtesy of Cumbria Library Service.

In common with most other sons of the gentry Braithwaite went on from the university to study law at the London Inns of Court where, on his own confession, he indulged in a life of drinking and debauchery: 'The day seemed long when I did not enjoy these pleasures; the night long wherein I thought not of them. I knew what sinne it was to solicit a maid to lightness; or to be drunken with wine, wherein was excess.'

When these roistering years were over Braithwaite, as Anthony Wood, the contemporary Oxford historian, recorded, 'receded to the north part of England, where his father bestowed on him Burneside... where living many years he became captain of a foot company in the trained bands, a deputy-lieutenant in Westmorland, a Justice of the Peace and a noted wit and poet.'

Braithwaite married twice: in 1617 to Frances Nesham of Darlington who died in 1633, and in 1639 to Mary Croft whose dowry included the manor of Catterick to which he moved in later life and where he died in 1673 at the age of 85. He had nine children by his first wife and one son by Mary Croft. An older son was killed in the Civil War fighting for the Royalist cause.

A contemporary portrait shows Braithwaite as a fashionably dressed gentleman of the Royalist persuasion wearing a dove-grey doublet, a wide lace ruff and lace cuffs, wide breeches, and a dark velvet cloak with a ruby fastening. He sports the flourishing moustache of his day and a pointed beard. A sword and crossbelt complete the picture of a man known to all as 'Dapper Dick'.

Braithwaite's prolific output of poetry is, unfortunately, no more than a footnote in English Literature, for it has to be said that he does not rate very highly even as a minor poet and, as one critic bluntly put it; 'in the essentials of a great poet… the mercury sinks well-nigh to zero.' Perhaps his best poems are his *Farewell to Poetry* and his elegy *The Fatal Nuptiall*, written in commemoration of those who died when the Windermere ferry sank in 1636. Forty-seven members of a party returning from a wedding in Hawkshead were drowned. It is on the strength of these poems that Braithwaite has been dubbed 'the first of the Lake poets' but if he is known at all it is as the author of *Barnabee's Journal*, published in 1638 and especially noteworthy for the high quality of the Latin verse in which it was originally written.

Polished Latin may have been meritorious in a gentleman-scholar in early seventeenth century England but it did nothing to ensure popular success and it was not until the author produced a lively English translation that *Barnaby's Journal* became a 'best seller'. It was reprinted several times in the eighteenth century under the title *Drunken Barnaby* and the phrase 'drunk as Barnaby' passed into the English language.

The English version belongs to quite a different literary world from the Latin original but it retains the author's often humorous observations on contemporary society and his empathy with his hero's rollicking romp through the shires of England.

Thus on his way from London northwards Barnaby, a horse-dealer addicted to liquor and womanising, arrives in Banbury where he relishes an opportunity to indulge in the Cavalier pastime of satirising the over-zealous practices of many Puritans:

> To Banbery came I, O Profane One!
> Where I saw a Puritane-one
> Hanging of his cat on Monday
> For killing of a mouse on Sunday.

The shortcomings of the clergy in some rural parishes also drew an occasional shaft of wit from Barnaby, notably at Garsdale where:

Richard Braithwaite by an unknown artist,
photograph courtesy of Cumbria Library Service.

> In an alehouse near adjoining
> To a Chapel, I drunk Stingo   *(a powerful malt liquor)*
> With a Butcher and Domingo
> Th'Curate, who to my discerning
> Was not guilty of much learning.

At Kirkland in Kendal, however, it was the parishioners rather than the priest who were found lacking. Though they lived in the shadow of the parish church they were:

> Far from God but neare the Temple;
> Though their Pastor give example
> They are such a kind of vermin,
> Pipe they'd rather hear than Sermon.

The hordes of beggars which infested English towns at that time also incurred Barnaby's scornful comment. Lancaster, for example, is described as:

> A seat anciently renowned
> But with a store of beggars drowned

while at Tadcaster he found:

> Beggars waiting:
> Nothing more than labour hating.

The hazards of travel are portrayed with touches of humour. Inns did not offer much in the way of restful sleeping quarters for such as Barnaby. In Wensleydale at Hardraw:

> Inns are nasty, dusty, fustie
> Both with smoake and rubbish mustie

but, more often than not, Barnaby seems to have found an accommodating companion happy to share her more comfortable bed:

> Thence to Mansfield, where I knew one
> That was comely and a trew one,
> With her a nak'd compact made I
> Her long lov'd I, with her laid I;
> Towne and her I left, being doubtfull
> Lest my love had made her fruitfull.

A succession of similar agreeable nights were spent at many other inns, some obviously quite enjoyable – as at Cowbrow which we know as

Lupton where:

> 'truth I'le tell ye
> Mine hostesse had a supple bellie;

all good tales to tell to the fellow roisterer he met with at Natland while
they drank the hours away:

> Till halfe-typsy, as it chanced
> We about the Maypole danced.

Indeed, Barnaby's partiality to liquor in large quantities is a constant
theme throughout his Journal. No sojourn at any inn was worthwhile
unless he could addle his brain with drink:

> Tipsy went I, tipsy came I
> Not a drop of wit remained
> Which the bottle had not drained,

a state of affairs which occasionally brought trouble. In Ingleton he un-
wisely broke the blacksmith's head in a drunken brawl:

> Which done, women rush'd in on me.
> Stones like hail showr'd down upon me.
> Whence amated, fearing harming   *(unnerved)*
> Leave I tooke, but gave no warning.

Occasionally it was neither amorous wenches nor irate womenfolk who
provided the excitement. At Wansford Bridge the River Nene took him
quite by surprise:

> On a Hay-cock sleeping soundly.
> The river rose and took me roundly
> Down the current...

Caught in another flood at Newark, he swam (by instinct one suspects):

> To a Cellar richly stored,
> Till, suspected for a picklock,
> Th'Beadle led me to the whip-stock.

And so Barnaby drinks his way steadily northwards, paying his way
with the profits from his dubious dealings as a horse-trader:

> Be he maim'd, lam'd, blind, diseased.
> If I sell him I'm well-pleased

while his own faithful Rozinante carried him along the rutted roads, travelling no more than about nine or ten miles each day, and often less.

At one overnight stop – 'a poore house' with 'poorer bedding' – his fellow lodgers suspect him of being infected with the plague which afflicted much of England in 1636 and demand that he prove otherwise:- characteristically, Barnaby makes use of the occasion for a little bawdy horseplay:

> Some there were had me suspected
> That with plague I was infected.
> So as I Starke-naked drew me
> Calling th'Hostesse straight to view me.

In due course Barnaby arrived at Nesham, near Darlington, a place:

> Deck't with tufty woods and shady.
> Graced by a lovely lady,

a lady whom our hero married soon afterwards:

> Thence to Darlington, there I housed
> Till at last I was espoused.

This episode has prompted some commentators to ask how far *Barnaby's Journal* is autobiographical. Braithwaite certainly took as his first wife, Frances Nesham of Darlington, and he certainly spent many years of his youth indulging in a life-style not too dissimilar from Barnaby's; but it is speculative and unnecessary to put too literal an interpretation on the events recounted in Barnaby's travels. Indeed, Braithwaite himself was very embarrassed whenever such suggestions were made.

After his marriage Barnaby presents himself as a reformed character:

> But I'm chaste, as doth become me.
> For the countrey's eyes are on me.

And perhaps they were, for his journey through his native county is described with unusual restraint. In just twelve lines he does little more than catalogue his route from Appleby to Lancaster – with not a pot of ale or a buxom wench in sight:

> Thence to native Appleby mount I
> Th'ancient Seat of all that County;
> Thence to pearlesse Penrith went I
> Which of Merchandize hath plenty;
> Thence to Roslay, where our Lot is
> To commerce with people Scottish.

By a passage crooktly tending.
Thence to Ravinglasse I'm bending;
Thence to Dalton most delightfull;
Thence to oaten Ouston fruitfull;
Thence to Hauxides marish pasture;
Thence to th'Seat of old Lancaster.

Ouston is the town we now know as Ulverston; Hauxides is an eccentric version of Hawkshead and 'marish' means marshy: all the places referred to in these verses were at that time major market towns where a horse dealer might expect to do good business.

It is not difficult to detect the poet's personal affection for Kendal – 'where I had my native breeding' – and for the countryside near his home at Burneside. Kendal, so Barnaby informs us, is famous not only for clothmaking, its Charter and its newly created office of Mayor, but also for, 'beauteous damsels and modest mothers' and for its prudent magistrates (of whom Braithwaite was one!):

Here it likes me to be dwelling.
Bousing, loving, stories telling.

But it is for Staveley that Barnaby reserves his real affection and it is here that he ends his tale:

Now to Staveley straight repair I
Where sweet birds do hatch their airy
Arbours, osiers freshly showing
With soft mossy rind o'er growing;
For woods, air, ale, all excelling,
Would'st thou have a neater dwelling?

Braithwaite's home, Burneside Hall,is now a farmhouse, well-preserved and still furnished with its fine oak panelling and ornate ceilings, but the great pele-tower is a shattered ruin, its jagged walls covered in strangling ivy and its medieval chambers filled with rubble. The original gatehouse is almost intact – even its studded oak doors still hang in place, but it is sadly neglected. There are traces of the fourteenth century barmkin or defensive enclosure; and a small lake with an artificial island is all that remains of the medieval moat and the ornamental ponds of a later age, now a playground for ducks and aerobatic swifts.

Braithwaite himself would probably agree wholeheartedly with the verdict of one recent observer that here is 'the essence of the picturesque… splendidly dilapidated' but he might also have wondered if the home of 'the first of the Lake poets' has not been allowed to suffer unduly from the hand of time.

7

Midsummer Murder

It was 19 June 1928. Thomas Wilson, a farmer from Grange-in-Borrowdale, was making his way home through Cummacatta Wood. The summer evening light filtered through the trees and sparkled on the waters of the Derwent just below. The first flush of spring flowers was almost over but the lush growth of high summer was yet to come and so an open umbrella lying near the river bank readily caught his eye. Curious to see such an object there, he stopped to examine it more closely. Underneath it lay the lifeless body of a young woman, strangled with three cords drawn tightly round her neck. She was richly dressed and appeared to be Chinese.

Wilson reported his alarming discovery when he arrived in Grange and with William Pendlebury, a Detective Constable from Southport who happened to be staying in the village, called in Inspector Harry Graham of Keswick Police. Accompanied by a local doctor, Dr Crawford, and Ralph Mayson, the Keswick photographer, the inspector visited the scene and compiled a detailed report of all the relevant evidence which Mayson also recorded on film. The doctor confirmed that death had been caused by strangulation at some time on the same afternoon, and noted that marks on the fingers of the left hand indicated that rings had recently been removed.

Visitors from China were not frequently seen in Borrowdale in 1928 and it did not take long for the inspector to discover that a Chinese couple had arrived at the Borrowdale Gates Hotel the day before. They had left for an afternoon walk on the following day but the husband had returned to the hotel alone, telling the staff that his wife had gone into Keswick to shop for warmer clothes. Not surprisingly Inspector Graham regarded him as the chief suspect and arranged for an immediate search of the room where the couple had stayed.

The missing rings were the vital evidence he hoped to find and he asked for the key to the lady's jewel case. Her husband insisted that he had never seen it and had no idea where it was kept. The search found it hidden in the folds of one of his shirts; but when the jewellery was examined the rings were not to be found. It was startlingly evident, however, that the young woman had brought with her several thousand pounds worth of valuable jewellery and almost certainly came from a very wealthy family.

Wai Sheung Sui was, indeed, a rich lady who had travelled to many countries far from her native China and was known internationally for her special interest in the role of women in western society. She had been presented to George V at Buckingham Palace and was a delegate at the International Women's Peace Conference in New York. It was here that she met Chung Yi Miao, a lawyer who had qualified as a Doctor of Jurisprudence in Chicago. A love affair developed between the two young Chinese and events moved so rapidly that in May, 1928 they were married in New York.

Wai proposed that they should spend their honeymoon in the English Lake District and so, three weeks after their wedding, they arrived in Borrowdale. Within 24 hours Wai was dead, strangled in Cummacatta Wood.

The evidence against Chung so far was too insubstantial to formally charge him with the crime. A jury would need more conclusive proof before they could be convinced that a young man would murder his beautiful rich wife on the second day of their honeymoon.

This proof was soon to emerge. The police search of the hotel room had revealed two exposed photographic films and these had been handed over to Ralph Mayson to be developed. When the wrapping foil on one of these films was removed Mayson discovered Wai's rings packed one at each end of the film. Chung was charged with Wai's murder and arrested, firmly maintaining his innocence. He was tried and found guilty at Carlisle Assizes in October 1928.

Rumours now began to circulate that two Chinese men had been seen in the Keswick area at about the time of the murder, and the inevitable corroborative witnesses made themselves known. There was never any scrap of evidence to link these nebulous visitors with the crime but on such dubious grounds Chung appealed against his conviction backed by a public petition. The sentence was upheld and Chung was executed on 6 December 1928.

Meanwhile Wai had been quietly buried in Crosthwaite Churchyard where she remained for only a short time before her body was exhumed and returned to her home country in a splendid coffin lavishly adorned with gold ornaments. She was reburied in her home town with a funeral appropriate to such a prominent and wealthy woman.

This remarkable episode in the history of Borrowdale was brought to a singular conclusion soon afterwards when Chung's mother revealed that her son was already married when he met Wai in New York and that his real wife was on her way to visit him in England. Chung quickly decided that he preferred his legal wife to the unfortunate Wai whose death was intended to rescue Chung from his self-inflicted dilemma. His mother also stated that, in a letter to her, Chung had confessed that he had indeed killed Wai.

Cummacatta Wood has few visitors; and fewer still know of the beautiful Wai Sheung Sui and the tragic fate she met there.

8

Mallerstang

You will find no signpost to direct you to Mallerstang. In the village of Nateby, a generous mile south of Kirkby Stephen, a sign informs you (with assured precision) that you are 266¼ miles from London, but there is no indication that in little more than a mile you will arrive in Mallerstang, one of the most secluded, secretive and unspoilt valleys in Cumbria. Recently described, with pardonable exaggeration, as 'A Northern Paradise' and as part of 'England's Last Wilderness', Mallerstang bears many of the features traditionally associated with such places: a green and pleasant valley, well-watered by numerous lively becks cascading over the gritstone crags as they flow into a river aptly named River Eden, and a habitat for some 200 species of flora and more than 100 species of birds; and, by contrast, looming 500 metres above the pastures on each side of the narrow valley's five-mile length are formidable crags and ridges marking the edges of vast areas of desolate moorlands, almost one hundred square miles of some of the wildest country in England, described by Dr Samuel Johnson as, 'a tract of solitude and savageness'.

Wilderness or paradise, Mallerstang offers those who venture there the bliss of solitude and quiet communion with Nature, an experience at once exhilarating and humbling whether one contemplates the gentle delights of the valley scene or the awesome loneliness of the trackless moors. Fortunately, neither the quiet joys of Paradise nor the hazardous challenge of the Wilderness have great appeal to most modern tourists, and Mallerstang has so far escaped all the mercenary trappings of tourism. And, indeed, it still retains a certain aloofness towards strangers and to the world 'outside'. The inscription (in Latin) over the doorway of a former inn perhaps expresses the spirit of the valley today as clearly as it conveyed the wishes of the innkeeper years ago:

'The landlord bids honest folk to enter and knaves to depart'.

Mallerstang was not always so isolated from the mainstream: an ancient track, known as Lady Anne's Highway, runs through the valley

Lammerside Castle, eighteenth century drawing,
courtesy of Cumbria Library Service.

from Kirkby Stephen and on into Yorkshire – and guarded by not one but two medieval castles, once of formidable construction. Along this highway for many hundreds of years travelled a steady stream of trade, in carts and wagons drawn by straining horses, in the panniers of pack-horse trains, on the backs of chapmen and pedlars, and 'on the hoof' as cattle-drovers took tens of thousands of Scottish and Cumbrian cattle to the markets of the Midlands and the South, a noisy clamour of commerce and humanity, day and night.

Medieval castles were rarely built primarily to protect the routes of trade and it was with military needs that the fortresses of Lammerside and Pendragon were concerned. Mallerstang was on one of the direct routes from Scotland into the heart of England and both Lammerside and Pendragon formed part of a strategic barrier stretching from Carlisle and Penrith, Brougham and Brough and through to Appleby and Mallerstang. Edward Balliol found a safe refuge in Pendragon when he was driven from the throne of Scotland in the 1330s but a few years later the castle was left in ruins by a vengeful Scottish raid, a destructive operation to be repeated in later Anglo-Scottish conflicts when Lammerside was also destroyed, but, unlike Pendragon, never restored.

Both Pendragon and Lammerside have found a place in the mysterious fables of the legends of King Arthur. Their idyllic situation by the River Eden in the heart of what was then the Forest of Mallerstang was a stage-set, ready made for romances of chivalric adventure. Lammerside was cast in the role of Sir Tarquin's 'Castle Dolorous' but Pendragon acquired a direct association with the great King himself. It was, so the story goes, Arthur's father, Uther Pendragon, who built the first castle here in the fifth century during the conflict fought between the British and the Saxon invaders.

The words 'pen' and 'dragon' mean 'chief warrior', and the eleventh century Chronicle of Geoffrey of Monmouth relates that at this time Uther Pendragon became Chieftain of the Cymri, the people of Cumbria. Among his other alleged feats Uther's attempt to change the course of the Eden is, perhaps, that most often recounted: to strengthen his defences, Uther planned to divert the river on to a course where it would act as a moat surrounding the castle, but the river thwarted all his efforts and so inspired the moralising couplet:

Let Uther Pendragon do what he can
Eden will run where Eden ran.

Uther died, we are told, when the enemy besieging his castle succeeded in poisoning the water in the well from which he drank a fatal draught.

Pendragon is certainly a place for the romantic imagination to be given full rein, an attribute given a gentle enhancement by its particular association with two redoubtable chatelaines: Lady Idonea de Vipont, who rebuilt the castle after its destruction in 1341 and made it 'her chief and beloved habitation', and Lady Anne Clifford, who restored it in the 1660s after yet another disaster and also did much to improve the quality of life in the valley, not least with an endowment for the teaching of 'the children of the dale to read and write English' and funds for the restoration of the chapel at Outhgill.

Pendragon Castle, 1735, engraving by S. Buck,
courtesy of Cumbria Library Service.

Lady Anne's formidable efforts to restore her castles were sadly a rather quixotic enterprise. The days of the medieval fortress were now over and it was not many years before Pendragon was once again little more than the 'great heap of stones' which William Camden had seen a hundred years earlier. Buck's engraving shows us how the castle appeared in 1735.

The economy of the valley no longer relied on the patronage of the castle: it was based firmly on a prosperous agriculture and on the proceeds from the constant flow of trade along the highway. The many fine houses from the seventeenth and eighteenth centuries scattered in such hamlets as Castlethwaite and Outhgill bear witness to a comfortable affluence at that time while services to passing commerce and to those employed in the quarries and in the coal, lead, copper and tin mines up on the moors provided sufficient income to support at least four inns – the Black Bull, the Checkers, the Gate, the King's Head and, further along the highway beyond Hell Gill, High Hall, none of which survives today.

The coming of the railway in 1876 turned the highway into a ghost road: the drovers disappeared almost overnight, as did the procession of carts and packhorse trains. Mallerstang was even denied a station of its own and yet the railway took away the commerce on which the prosperity of the valley depended. It was not long before the mines closed too. Mallerstang had been by-passed. The main motor roads of a later generation also passed by on the other side, just as the Romans had done almost 2,000 years before.

In Mallerstang the end of the busy 'traffic' along the highway also put an end to the lively gatherings at meeting points such as the bridge over Hell Gill where, for many generations, drovers and travellers were met by an array of stallholders selling local products such as cakes, herb beer and blue-milk cheese, besoms, knitwear and baskets, and (to tempt those on their way home to wives and lovers) ribbons, lace and other trifles. A great effort of imagination is required to conjure up a scene such as this in the wild, empty landscape which surrounds Hell Gill today.

Communal gatherings and festivities form part of Mallerstang's tradition. One such occasion was the annual 'riding of the parish boundary' when not only the bounds of Mallerstang parish were defined but also the limits of grazing rights and any other estate boundaries. It was all very homespun and practical: initials carved on a tree trunk indicated both boundary and ownership; where the course of a beck acted as a boundary this was enshrined in the quaint phrase 'as Heavens-water deals' intended to convey that the line began at the very source of the beck. These ridings were made an occasion for all forms of sports and entertainments and were one of the highlights of the valley year. The last riding of the boundaries was held in 1904.

As in many other rural communities Mallerstang enjoyed the well-established custom of 'barring out the schoolmaster'. Each year when the time came for the school to break-up for the Christmas and Summer holidays the pupils barred up the doors and windows of the school to prevent the schoolmaster from entering. A good-natured exchange took place until a bargain was struck regarding such issues as holiday work, free time and the length of holidays. At the school in Mallerstang this negotiation became a rather erudite affair with the exchange of demands and offers made in lines of impromptu verse. Thus in 1740 one part of the pupils' 'terms for settlement' was set out in the following lines:

> *This day to play we think it is our due*
> *And hope it may not be offence to you,*
> *A month at Xmas we now require,*
> *A week at Shrovetide and at Easter we desire.*

The schoolmaster was also reminded that they expected to be given two extra days holiday to leave them free to attend the great Autumn Fair at Brough Hill:

> *Two days at Brough Hill we hope you'll remember*
> *The first of October and the last of September*

The schoolmaster replied in similar poetic terms expressing certain reservations but the pupils' requests were usually met and good humour prevailed – accompanied by appropriate seasonal entertainment.

This traditional (and amicable) confrontation also faded away as did many other customs no longer considered appropriate in the twentieth century. The distribution of two loaves in the chapel each Sunday to elderly folk likewise came to an end but to uphold the terms of Middleton's Charity the loaves could be collected from a shop in Kirkby Stephen. Similarly, the ancient payment of feudal obligations came to an end when in 1929 Elizabeth Orwell paid the sum of £6 to the Veteripont Estates for her property at Thrang.

These obligations, in Mallerstang as elsewhere, had been a constant cause of irritation and conflict for centuries and in 1537 were responsible for a body of frustrated Mallerstang men making the ill-judged decision to join the general uprising in the North usually referred to as the Pilgrimage of Grace. In the judicial carnage which followed 74 men from the area were found guilty and ten of them were hanged at Boggle Green by the highway (boggle is a northern word for a ghost so their fate may well be recorded in their place of execution).

This was not the last time men from Mallerstang were tempted to become involved in rebellion against the Crown. In 1663 Robert Atkinson from Blue Grass (now called Dale Foot) became the leading figure in what is known as the Kaber Rigg Plot. This was part of an enterprise hatched by discontented elements in the North to overthrow the recently restored government of Charles II. Atkinson's plan was to gather his force of malcontents at Kaber Rigg, just north of Kirkby Stephen, where they were to link up with a greater force from the Kendal area and proceed to besiege and capture Appleby Castle.

This bizarre scheme, which had no remote chance of success, fell completely apart when the expected reinforcements failed to materialise. Atkinson was arrested and imprisoned in the very castle he had hoped to capture and was subsequently hanged, drawn and quartered – a grisly fate but Atkinson had already escaped punishment for the murder, fifteen years earlier, of a Robert Daly on the highway near Pendragon Castle.

This was not an isolated criminal act on the highway. Such a busy and remote trade route was sure to be a temptation to that scourge of eighteenth century travellers: the highway robbers. Mallerstang at that time was the playground of a trio of these outlaws. Of these the most romanticised was Ned Ward, alleged to be cast in the tradition of Robin Hood, robbing only the rich and, therefore, a 'good' highwayman whose status as a local 'hero' was enhanced when he escaped arrest by persuading his horse to leap clear over Hell Gill. The feat is also often attributed to Dick Turpin.

Perhaps more worthy of a place of honour in the valley's history is George Birkbeck, son of a Quaker family of Deepgill, Professor of Natural Philosophy in Glasgow, and founder, in 1824, of the Birkbeck Mechanics Institute (later Birkbeck College) and, in 1827, of the University of London.

Mallerstang has connections with the genius of Michael Faraday, the scientist and pioneer of electrical power. His family lived and farmed in the upper Eden Valley for many years. His father, James Faraday, lived and worked as the blacksmith at Outhgill, but moved to London before Michael was born in 1791.

You may drive through the five mile length of Mallerstang, pause to visit Pendragon Castle and admire the scenery, in no more than half an hour but in so doing you will join those admonished by William Green in 1819 in his *Tourist's New Guide*: 'What enjoyment can be experienced', he asks, 'by those who, lolling in their chariots, confine themselves to the glimpses to be obtained from their windows?'

On foot you may see all the interesting detail in the landscape: the awesome power of Hell Gill Force in spate; the seventeenth century houses at Castlethwaite and also at Outhgill, where part of James Faraday's smithy still exists; the prehistoric lynchets near Wharton Hall;

Mallerstang riding the boundaries for the last time in 1904
(photograph from publisher's private collection).

Lady Anne's Chapel: the restored Jew Stone destroyed by men building the railway because it bore a Star of David; and the waterfall known as 'The Auld Wife's Kitchen' where much of the water is caught in an up-draught of air and appears to be flowing upwards.

You may walk along the highway, now known as Lady Anne's Way, a 100 mile recognised footpath and view the large sculptures recently erected there. You may glimpse several of the rare birds found here, or, at the right time of the year, see one of the finest displays of globeflower in Cumbria. You may hear the story of the last wild boar in England killed on Wild Boar Fell 200 years ago by Sir Richard Musgrave of Kirkby Stephen. Or, if you collect unusual ghosts, you may come across the apparition of the black hen of Pendragon Castle.

However long or short a time you spend in Mallerstang it seems unlikely that your impressions will be the same as the Domesday Book Surveyors who in 1086 found it 'all spoilt and good for nothing', or as William Camden's who 500 years later saw it as 'waste, solitary, unpleasant and unsightly.' On the contrary you will not be at all surprised that in 2016 Mallerstang became the Westmorland Dales part of the Yorkshire Dales National Park.

9

Jonas Barber: Clockmaker

For medieval folk the day began at dawn and ended at sunset: a precise division of the hours of daylight was of little interest. So long as life was governed by the sowing, tending and harvesting of crops and by the needs of farm animals, it was the succession of the seasons rather than the passing of the hours which determined their concept of time. It was not until the sixteenth and seventeenth centuries that any enthusiasm was shown for a more accurate measurement of time than that achieved by the Egyptian water-clock, sandglass or shadow-clock 2,000 years before. In some towns the new mechanical clocks had been installed, often in the cathedral, and bells rang out to indicate the time of day; thus three chimes meant it was '3 of the clock'.

In 1581 Galileo's observation of a lamp swinging in Pisa Cathedral revolutionised completely the technology of time-keeping. Within less than 100 years the regular movement of the pendulum combined with a simple escapement mechanism had made possible the construction of reliable and accurate clocks, above all the popular longcase clock with its 39 inch pendulum beating one second. Mechanical refinements such as the balance spring quickly followed and by 1700 clockmakers had created the first precision lathe.

So great was the demand for these new 'time-pieces' that almost anyone who could call himself a craftsman tried his hand at their construction – gold and silver smiths, jewellers, gunsmiths, blacksmiths, whitesmiths, even dentists and opticians. The foundation of the Clockmakers' Company and an Act of Parliament aimed to impose standards and to regulate the craft and by 1700 every clock had to bear the name of its maker and the town or village where he practised his trade. Even so there were a remarkable number of clocksmiths at work in almost every part of the country – and Lakeland was no exception for here supplies were readily to hand of the white metals so essential to clockmaking (tin, lead and refined steel) and of good oakwood for the all-important cases designed to impress visitors and to demonstrate the affluence of their owners.

From the early eighteenth century onwards longcase clocks became an essential adornment in almost every yeoman's house in Lakeland, and it was in these years that the clockmakers flourished. No fewer than 150 are known to have worked in Kendal and another 150 are recorded in Furness and Westmorland – 50 in Ulverston, 24 in Kirkby Lonsdale, twelve in Ambleside.

Among these clockmakers, not all of whom were naturally gifted in this craft, there appeared in a remote corner of a remote Westmorland valley a man of genius: Jonas Barber of Winster, a superb master of his craft whose clocks are, 250 years on, regarded as masterpieces of fine, precision engineering. In the fifty years of his active working life Barber produced no fewer than 1,435 clocks, each one numbered and named, each one a tribute to his skills and to his extraordinary ability to improve in design, mechanical ingenuity and accuracy.

If such a man had lived in London or Liverpool or any other major centre of clockmaking his achievements would not perhaps seem quite so extraordinary, but to have produced so much high-quality work and to have shown so much constant imaginative

Jonas Barber clock, photograph courtesy of Bowes Musuem

flair in its design and precision in such rural isolation is nothing less than astonishing. For it must be   remembered that Winster was 300 miles from London and ten from the nearest town, Kendal, to which it was linked only by packhorse tracks which were always rough and deeply rutted and often muddily impassable, conditions which were never conducive to the easy conveyance of delicate goods or to the communication and acceptance of new ideas.

Jonas Barber was born in 1688, the son of John Barber, clockmaker of Skipton, and nephew of Jonas Barber, also a clockmaker,of Ratcliff Cross in London. We know almost nothing of his early years but it is self-evident that he would have received a childhood introduction to the intricacies of the craft which was eventually to be his life's work. His first known clock is now referred to as the Barrow clock and it was probably made when he was only seventeen years of age, an apprentice piece which students of horology accept as the first achievement of a craftsman of rare genius on his fifty year progress to the sophisticated design of the Keswick clock in his later years.

Parish Registers tell us that in 1717, at the age of 29, Jonas married Elizabeth Garnett of High Mill in the Winster Valley, the daughter of a wealthy yeoman. In 1727 Jonas, Elizabeth and their two surviving children moved from Bowland Bridge to Bryan Houses Cottage, and later on to Bryan Houses farmhouse next door, a house which they probably built – a conclusion apparently confirmed when a stone slab such as adorns many Lakeland farmhouses was recently recovered bearing the initials 'JB' and the date 1737 with a 'pig-tail' decoration of the same design as that which appears on so many Barber clocks.

Across the lane from Bryan Houses there still stands the small bam which was Jonas Barber's workshop. So improbable does it seem that some of the finest longcase clocks made in the eighteenth century were actually created in this simple Lakeland barn that for many years doubts were cast on the very idea. Such doubts were dispelled when the farmer who worked the land here in the 1930s and 40s related that when he had to re-roof and repair the building a large assortment of brass clock-parts were discovered in almost every crevice of the stonework. Sadly, he added that all these were buried in a trench then being dug for a new drain!

It is appropriate, too, that we bear in mind that Barber was working

Jonas Barber's barn, drawing by M. Woods, 1999.

in the days before machine tools and machine-made parts were available to clockmakers. All the parts of his clocks were hand-made: the only 'machine tool' he may have had in his barn was the recently invented clockmaker's lathe but even this had no tool-holding carriage and so accuracy still depended on the eye and skill of the craftsman. The clockcases would have been made by local joiners using local oakwood and so display little of the elaborate ornamentation and inlay which by the late eighteenth century were expected by fashionable customers for whom the case was at least as important as the clock itself.

For these few affluent landowners and tradesmen Barber was happy to add such mechanical contrivances as lunar dials, tidal dials and even seconds hands – all then a feature of clocks made in London – but otherwise his yeomen clients were content with his reliable if unsophisticated 30-hour clocks with simple chain-driven movements housed in simple, unpretentious oak cases. Barber and the dalesmen of Lakeland continued to ignore (or be oblivious to) the whims of London fashion in most other respects too: square dials were 'out' in London while Barber was still a young man but his workshop had a ready market for them long after Barber's death in 1764; the longcase clock itself was falling out of favour by this date as 'modern' homes turned more to mantelpiece clocks or bracket clocks but in rural areas of the North the longcase remained popular until the late nineteenth century and Barber's successors in Winster continued to produce them in significant numbers.

The third generation of the Barber family of clockmakers was represented by Jonas Barber's son, Jonas, who took over the business when his father's health began to fail in the late 1750s and inherited it, together with Bryan Houses, in 1764.

Jonas senior's will appears to indicate that Jonas junior was a somewhat wayward character in whom his father had less than complete confidence. For the will states that if Jonas refused to pay his sister her stipulated legacy of £150 he would forfeit Bryan Houses to her and her heirs, and that if he failed to make his mother a new 8-day clock she would be entitled to have the 8-day clock already in the house!

We do not know whether these domestic issues were amicably settled but in his clockmaking young Jonas continued his father's work industriously until his death in 1802. Although he actually produced more clocks than his father he appeared to lack his touch of genius and inventiveness with the result that his work became increasingly conservative and failed to keep up with new developments both in technology and in design. He did, however, leave a flourishing industry to John Philipson, heir to the John Philipson who had been apprentice to Jonas senior in 1748 and created many fine clocks including the outstanding musical clock now in Abbot Hall in Kendal.

Both the Philipsons and Jonas Junior had the advantage of manufactured machine tools and machine-made clock-parts to assist their work and, while this does not diminish the value or significance of their remarkable achievements, it does serve to underline the extraordinary vision, dedication, skill and genius of Jonas Barber senior, clockmaker of Winster in Westmorland.

10

A Cumbrian Alphabet

Cumbria has a particularly interesting heritage of place-names reflecting the history of diverse human settlements in this corner of Britain. Celtic Britons, Angles and Saxons, Danes and Norwegians, Irish and Norman French, all have left their mark on the place-names of Cumbria – all except the Romans who, in spite of their 300 year occupation, left no obviously Roman place-names – who now asks the way to Galava, Mediobogdum or Glannaventa? Much has been written and many lectures have been given on the subject of Cumbria's place-names and fewer tourists from southern counties now exclaim at such 'outlandish' words as *beck, fell, thwaite* and *ergh*. Many Cumbrian place-names can be partially understood from a dozen such simple elements but there are in the county many more complex and exotic-sounding names which can happily compete in their colourful singularity with the southern charm and idiosyncrasy of Piddletrenthide, Chipping Ongar and Toller Porcomm. A simple alphabetical guide may serve to illustrate this.

A

Aughertree (pronounced Affertree) This small hamlet on the northern fringe of the National Park is recorded in the sixteenth century as Alcotewraye, a name derived from the Old English words *eald* and *cot* meaning old cottage; the final element is the Old Norse word *vra* meaning a nook or secluded corner.

B

Bretagh Holt (pronounced Bretter Holt) This once quiet spot is now well-known as a major road junction a few miles south of Kendal. It was once a summer pasture and woodland of a local tribe of Britons as its component elements are the Old Norse words *Breta* (meaning Britons), *erg* (summer pasture) and *holt* (wood).

C

The Carles The Castlerigg Stone Circle near Keswick is also known as The Carles, a name probably derived from the Norman-French word 'carole', a circle or a ring-dance, the original meaning of the word 'carol' and often given to ancient stone circles including Stonehenge. In 1725 William Stukeley stated that there were two circles on this site but no trace of a second circle has been found.

D

Doctor Bridge (Eskdale) According to tradition this seventeenth century packhorse bridge over the River Esk received its name when a Dr Edward Tyson of nearby Penny Hill had the original narrow bridge widened to accommodate his trap. There is no doubt that Dr Tyson lived in Eskdale at that time – the parish registers confirm this – but the recent discovery of a document dated 1817 setting out in detail the terms of a contract for the widening of the bridge casts doubt on the story. From this it is clear that the bridge may not have been widened in Tyson's day (he died in 1755); and, significantly, the name Doctor Bridge does not appear on any map until the first Ordnance Survey Map of 1860. The name Doctor Bridge may be derived from this Eskdale surgeon but there seems to be no evidence to support the tradition that he had its structure changed.

E

Eamont Bridge (pronounced Yamont) The earliest written reference to this historic spot is in the Anglo-Saxon Chronicle which calls it *Ea motum*, meaning 'the meeting of the rivers' from the Old English word *ea-mot* (later replaced by the Old Norse *a-mot*). The Rivers Eamont and Lowther converge near this bridge. If historical tradition is to be believed, it was here that in 927 the Kings of England, Scotland and Strathclyde met to resolve their differences.

F

Flaska, Flaskew, Flusco. The early forms of these names – Flatscogh and Flatsco – point to a derivation from the Old Norse *flatr-skogr* meaning a level woodland. The woods were felled and much of the underlying peat removed to supply fuel for the great smelting furnaces at Brigham near Keswick in the sixteenth and seventeenth centuries. At Flusco just north of Ullswater a splendid Viking silver brooch from the tenth century was found and is now in the British Museum.

G

Goldscope In 1564 Queen Elizabeth I established the Company of Mines Royal to exploit the mineral deposits in her realm and, most importantly, to mine the recently discovered veins in the Newlands Valley near Keswick. Skilled German miners were imported but at first they had little success. In 1566 they struck a rich vein of copper and lead with significant quantities of silver and some gold. This they jubilantly dubbed *Gottesgab*, God's Gift, and, in the way the English have with foreign names, this was soon corrupted to Goldscope.

H

Helvellyn This, the most popular of Lake District mountains, has no written record before 1577,and the meaning of the name remains obscure. A recent attempt to solve the mystery seems more convincing than any of the earlier suggestions. Richard Coates (1988) suggests a derivation from 'a Cumbric *hal velyn*' meaning 'yellow upland moor', referring to the colourful lichen or dry yellow *Nordus Strictus* grass which may at one time have carpeted the summit plateau.

I

Isthmus This promontory at the northern end of Derwentwater was originally called Espness, a name now corrupted beyond recognition. Espness is derived from the Old Norse *espi* (aspen tree) and *nes* (a promontory).

J

John Bell's Banner This is one of the alternative names given to Caudale Moor, a 2,500 feet fell towering over the Kirkstone Pass. John Bell was curate of Ambleside from 1585 to 1630 and he seems to have been very active in local affairs. There were ongoing disputes between the parish of Ambleside and the township of Troutbeck over grazing rights on the vast area of 'wasteland' to the north where no clear boundary had been established. Furthermore, the 1598 Poor Law with its Statutory levy of Parish Poor Relief made it essential that parish boundaries should be permanently and indisputably fixed. John Bell, it seems, planted a boundary mark (a banner) to mark the limits of the rights and responsibilities of the inhabitants of Ambleside, Hartsop and Troutbeck.

K

Keswick The town's name is derived from the Old English words *cese* (cheese) and *wic* (buildings used for a particular purpose or activity, often a dairy farm). *Wic* has linguistic links with the Latin *vicus* referring to settlements which grew up close to Roman roads and forts. No Roman road near Keswick had been traced until 1994 when the route from Penrith to Keswick was fairly convincingly established together with a suggestion that a Roman fort once stood near the River Greta on the site of Keswick School, The *vicus* nearby would be the dairy farm supplying this garrison.

L

Lanty's Tarn Lanty is a pet form of the name Lancelot and here refers to a Lancelot Dobson who, in the nineteenth century, lived with his family in a cave nearby. He died aged 95 in 1865. Tarn is derived from the Old Norse *tjorn*, a small lake; this particular tarn was made as a reservoir to supply fresh water to Patterdale Hall. An ice-house is built into its bank. The views from the pine-clad summit of Keldas above the tarn are among the finest in Lakeland.

M

Mungrisdale Grisedale is derived from the Old Norse words *griss* (pig) and *dalr* (valley). It is not possible to be sure whether the pigs concerned were domestic animals or wild boar which were common in England in early medieval years. The first element refers to St Mungo, a missionary of the Celtic church, also known at St Kentigern, who travelled through Cumberland to convert the local people to the Christian faith. Several churches in Cumbria are dedicated to him, including the eighteenth century church here in St Mungo's valley of the pigs.

N

Nan Bield Pass This high level (2,100 feet) pass at the head of the Kentmere Valley is one of Lakeland's finest mountain passes, at the summit of the ancient packhorse route linking Kendal and Penrith. The old word *bield* indicates that at one time there was a shelter on the pass, a welcome refuge no doubt for many a weary traveller. A common explanation for Nan is that it is a pet form for the name Anne.

O

Orrest Head This viewpoint above Windermere stands near the route of the important Roman road from Watercrook, near Kendal, to Ravenglass. It is close to the junction with the Roman road to High Street and Penrith. The name is derived from the Old Norse *orrusta* meaning a battle. There is no record of a battle here but such a spot would be of great strategic importance. Orustudalr in Iceland is the site of a known battle.

P

Portinscale A twelfth century document records this name as Portquenescales. *Portcwene* is the Old English word for a prostitute and Old Norse *skali* means a hut. This is the only place-name in England which refers to prostitutes and for this reason there are those who would redeem the reputation of the ladies of this settlement across the Derwent from Keswick by substituting the term 'townswomen' as a more suitable translation.

Q

Queneldeskore This lost medieval name refers to Cwenehild, an English lady who owned land near Windermere with a distinguishing deep gully or crag with a deep cleft (Old Norse *skor*).

R

Robinson This uninspiring fell, (rising above Buttermere but best seen from the Newlands Valley) belonged to a Richard Robinson who bought it as part of a land purchase in the great redistribution of monastic property following the Dissolution of the Monasteries in the reign of Henry VIII. The mountain formerly belonged to Fountains Abbey.

S

Sizergh (pronounced Sizer) The origin of this name is found in a twelfth century version: Sigaritherge. The first element is a Norse feminine personal name, Sigarithr (Sigrid), and the second the Norse word *erg* – a summer pasture or shieling – a common feature in areas of Norse settlement.

T

Torpenhow (pronounced Trepenna) The three elements in this name appear to be *tor* (a rocky hill), *pen* (a hill), and *haugr* (a hill). This triple emphasis on a prominent hill at Torpenhow defies the local topography: there is no hill in the vicinity of this village on the north-west Cumbrian plain. A more probable explanation of the name might lie in the Norse personal name, Thorfinn, which appears in other Cumbrian place-names. *Haugr* is also used in the sense of a burial mound – Thorfinn's mound.

U

Uzzicar A thirteenth century version provides the key to this name. Husaker (1210) is derived from the Old English *hus* (a house) and *aecer* (an acre or a plot of cultivated land). The precise size of an acre varied until it was fixed by Statute in 1284. This house in its acre of land gave the name to Uzzicar Tarn nearby which was drained in early medieval times.

V

Viver A vivary or vivarium was an enclosed area, usually a fish-pond, for the breeding of fish for the table. This particular vivary, at Hincaster a few miles south of Kendal, is referred to in the early thirteenth century. Fish constituted an important part of the diet in medieval times and manor ponds were regularly restocked with eel, perch, roach, tench and other freshwater fish.

W

Watendlath The name of this much photographed hamlet presents a linguistic puzzle. The simple explanation takes the three Old Norse elements *vatn* (lake), *endi* (end) and *hlatha* (barn) to give 'the barn at the end of the lake'. But this does not account for the very early (1211) version Wathendelan which could refer to land (at the end of the lake). A more fanciful interpretation would derive the middle element from a Celtic personal name such as Gwenddoleu which the newly-arrived Norsemen had some difficulty in pronouncing. Watendlath would thus mean 'Gwendolen's lake'.

X

Crosscanonby In 1285 this is recorded as Crosseby Canoun reflecting the fact that this part of the parish of Crosby in Allerdale had been gifted to the canons of Carlisle. The numerous place-names with the word cross indicate either a religious symbol to mark a preaching place or a simple landmark.

Y

Yotton Fews (near Sellafield) 'Fews' is almost certainly the Norse word *fe-hus*, a cattle shed but the only recorded version (thirteenth century) of Yotton (yoton) is unhelpful. It may be a lost personal name but the local topography points strongly to the Old English *ea-tun*, the farmstead by the river.

Z

(Sellafield) Very few English place-names begin with Z and there are none in Cumbria, but two places in Devon called Zeal have the same origin as a number of places in Cumbria. Zeal is derived from the Old Norse *selja*, a willow tree, which may also be the origin of Selside, Selker, Sella and Sellafield. The willow was one of the most common species in Cumbria before extensive land drainage took place. The Old English word *feld* refers to open country or to land which has been deforested. An alternative and equally possible origin may be the Old Norse word *sel* meaning a shieling, although this is rarely found in Cumbria. Sellafield could thus mean either open country where willow trees grow or open country with a shieling.

11

Ann Macbeth

For at least two hundred years the Lake District has been the retirement sanctuary of eminent figures from all walks of life. Poets, painters, professors, politicians, novelists, bishops and business tycoons have all sought here refuge from the pressures of the lives which brought them fame, wealth or other rewards of success. Many contributed much to the community in which they settled, even if it were no more than an imposing residence set in extensive and well-ordered grounds. Unique among these 'off-comers' was Ann Macbeth, a lady of extraordinary talent and energy whose work was nationally and internationally honoured. In the Lake District, she is virtually unknown outside the parish of Patterdale where she spent the last 27 years of her life.

Ann Macbeth was bom in 1875, the first of nine children in the family of a Scottish engineer living in Bolton, Lancashire. Her grandfather was a member of the Royal Scottish Academy as were three of his sons and this artistic aptitude was continued among most of Ann's brothers and sisters. The family moved to St Anne's and the children attended a Dame School run by an Aunt and six Scottish sisters and appear to have received a good education in literature, languages, mathematics, music and art.

One might have expected that this strong Scottish Presbyterian childhood influence would have had an inhibiting effect on the ambitions of the daughters in the family, particularly in an age when it was considered socially unacceptable for women and girls to contemplate a career or even to earn their own living, largely because this would reflect on their father's or husband's ability to keep them. But Ann Macbeth and her sisters were clearly not so easily swayed by the conventions of the late Victorian age: Ann was allowed to enrol on a course at the Glasgow School of Art where for over twenty years she followed a distinguished career; Alison qualified as a Doctor of Medicine; and the colourful career of Sheila included being torpedoed when she was a nurse on board the hospital ship *Britannic* in 1916 and many years later, at the age of 88, visiting the wreck of the ship on one of Jacques Cousteau's underwater expeditions. Without the publicity and melodrama of the Suffragettes (whose cause they supported) the Macbeth sisters were unquestionably in the vanguard of the twentieth century movement for the liberation of women.

Ann joined the Glasgow School of Art at a remarkable time in its history when under the guidance of Francis Newbery and his wife, Jessie, it became the focus of European and, indeed, world attention by their pioneering work in new concepts of design and technique and also in the positive encouragement given to their women students. The Newbery's educational and artistic innovations received great impetus through the close involvement of the renowned Scottish architect, Charles Rennie Mackintosh who not only designed the Glasgow School of Art but also played an active role in gaining international appreciation of the 'Glasgow Style', an avant-garde form of art and design created by the work of the 'Glasgow Boys' and the 'Glasgow Girls' at this time – although until very recently the female contribution to this remarkable movement received scant recognition. Little more than fifty years ago this strange reluctance to acknowledge the achievements of women artists was blatantly apparent in a review of an artist's exhibition:

> We learned the artist is a woman in time to check our enthusiasm. Had it been otherwise we might have hailed these expressions as surely by a great figure among moderns.

Against this background of professional enthusiasm and public disapproval Ann Macbeth and her colleagues developed their talents and their unique style. Ann's skills and imaginative approach to her art made an immediate impact and only four years after entering the Glasgow School of Art her work was awarded medals and prizes at the Turin International Exhibition of Modern Decorative Art and was praised in the most prestigious art journals of the time. She had already mastered the essential skills of drawing and design and had moved on to the techniques of metalwork, ceramics, jewellery, bookbinding, leather-work and carpet design. But her personal specialism was embroidery which became her life-long passion, an enthusiasm which inspired her to revolutionise the teaching of needlework in schools, not only in the United Kingdom but in America, Africa, India, and in many countries across Europe.

Ann Macbeth's books *Educational Needlecraft* and *The Playwork*

Book gave a new direction to the teaching of arts and crafts in schools by the emphasis she gave to the individual child's involvement in the design and practicality of the needlework, to the use of coloured thread to develop a sense of colour and to the progressive learning of new

Ann Macbeth, courtesy of Glasgow Museums.

techniques. The dull chore of fine hemming and the cross-stitch sampler so beloved of earlier generations was replaced by coloured appliqué and needleweaving, and each lesson resulted in a completed article: an embroidered cushion, table mat, tea-cosy, pillow case or a simple bag. Imagination, creativity, and drawing skills were developed by encouraging the children to plan their own designs; and to this end motifs from nature were considered important: flowers, plants and foliage were studied in detail.

Special Saturday morning classes were held at Glasgow School of Art to instruct teachers in these new techniques and often as many as a hundred teachers were enrolled, such was the charismatic and yet down-to-earth practicality of Macbeth's teaching. She instilled into all who followed her methods – both women and children – that they were capable of making and decorating with their own embroidered designs household articles which were more attractive to look at and cost very much less than any which were mass produced. Long before she became Head of the Needlework and Embroidery Department in 1908 or had been honoured in Paris, Budapest, Turin, and Chicago, a leading art journal could confidently assert that Ann Macbeth had convincingly shown that 'embroidery is a thing that lives and grows and is therefore of greater value and interest than a display of archaeology in patterns and stitches.'

Soon the major manufacturers of textiles were clamouring for Macbeth designs – Paton and Baldwins, Clarks, Liberty's and Donalds of Dundee among many others – and she received commissions to create designs for such diverse institutions as the Nottingham Tearooms, Glasgow Cathedral and other churches, the British Association, and the famous Glasgow Tearooms of Miss Kate Cranston. In 1916 she was appointed Lecturer at Bangor University in North Wales and travelled widely throughout the United Kingdom and in Europe gaining enthusiastic support for her educational ideas and collecting awards and diplomas on the way.

In 1921, at the age of 46, Ann Macbeth retired to live in the Lake District making her home first in the hamlet of Hartsop and later in Patterdale. Here she took an energetic part in the life of the local community: indeed it might be said that she brought new life to that community. One of her first achievements there was to enlist support in the valley for the creation of a Patterdale Women's Institute whose members she immediately began to inspire with her enthusiasm for practical arts and crafts. As with the teachers and schoolchildren whom she had encouraged in the past, she convinced the women of Patterdale that they too could design, make and decorate beautiful and useful craftwork: 'Try it, ladies, of course you can do it.'

In 1981 to mark the Diamond Jubilee of their WI the ladies of Patterdale paid tribute to their founder by producing a booklet entitled *The Life of Ann Macbeth, Embroideress Extraordinary.* Perhaps one of Macbeth's most valuable contributions to the Patterdale community – and probably to rural communities well beyond Patterdale – was her effort to seek a practical alleviation of the hardships suffered by so many dalesfolk as a result of the agricultural depression of the 1920s. She saw that the tough, coarse wool of the Herdwick sheep made extremely durable and not unattractive rugs which could be woven on a simple cottage loom. So first of all she invented an easily constructed loom built from materials to which every cottager had ready access – basically, two spars of wood weighted with stones – and arranged with the Cumberland Tweed Mills at Wetheral, near Carlisle, for the wool to be mechanically spun. She then instructed the villagers how to weave it on her looms and produced a book, *The Country Woman's Rug Book*, with full details and suggestions for various' designs. Armed with this and her own special charisma she gave talks up and down the country extolling the virtues of the wool of the Herdwick sheep.

In Hartsop, Ann Macbeth had a house – High Bield – built on a rock shelf high above the village but she spent only a short time there and joked that it was really there for her nephews and nieces 'to escape from their parents'. She soon moved to the cottage down in the valley always known as Wordsworth's Cottage, (a house where Wordsworth never lived although he did own the land). A small building adjacent to the cottage Ann used as her workshop, complete with a kiln where she fired the numerous items of pottery she created.

From this 'studio' emerged the many beautifully decorated ceramics which she made for almost every family in the dale. Every child received a Macbeth christening plate or mug; every important wedding anniversary would be commemorated by a Macbeth teapot or jug. Sometimes a family would receive a 'family-tree' with the new-born baby depicted as a tiny leaf on one of the branches. Many of these gifts may still be found in Patterdale and are treasured heirlooms.

It was in the fields near to Wordsworth's Cottage that Ann found the inspiration for two large and famous embroidered wall-hangings for which she is especially revered in Patterdale. One, given the title 'The Good Shepherd' and embroidered in wool and silks, shows Christ as a shepherd tending Herdwick sheep and surrounded by flowers found in the valley, with Deepdale, Hartsop and Kirkstone in the background. Below the landscape are embroidered two lines of music from the score of Hubert Parry's setting of Blake's *Jerusalem* (there is said to be a wrong note in Bar 11!)

Smaller embroidered panels made by Ann Macbeth include a bowl of flowers originally given to Bishop Gorton of Hartsop and several embroidered 'Peace Panels' she made bearing the words 'Peace when thou comest and when thou goest may thy footsteps echo peace.'

The second major wall-hanging is entitled 'The Nativity'. According to Ann Macbeth's own account the inspiration for this came one day when she discovered in a ruined farm building near her cottage 'a tiny manger, made I should think for a goat. It was just large enough to hold a tiny baby comfortably... and this set my needle working.'

Against a background of Patterdale with Helvellyn in the distance, the Virgin Mary is shown with Christ in a manger watched by the Angel Gabriel apparently amusing the child with a dandelion puffball. A colourful array of valley flowers surrounds them. This panel is one of Ann Macbeth's most important works and it is characteristic of the generosity for which she was so admired that she should present such a fine example of her art to the parish church of a remote Lakeland dale.

It is not to be wondered at that she is still remembered in Patterdale with warmth and great respect nor that to commemorate her life there the parishioners planted a tree which would perpetuate her memory for generations to come. She must have seemed like a being from another world when she descended on Hartsop and Patterdale in the 1920s – a tall, slim formidable figure dressed in skirts of bright vivid colours, long necklaces swinging and her crimson cloak flowing in the breeze: one of the great and neglected women of the twentieth century.

12

Margaritifera margaritifera

Chapter 6, Paragraph 3, sub-section 5a of the 1994 National Rivers Authority *Catchment and Management Plan for Derwent and the Cumbria Coast* bears the title: 'Unknown Status of the Nationally Rare Freshwater Pearl Mussel (Margaritifera margaritifera)'. We are then informed that 'This nationally rare species receives special protection under the Wildlife and Countryside Act, 1981. It is known to be present in the Rivers Ehen and Irt, though its exact distribution and status remains a mystery... It is... a conservation priority to find these sites so that the species can be fully protected in this catchment.' Thus, in the cold (but unequivocally encouraging) language of bureaucracy, is the long and elusive story of the Cumbrian pearl brought up-to-date.

Margaritifera margaritifera, known to Cumbrians as the horse mussel, was found by the Romans on the sandy, gravelly bed of the rivers Irt and Ehen. It is about fourteen cms long and has a lifespan of up to

The River Irt, photograph courtesy of Ian Brodie.

100 years, a longevity no doubt aided by the fact that when lying on the river bed it is very difficult to find. The Roman historian, Tacitus, clearly regarded the pearls of Britain as a noteworthy part of the 'wages of victory' although he wrote disparagingly of their quality describing their colour as 'brownish', a slur on stones which vary in colour from an iridescent pink to a silvery grey or a velvety cream.

It is difficult to believe that the pearls which were set in the breastplate presented by Julius Caesar to adorn the statue of his divine ancestress, Venus Genetrix, and which he was at pains to emphasise came from Britain, were no more colourful than merely 'brownish'. The Venerable Bede, writing in the eighth century, refers to the mussels as having 'excellent pearls of various colours', and, according to legend, they were considered fine enough to embellish the Crown of Saint Edward, the most precious of the Crown Jewels of England.

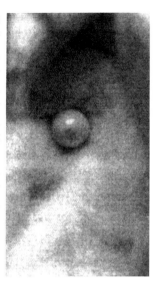

A pearl found in the river, photograph courtesy of W. R. Mitchell

By the reign of Queen Elizabeth I the County of Cumberland was renowned as much for its pearls as for its copper mines. Sir John Hawkins, the great Elizabethan seaman, secured from the Queen the monopoly of pearl-fishing in Cumberland, and, it would seem, made quite a useful profit from the enterprise, for in, 1586, William Camden, on his travels through Britain, records that the jewellers bought the pearls 'of the poor for a trifle' and sold them again 'at a very great price'. Mary, Queen of Scots, was proud to wear a necklace of 52 Cumberland pearls, a sure indication that they were regarded as more than mere baubles and were, indeed, highly valued.

Some idea of this value – and a certain pointer to the continuity of pearl fishing in the Ehen and Irt – is given in 1693 when the Company of Pearl Fishers was formally incorporated, with control firmly in the hands of the Governor, Thomas Patrickson of How Hall in Ennerdale who, we learn, set the 'poor inhabitants' to wade waist deep in the cold waters to search for the mussels, scores of which might have to be slit open before someone's icy thumb probing through the fleshy part would earn the reward of finding one of the precious pearls. Patrickson paid them a pittance for their efforts while he persuaded London jewellers to pay him £800 (about £150,000 in modern values) for the pearls he sold them.

It is strange that when Daniel Defoe toured this area a few years later and 'enquired much for the pearl fishery here... which has made a kind of bubble lately' he 'could discover no trace of it'; he reported that 'not even the fishermen could give us an account of any such thing.' One has to suspect that the canny natives were merely discouraging prying foreigners from meddling on their patch – just as a party of Japanese 'fishers' were put off in more recent times.

There seems to have been a decline in the fortunes of the Cumbrian pearl fishers from the mid-eighteenth century onwards. Nicolson and Burn, writing in the 1770s, commented only on the activities of Thomas Patrickson, while the 1829 Directory stated that no pearls had been gathered for many years. Indeed, the local adage 'Fair as an Irton Pearl', once a charming compliment, had acquired quite another meaning and was intended to suggest that the lady in question was not quite as unblemished as she appeared to be.

This fall from grace for the Cumbrian pearl was probably connected with the greater availability of the superior pearls from the Orient which came to dominate the fashionable market in these years. Whatever the virtues of even the finest Irton pearls they could not compete with those now flooding in from Britain's new Empire in the East.

It would appear, however, that the local folk continued to patrol the river beds from time to time and were occasionally lucky in their quest. But, as Eliza Lynn Linton noted in 1864, 'Poor people getting them... sell them to jewellers for pence what they sell again for pounds.' Before long fishing for pearls became a pastime for tourists. One Victorian enthusiast informs us that, 'A more agreeable pursuit of the manual order can scarcely be imagined, and it is, in point of fact, as pleasant as trout fishing, and infinitely more profitable.' And only half a century ago a Windermere lady wrote a letter to the magazine *Cumbria* describing how as a girl she used to don her bathing 'dress', wade into the waters of the Irt armed with a canvas bag and a pointed stick, and 'after long hunting went back to the bank to sit and open the shells with a tin opener.' On many days she drew a blank but soon 'grew wise about the type of spot where we were most likely to find pearls' and she clearly treasured the ring she had set 'with three of the pearls she found'.

It is encouraging to know that these rare Cumbrian pearl mussels are now protected by Statute and that the Environment Agency which is now responsible for them is undertaking a comprehensive study of the numbers and distribution of the species as part of a programme of conservation.

13

Admiral of the Red

The tall Anglian cross has stood in Irton churchyard for more than 1100 years. It is one of Cumbria's most important historical monuments, a place of pilgrimage, with its carved motifs recalling a generation's ambivalent transition from Paganism to Christianity. But few of the hundreds of visitors whose sense of history is touched by this lonely monument give more than a passing glance to an unremarkable memorial inside the church, erected in honour of an Admiral of the Royal Navy who served with Lord Nelson and whose home was less than a mile away at Holmrook Hall.

Skeffington Lutwidge was born in 1723 into a family of West Cumbrian merchants and shipowners based in Whitehaven who had in a single generation acquired wealth and influence enough to cross swords with the all-powerful Lowthers. Thomas and Walter Lutwidge moved from Ireland in the late seventeenth century and quickly established a thriving business in shipping and merchandise. Thomas became Whitehaven's principal tobacco merchant and Walter handled any commodity which would make a profit – he imported 1200 hogsheads (approximately 75,000 gallons) of wine each year, in addition to great quantities of brandy, rum and tobacco and plentiful cargoes of textiles, hats, timber, potatoes, shipping gear and armaments.

His agents were in almost every large port in Britain, Ireland, America and the Netherlands – even in Kendal where he monopolised the trade in snuff. At a time when Whitehaven was second only to London in the tonnage of English ships cleared each year, it is not surprising that their affairs prospered. The nature of this prosperity is evident from Walter's boast (he was never known for his modesty) that on his retirement in 1746 he was 'a man of opulence' with a fortune of £30,000 the equivalent in modern currency values of more than six million. He also weighed 19 stones.

The Lutwidges were anxious to achieve some social standing, but trade, and the money made from trade, were still regarded with some disdain by the landed gentry. But these were also expensive times for gentlemen. So it was a mutually beneficial union when Thomas married the daughter of Sir Henry Hoghton of Hoghton Hall whose wife, Mary, was the daughter of John Skeffington, Viscount Masserene. It was clear that Thomas had secured his position in society when in 1726 he was appointed High Sheriff of Cumberland, a prestigious post to which his brother Walter succeeded in 1748.

Thomas's sons continued to consolidate the family's wealth and status by business acumen, public service and the acquisition of landed property. Their country seat was Holmrook Hall, a fine Georgian mansion near the River Irt, beautifully designed and tastefully decorated in the style of Robert Adam. This estate in remote Cumberland held no appeal for Walter's grandson, Charles, who gladly sold it to his uncle, Skeffington Lutwidge.

A well-proven avenue to social advancement for those who had acquired wealth but had not inherited land or a coat of arms was to follow a career in the Army or the Navy. Skeffington Lutwidge chose the Navy, and in 1773 he was appointed to accompany Commander C. J. Phipps (later Lord Mulgrave) on an expedition to the Arctic in an attempt to discover the North-East Passage. Two bomb-vessels (ships carrying mortars) were commissioned for this enterprise, HMS *Racehorse* and HMS *Carcass*. The latter was commanded by Captain Lutwidge and had on board a young midshipman who, at the age of fourteen, had no right to be there at all, but young Horatio Nelson was not to be deterred by rules and regulations – even then.

In his *Sketch of my Life* he wrote:

Although no boys were allowed to go in the ships (as of no use) yet nothing could prevent me using every interest to go with Captain Lutwidge in the *Carcass* and as I fancied I was to fill a man's place, I begged I might be his coxswain; which, finding my ardent desire to go with him, Captain Lutwidge complied with, and has continued the strictest friendship to this moment. Lord Mulgrave, whom I then firstly knew, maintained his kindest friendship and regard until the last moment of his life.

In the course of this expedition Nelson was involved in a dramatic incident which was famously commemorated in a painting by Richard Westall. Captain Lutwidge wrote his own account of the event:

Holmrook Hall

'(Nelson had) a daring shipmate to whom he had become attached. One night during the mid-watch it was concerted between them that they should steal together from the ship and endeavour to obtain a bear's skin. The clearness of the nights in those high latitudes rendered the accomplishment of this object extremely difficult; they, however, seem to have taken advantage of the haze of an approaching fog and thus to have escaped unnoticed... It was not long, however, before the adventurers were missed by those on board, and as the fog had come on very thick the anxiety was very great. Between three and four in the morning the mist somewhat dispersed and the hunters were discovered at a considerable distance attacking a large bear. (Nelson had gone out on to the ice armed only with a rusty musket). The signal was instantly made for their return but it was in vain that Nelson's companion urged him to obey it. He was at this time divided by a chasm in the ice from his shaggy opponent: which probably saved his life: for the musket had flashed in the pan and their ammunition was expended. 'Never mind,' exclaimed Horatio, 'do but let me get a blow at this devil with the butt-end of my musket and we shall have him.' His companion, finding that entreaty was in vain, regained the ship...'

(Captain Lutwidge thereupon ordered the ship's guns to fire a blank charge and the startled animal slunk away. Nelson returned to his ship, where the Captain severely reprimanded him demanding to know what had been the purpose of his rash action).... Nelson, pouting his lip as was his wont when agitated, replied 'Sir I wished to kill the bear that I might carry its skin to my father.'

The whole expedition came to an end when at a latitude of 80° 48 northwest of Spitzbergen the two ships became trapped in the ice. Plans were made to abandon ship and to slide the boats across the ice to open water. Nelson exerted himself, as he put it, 'to have command of a four-oared cutter... which was given me with twelve men: and I prided myself in fancying I could navigate her better than any other boat in the ship.' Lutwidge clearly recognised the potential of his impulsive young midshipman but he must, even so, have been relieved when the expedition arrived back in port and the impetuous youngster was safely paid off. He could not then guess that his protégé was to be the victor of the Nile, Copenhagen and Trafalgar, and become the most famous naval hero in British history.

Lutwidge's own progress in his naval career was notable for steady achievement but without any of the maverick genius of Nelson. There is no biography of Lutwidge and the details of his record still lie virtually untouched in the archives of the National Maritime Museum and the Public Record Office. Admiralty records show that after the Arctic expedition he was appointed Captain of HMS *Triton* (26 guns), HMS *Perseverance* (36 guns) and HMS *Terrible* (74 guns), and in the 1790s he was promoted successively to the rank of Rear Admiral and Vice Admiral. On New Year's Day 1801 he became an Admiral of the Blue.

These were years of almost uninterrupted action by the Navy: the War of American Independence and the long wars against the French Revolution and Napoleon occupied more than 30 years between 1773 and 1815. Skeffington Lutwidge's part in naval operations in these years is still largely buried in the archives but he never achieved the eminence of Rodney, Hood, Duncan, Jervis and Nelson.

It is well known that as Commander of HMS *Terrible*, he participated in the action which led to the capture of Toulon and Corsica in 1793 – an operation which, but for the inertia of the politicians, could have had important effects on the course of the war against France. It seems probable that Lutwidge was not a natural naval tactician cast in the mould of Nelson or Hood but one of those reliable and efficient organisers and administrators who play so important a part in the successes of those

Above, High Borrowdale, photograph by J. Darrall and below, juniper at Silver Howe photograph by Ian Brodie.

Ann Macbeth: The Nativity, detail, in Patterdale Church,

courtesy of Angus Mitchell, photograph by Ben Stephenson

A columnar juniper, Loughrigg Fell, photograph by the author.

Above, Millican Dalton's cave, photograph by Ian Brodie and below, Fawcett Mill Bridge, photograph by the author.

Above Hollow Gill Bridge, and below, Sosgill Bridge, photographs by the author.

Rowantreethwaite Bridge, photograph by the author.

The Nine Standards, photograph courtesy of Val Corbett.

Aira Force, photograph by Val Corbett.

who gain all the glory.

It may well have been such abilities which led to his appointment as Flag-Officer the Nore (1798-99) and the Downs (1800-01) in the uncertain period following the mutinies at Spithead and the Nore. At the age of 64 these were his last official Active Service postings, although he was promoted to the rank of Admiral of the White shortly after Trafalgar and to Admiral of the Red in 1810, four years before he died.

Admirals of the Red, White and Blue were so named in accordance with the colour of their flags. The Blue commanded the van of the fleet in any engagement; the White commanded the rear; and the Red commanded the centre and was thus the Admiral in command of the Fleet and Senior Flag Officer of the Navy. All these ranks were abolished in the course of the nineteenth century.

Skeffington's steady progress in the naval hierarchy encouraged other members of the family to follow a career in the Services. His nephew, Harry, entered the Navy as his uncle's servant on HMS *Terrible* and subsequently saw action on many stations. Another nephew, Charles, served for some years as a Major in the Royal Lancashire Militia, became Collector of Customs for the Port of Hull and attained a kind of social cachet by having his portrait painted by John Hopper, painter to the Prince of Wales. A third nephew, Skeffington, made a successful career in the Madras Army and eventually became his uncle's heir to the family estates. It was this generation of Lutwidges who applied for and obtained a coat of arms bearing the motto *Pro Patria Amicis.* The Lutwidges had progressed in almost exactly one hundred years from immigrant Irish merchants to minor English landed gentry.

The Admiral's descendants remained prominent figures in the County of Cumberland for some years serving as High Sheriffs, Lieutenants, and JPs. It was, however, the Admiral's great-niece who brought the family name a much wider and very different fame. In 1827 Frances Jane Lutwidge married the Venerable Charles Dodgson and in 1832 gave birth to Charles Lutwidge Dodgson, better known to the world as Lewis Carroll, mathematical scholar and author of *Alice's Adventures in Wonderland.* One wonders what the Admiral of the Red would have made of the Lobster Quadrille, the Dormouse's Treacle Well and the Mad Hatter's Tea-party.

At least he may not have been displeased that his house at Holmrook was put to valuable use by the Navy during the Second World War; but he may well have felt justifiably indignant when in 1956 this fine building was summarily demolished and the Lutwidge link with Cumberland effectively came to an end.

14

The Immortal Yew

The earliest record of a yew tree is a fossil 140 million years old. The world's oldest wooden artifact is a yew spear found at Clacton and estimated to date from about 250,000 BC. A yew longbow found in the wetlands of the Somerset Levels belonged to a Briton who lived 5,000 years ago.

Perhaps more immediately impressive than these statistics is the simple fact that the yew tree is the oldest living thing on Earth: left to itself the yew is virtually immortal. Despite the ravages of Time and Man there are in Britain today well over a dozen yew trees estimated to be over 4,000 years old, and more than 50 others were here when the Romans arrived 2,000 years ago. Perhaps one of the most imaginative projects to emerge from the welter of schemes dreamt up to mark the 2000 millennium was the national 'Yew Trees for the Millennium' programme to encourage the planting of yew trees throughout the country to replace the innumerable yews destroyed, mainly by people, in the course of past centuries. Many thousands of yew seedlings have been planted; some of them could be venerable features of the countryside at the dawn of the Third Millennium.

Cumbria has an impressive number of these remarkable trees, and with the revival of interest in native tree species they have received more respect in recent years than has been their lot for nearly four hundred years. The yew is one of the truly native trees of Britain and, with the juniper and the Scots pine, is one of a select trio of native conifers. But the yew is unique, and not only on account of its extraordinary longevity.

A primary concern of any woodland tree is to maintain its territory and its access to light and water against competition. Almost all parts of the yew tree are poisonous – roots, bark, leaves and the seeds at the heart of the bright scarlet berries – only the fruit surrounding the seeds is not. The yew therefore has the means to inhibit the growth of other plants within its territory and to repel attacks by animals, insects and fungi. It ensures the successful dispersal of its seeds by making its fruit sweet-tasting, non-toxic and attractive to birds, which void the seeds well away from the parent tree. Daredevil humans may also eat the luscious fruit but if they fail to spit out the seed there is no antidote to the poison and death follows quickly. Some animals, such as deer, can survive a modest browsing on yew foliage but any temptation to gorge can easily have fatal results. The tree itself merely calls up dormant buds to repair the damage.

The yew tree's remarkable ability to renew itself largely accounts for its longevity and it is demonstrated in a variety of ways. Perhaps the most obvious is the process known as 'aerial rooting' whereby the parent tree puts out low, hanging branches which slowly grow towards the ground where they eventually take root. A single tree can, in the course of a few centuries, create a circle of new trees. Cumbria has one of the most curious examples of this: at Armathwaite Hall, near the foot of Bassenthwaite Lake, a 2,000 year-old yew is encircled by a clipped yew hedge which has, in fact, been created from the 'grounded' branches of a massive parent tree, a notable if somewhat bizarre piece of horticultural architecture. Other forms of yew tree artistry may be seen in the fine yew hedges at Muncaster Castle, Holker Hall and Acorn Bank, and, pre-eminently, in the world famous topiary at Levens Hall.

The main trunk of old yew trees is often hollow and this can give the impression that the tree is dying. Yew trees do not give up so easily. 'Aerial rooting' often occurs within the hollow trunk and there are many examples of these 'new' trees growing inside the parent tree. A 4,000 year-old yew at Linton in Herefordshire has a 'new' tree within its hollow trunk which is itself seven feet (around two metres) in circumference. At the Old Church Hotel on the shore of Ullswater a 1,500 year-old yew with a girth of 22 feet (6.7 metres) can offer shelter within its hollow for several people. Aerial rooting here has been prevented by vandalism some years ago.

Ancient yew trees, which have suffered damage and, to all appearances, appear to be dead or dying, are almost certainly neither. If left undisturbed most yew trees will, in time, sprout new shoots and even grow a new casing over the 'dead' wood: the process may be slow but where a yew is concerned we have to think in terms of centuries rather than decades. Occasionally, the damage can be catastrophic as clearly happened at Seathwaite in Borrowdale where one of Wordsworth's

The Armathwaite yew, photograph by Ben Stephenson.

'Fraternal four, joined in one solemn and capacious grove' was totally uprooted in a storm in 1883. Today it still lies shattered, bleached and decaying beside the three gnarled and venerable survivors. It is sad that through irresponsibility or ignorance campers still light fires inside the hollow trunk of the largest of these famous trees which have been growing here for at least 2,000 years – and, according to some authorities, for perhaps twice as long. Justifiably, they are the only trees in Lakeland to be honoured by name on the Ordnance Survey maps.

The great age of many yew trees and their apparent immortality gave them particular importance in pre-Christian religious beliefs. The Celts, the Saxons and the Norsemen planted yew trees on or near their burial mounds, and the yew featured prominently in the Celtic Spring and Autumn Festivals of Beltane and Samhain and also in the Mid-Winter Festival of all the peoples of Northern Europe: its evergreen foliage held the promise of eternal life and its red berries were powerful protection against evil spirits.

At the heart of the mythology of these people was Yggdrasil, the World Tree, the Tree of Life, the source of all Wisdom; this is usually described as an ash tree, but its Norse name is 'barraskr' meaning 'needle ash' and there are many references to its evergreen needles. But the ash does not have needles, evergreen or otherwise, – nor is the ash at all long-lived – so it is very probable that Yggdrasil was not an ash, but a yew. These traditions and beliefs led to the planting of innumerable yew trees throughout Britain. It is no accident that so many of our ancient yews are 1,000-2,000 years old.

The question is often asked: 'Why were yew trees planted in church-yards?' We should rather ask: 'Why were Christian churches built near yew trees?' Pope Gregory exhorted St Augustine 'not to destroy pagan temples but rather… sprinkle the old precincts with holy water and rededicate them, because people come more readily to the places where they have been accustomed to pray.' Yews were not planted in church-yards: churches were built on sites already made sacred by an earlier religious tradition.

It is still widely believed that the yew trees in our churchyards were planted there as a protected source of the yew wood required to make the longbow which was the dominant weapon in medieval warfare from the time of Edward I through the Hundred Years' War and well into the Tudor period – 139 yew longbows were recovered from Henry VlII's flagship, Mary Rose, when she was raised in 1982. But there was never any truth in the story; in fact, church yews were exempt from the axe, and the author of the most important book on archery commented 'Is it not absurd to suppose that men would plant within these contracted bounds, a single tree of such slow growth that in the space of a century its height and substance are scarcely sufficient to supply half a dozen bow staves?' It was not churchyard yews which were plundered to meet the demand for yew wood for longbows but the yew trees of England's medieval forests. So great was the destruction that by the fifteenth century there was an acute shortage and yew bows had to be imported from Europe.

One of Cumbria's most venerable churchyard yews stands in the heart of what is still a remote and tranquil Lakeland dale. Martindale Chapel has been the site of a Christian church for at least 700 years, but its yew tree was there long before the Christian missionaries arrived, for its age is estimated to be well over 2,000 years and it may mark a site sacred to a Celtic tribe. Other fine church yews in Cumbria may be seen at Muncaster, Greystoke, and Morland, all about 1,000 years old, while Witherslack, Kirkoswald, Patterdale, Kentmere and Lanercost Priory have impressive yews planted in the thirteenth century. The 1,500 year-old yew at Old Church by Ullswater lost its church long ago.

Another of Cumbria's famous yew trees also has an historical link with religious faith; this is the High Lorton yew, 'the pride of Lorton Vale', immortalised by Wordsworth's poem but first recorded in 1652 when George Fox came here to use the tree as his pulpit to bring the message of Quakerism to a large gathering of dalesfolk. Wordsworth considered this tree to be 'too magnificent to be destroyed', but destroyed it almost was when in 1865 it was sold for £15 to a cabinet maker but 'a gentleman from Cockermouth' saved it from the axe at the last moment. It seems probable that a great storm in 1885 inflicted severe damage for in 1898 Edmund Bogg found it to be 'only a wreck of its former glory'. The mayors of Cockermouth take great pride in a splendid mayoral chair made from the fallen timber. Whatever its state a century ago, the Lorton yew is healthy enough today with a girth of over seventeen feet (5.2 metres) and over 1,200 years of history behind it.

Yew trees are most frequently referred to in the context of a single tree; but, except for church yews, these are mainly the isolated survivors

The Lorton yew, photograph by Ann Jones.

from the forests of yew trees which were a feature of the English landscape before the extravagant demands of medieval warfare brought about their virtual destruction. Remnants of these forests remain in small groves scattered about the countryside, mainly in the southern chalkland counties, but also in the limestone areas of southern Cumbria, as may be seen on Arnside Knott, Haverthwaite Heights and Whitbarrow; and Norman Nicholson reminded us that 'there is a wood of them near Beetham, dark and Gothic, like a crypt with red pillars and blue-green fan-vaulting.'

The groups of yew trees by Derwentwater described by Wordsworth have vanished, but the poet himself planted a number at various places in Lakeland. He was not alone in his enthusiasm, for his contemporary, the farmer at High Yewdale near Coniston, must take the credit for the fine array of fifteen yew trees there, each commemorating the birth of one of his children.

Modem science has recently begun to restore the yew tree to its former status as the Tree of Life. Just a few years ago two important anti-cancer drugs were derived from this tree: taxol, produced from the bark of the Pacific yew, has had proven success in the treatment of ovarian cancer and, perhaps more promising, because the process is less damaging to the trees, the drug baccatin has been extracted from the needles of the European yew. Work is now in progress to carry forward these exciting developments in the long fight against cancer.

The Conservation Foundation and its campaign 'Yew Trees for the Millennium' has set in train a project which will, in time, restore to the English landscape a prospect not seen for some 600 years – groves and woodlands of yew and distinctive single trees, many of which will be admired and appreciated by those who celebrate the Third Millennium. Cuttings from the yew trees in Martindale, Lorton and Borrowdale are now tiny saplings, which may even outlive the human race itself.

15

Millican Dalton, Professor of Adventure

Long before our modern universities began to award degrees in such bizarre subjects as beauty therapy, automotive retail management and golf, the Lake District had acquired its own eccentric professorship. In the 1920s and 30s, Millican Dalton, self-styled 'Professor of Adventure, Camping Holidays, Mountain Rapid Shooting, Rafting and Hair-Breadth Escapes', established his 'study' (and his residence) not in the plate-glass comfort of twenty-first century university architecture but in a cave on Castle Crag in Borrowdale. His teaching was essentially pragmatic and not overly concerned with rules and theories; but he imparted his own enthusiasm for and knowledge of the mountains and the countryside to all those whom he escorted on expeditions not only into the Lakeland fells but also into the mountains of Scotland and Switzerland. His methods may have been unorthodox and his skills somewhat empirical – hence, no doubt, his promise of 'hair-breadth escapes' – but he introduced many a 'student' to the joys of adventure in the hills and on the crags.

Those who accompanied Dalton on his excursions were sure to become involved in companionable discussion of some of his highly individual, even idiosyncratic, views on life, current events and politics. He was a keen disciple of the 'subversive' writings of Bernard Shaw and an avid reader of the left-wing *Daily Herald* newspaper, a convinced socialist and pacifist, a vegetarian and a teetotaller. And in a society rapidly adopting uniformity and materialism as its totems, Dalton believed passionately in the pleasures and satisfactions of the simple life, in self-sufficiency and individual inventiveness, and in a respect for nature and the environment.

Millican Dalton was born in April 1867 in the isolated mining hamlet of Nenthead on the north-eastern Pennine fringe of Cumberland. His mother's family came from nearby Alston and it was from her that he acquired his unusual first name. Little is known of his childhood other than that he spent some time at the Friends School in Wigton before the family moved south to a house on the edge of Epping Forest. As soon as he left school, presumably at the leaving age of thirteen, Millican was set to work in an insurance office, an employment he obviously found totally uncongenial, for soon afterwards he built himself a hut in the forest where he began to design, make and sell lightweight camping tents and equipment. He supplemented the modest income this brought him by organising and conducting his first touring parties into the mountains.

Like so many before and since he fell under the spell of the Lakeland fells and he was, no doubt, overjoyed when he was offered employment as secretary to the Holiday Fellowship organisation in the Newlands Valley, a post he managed to persevere with for no more than a few seasons.

For a while Dalton lived in a tent at High Lodore in Borrowdale but as he approached his fortieth birthday he sought out a more comfortable abode. This he discovered in the cave on Castle Crag which now bears his name, a place now visited by scores of walkers each year, curious to see where this extraordinary fellow had his abode, and to decide quite firmly that it would not do for them.

Partly obscured now by the growth of woodland, the view from the 'terrace' in front of the cave included a splendid vista along Derwentwater and a fine prospect of the Bowderstone Pinnacle over on the far side of the valley. Inside the cave is a spacious and unexpectedly dry area which Dalton used as his 'living-room' and bedroom, an upper level 'attic' for the use of guests, and a wide entrance space for cooking and other domestic activities. The surrounding woods provided a plentiful supply of fuel and a source of never-failing clear spring-water dripped through a crack in the cave roof. Heather and bracken were readily available for bedding – although on chilly nights (most nights one imagines...) he would have been glad of the down quilt or the Scotch plaid which always accompanied him in cold weather on expeditions to the fells or to the shops in Keswick.

Not that Millican contributed greatly to the tills of the Keswick shopkeepers. His vegetarian needs were simple enough, and he baked his own bread and grew his own potatoes on the broad 'terrace' in front of his cave. It is said that his household implements and his kitchen hardware were mostly fabricated from the booty selectively pillaged from raids on a tip at nearby Grange. Nor did the 'gentlemens outfitters' see

Millican Dalton, image courtesy of
The Dalesman.

much of this unkempt, fiercely mustachioed and bearded figure in his home-made and well-patched clothes, trousers rolled up, socks rolled down, and a jaunty feather stuck defiantly in his broad-rimmed hat. If any shops greeted his arrival with commercial enthusiasm it would have been the coffee merchant and the tobacconist: for our thrifty ascetic had an unwavering addiction to strong, black coffee and to cheap Woodbine cigarettes. (To mark the occasion of his 50th ascent of Great Gable's formidable Napes Needle he lit a fire on the undeniably limited area of the summit rock, brewed a billycan of coffee and smoked, happily at peace with the world).

It was not only his distinctive appearance which made Dalton so well-known in Keswick and Borrowdale. He sported an unmistakable blue bicycle to convey himself and his goods. Even more eye-catching was his water transport: this was a remarkable raft constructed from odd pieces of timber, an assortment of sticks, a paddle for a rudder, drums and cans for buoyancy, and a tattered piece of cloth for a sail. A makeshift name-plate attached to the prow announced that this ship had been baptised the Rogue Herries, (Hugh Walpole's novel had been published in 1930). The sight of this unlikely craft on the Derwent, navigated by its equally improbable captain, must have caused many a visitor to Borrowdale to rub his eyes in disbelief.

So, indeed, must any casual walkers have done if they had been passing by on the path just below the cave on the day when Millican acted as best man for a wedding in the dale. The party were invited to the Castle Crag venue for the wedding breakfast, all no doubt arrayed in their best suits and dresses, to be welcomed by Millican in nailed boots and climbing gear (but unusually smart in a pair of neatly pulled-up knee-length stockings). As the rock-seated guests tucked into their chicken, cooked to a succulent turn in the best man's recycled kitchen-ware, this must have become a memorable and lively happening, the most extraordinary wedding reception ever held in Borrowdale – or anywhere else.

We have no details of other items on the menu on this occasion but we are given a hint, from another of Millican's 'parties', that he could concoct inventive and somewhat unorthodox recipes. One moonlit night he cajoled three holiday-makers camping near his cave to accompany him on a midnight adventure to Derwentwater. He took them in a boat to the lake, where they landed on an island, kindled a fire and watched their host heat up, in a suitable can, a 'porridge' of chocolate, oatcake and water – a recipe the writers of cookery books seem to be unaware of. It is not recorded how this delicacy was eaten – or appreciated. Such a spontaneous act of lighthearted adventure, as this nocturnal expedition seems to have been, suggests that Dalton was not entirely the austere recluse his rather spartan lifestyle might lead one to believe. On the contrary, he positively promoted the virtues of companionship, hospitality and conversation. Although he held independent views on many topics, he was a man of wide knowledge and shrewd intelligence.

Unlike so many others who have, for shorter or longer periods of time, lived the life of a hermit, Millican Dalton did not feel impelled to write about his experiences or to spell out his philosophy of life. He was not in any way a proselytising evangelist; he was his own man, steadfast in his views but concerned neither with the approval or disapproval of others. The only words of 'advice' offered to the world are carved on the wall of his cave – and these, it is believed, were inscribed not by Dalton himself but by a Scottish friend whose rolling 'r's Dalton had found amusing, although the ambiguity of their meaning might well have had its origin in his inventive mind:

'Don't! Waste Words Jump to Conclusions'

Millican Dalton died in Amersham hospital in 1947 at the age of 80. In his obituary a close friend paid tribute and summarised his life as follows:

'He was respected by all who knew him. A man of simple pleasures and tastes… a mind at peace with the world… After a day on the hills with him, or just pottering about, one had a feeling of contented happiness and peace of mind'.

16

Tales from Small Islands

Thomas West published his *Guide to the Lakes* in 1778 and set the fashion for 'scenic tourism' which has flourished ever since. This is perhaps not surprising in an area so widely renowned for its natural beauty: what is surprising is that while so many viewpoints have had their moments of artistic or literary glory, the islands in the lakes have been largely neglected. Yet Thomas West himself chose Belle Isle for two of his 'stations' on Windermere 'where you will see all that is charming on the lake or magnificent and sublime in the environs, in a new point of view'; and for the fourth of his 'stations' on Coniston Water (there being no suitable island available) he advised his readers to row to a point in 'the centre of the lake opposite to Coniston Hall' for 'one of the finest views on the lake'.

Perhaps islands hold a greater fascination for children than for grown-ups, for it is in modern children's literature that the Lake District islands come into their own. St Herbert's Island in Derwentwater became Beatrix Potter's Owl Island in *Squirrel Nutkin*; Marjorie Lloyd in *Fell Farm Campers*, gives a wonderful description of Tarn Hows Island where Jan and Hyacinth were marooned; Arthur Ransome combined features of Windermere's Blake Holme Island and Coniston's Peel Island for the adventures of the *Swallows and Amazons* on Wild Cat Island.

The long sweep of Windermere is dotted with more than twenty islands, the largest, Belle Isle, has a shoreline one and a half miles long; the smallest are little more than rocky crags protruding above the surface of the lake – Chicken Rock, Curlew Crag, Hen Holme, Hen Rock and Seamew Crag, and, of course, Silverholme, or Cormorant Island to the Swallows and Amazons.

Belle Isle has had several changes of name over the years. In the Middle Ages when the de Lindeseys and the de Courcys had their manor houses here it was known simply as The Holme – the island – but in the seventeenth century when the Philipsons were besieged there by Colonel Briggs and his Parliamentary troops it was called Longholm. Fifty years later Celia Fiennes wrote that 'very good barley and oats' grew on the island, and in 1772 William Gilpin declared that he could not easily conceive of 'a more sequestered spot... excluded from the noise and interruption of life.'

Soon after this the island acquired its most renowned feature, the first circular house in the country, set in elaborate formal gardens. The Mr English whose creation this was became the object of universal condemnation; William Gilpin commented that 'the proprietor [has] spent six thousand pounds upon it; with which sum he has contrived to do almost every thing that one would wish had been left undone'; while William Gell fumed that the house 'wants only a little green paint and a label of Souchong or fine Hyson to make it exactly like a large shop tea canister.' Dorothy Wordsworth exclaimed, 'And that great house! Mercy upon us! If it could be concealed, it would be well for all...' Today, of course, it is much admired.

In 1781 the island was purchased by the wealthy landowner and industrialist, John Curwen who renamed it Belle Isle in honour of his wife, Isabella.

A little to the west of Belle Isle lie three small islands, the largest named rather prosaically after the Thompson family who lived 600 years ago at Undermillbeck; the two tiny ones bear the charming name Lilies of the Valley and appear in Book II of Wordsworth's *Prelude*.

North of Belle Isle is an island called Lady Holme but for many centuries known as St Mary's Holme named, as medieval records tell us, from 'our ladie chappel of Tholme'. A few roughly cut steps in the rock may be a relic of this former shrine but otherwise no trace is now to be found.

To the south, among a scattering of tiny rock-islands, are Crow Holme, a stone's throw from the ferry, and presumably a haunt of crows; and Ramp Holme, known throughout the Middle Ages and until the late eighteenth century as Roger Holm – possibly after a thirteenth century Roger the Marshal. For a brief period it then took the name of Berkshire Island when it came into the possession of the Earl of Suffolk and Berkshire, but in 1793 it had already acquired its present name.

Coniston Water has two notable islands: Fir Island with its fine group of pine trees; and Peel Island, with its little 'harbour' made famous by the adventures of the Swallows and Amazons. Peel Island also appears in W. G. Collingwood's novel of Viking times, *Thorstein of the Mere,* when Thorstein and Raineach find refuge there from their pursuing enemies. From the craggy knolls of this idyllic island Arthur Ransome took a sprig of heather on his assignment to Russia to remind him of the happy picnics he had enjoyed there with the Collingwood family.

Picnics also feature prominently in the story of the island in the middle of Grasmere. Dorothy Wordsworth refers on a number of occasions to their visits to the island, taking a kettle to boil water from the lake and cooking the pike and bass they caught from a rowing boat. On one of these outings they were accompanied by Samuel Coleridge who wrote a glowing account of the experience, joyfully recalling how the 'kettle swung over the fire hanging from the branch of a fir tree' and the 'glorious bonfire on the margin' round which they all danced, 'ruddy laughing faces in the twilight'. The contemporary print of the island, by William Westall, now in Rydal Mount, shows that in Wordsworth's day there were more trees and many more sheep and that the stone building, a familiar sight today, was there also. Indeed, Wordsworth inscribed a superior form of graffito on its wall with his lines 'Written with a Pencil upon a Stone in the Wall of the House on the Island of Grasmere' which begin:

> 'Thou see'st a homely Pile, yet to these walls
> The heifer comes in the snow-storm, and here
> The new-dropped lamb finds shelter from the wind.'

Derwentwater has four main islands, a number of tiny islets, two named, significantly, after the otter; and an elusive island which makes brief and irregular appearances.

Derwent Island, the largest of all, has a varied and somewhat melodramatic history. In the earliest records it is known as Hestholme (stallion island) but when, in the twelfth century, it became a property of Fountains Abbey it was assigned to the Vicar of Crosthwaite and became Vicar's Island. It passed to the Crown at the Dissolution in 1539 but was quickly disposed of and by 1569, when Queen Elizabeth was anxious to exploit the rich copper deposits of the Newlands Valley, it had been acquired by the Company of Mines Royal to accommodate Headquarters Staff and their families. The 'wilderness of trees' was cleared, a brewhouse, a bakehouse, a dovecote, a pigsty and a windmill were built, gardens were created and 300 fruit trees planted. It is also possible that the

Belle Isle and the Round House, T. Allom, image courtesy of Cumbria Library Service.

low wall which still encircles the shoreline may have been constructed at this time – the German miners were not universally welcomed by the native population.

There were several changes of ownership following the collapse of the mining venture until in 1778 the island came into the hands of Joseph Pocklington, a wealthy banker from Nottingham, who made up in eccentric enterprise for his remarkable lack of taste. Vicar's Island soon became Pocklington's Island; a Palladian mansion was built to Pocklington's own strange design; this was followed by a boathouse built to resemble a chapel, a mock church complete with a bell-tower and furnished to serve as a dining room, a sham fort sporting real cannon fired to create thunderous echoes from the surrounding fells, and a 'Druid's Circle' modelled on Castlerigg Stone Circle. It was Pocklington who introduced to Derwentwater the annual event of the Keswick Regatta which involved an attack on 'Fort Joseph' by numerous rowing boats. Musket fire and the roar of cannon, the shouts of 'battle' and the cheers of the crowds who came to watch brought to the island all the noisy clamour of the circus.

Normality was restored in 1797 when Pocklington sold his island to General William Peachey who quickly, as Wordsworth put it, 'ridded the spot of its puerilities', demolishing the follies except the mock church which became a genuine boathouse and still survives.

In 1843 Derwent Island, as it now became, was bought by the Marshalls, Leeds textile manufacturers who were rapidly establishing an extensive landed estate in the Lake District. They employed the architect, Anthony Salvin, to redesign Pocklington's house to create an elegant Italianate mansion, with landscaped gardens, lawns, terraced walks, and fine shrubs and trees. In 1951 the Marshalls gave Derwent Island to the National Trust and on rare occasions each summer the house and island are open to the public.

The Marshall family also donated to the Trust the island known as Lord's Island. In 1539 John Leland had described the manor house on this island as 'the head place of the Radcliffes' who became the Earls of Derwentwater and achieved the dubious fame of execution for treason for their part in the Jacobite rebellions of 1715 and 1745. Few traces now remain of their house but a twentieth century archaeological survey revealed a number of features which suggest that the original house may have been built in the fifteenth century with later extensions. Also found was a trench 76 metres long marked on the O.S. map as 'The Butts' on the assumption that it was used for archery.

The history of St Herbert's Island goes back to the seventh century when we learn from Bede's *History* that 'There was a priest of praise-worthy life named Herebert… who lived the life of a hermit on an island in the great lake which is the source of the river Derwent.' Herbert was a close friend of St Cuthbert and the two visited each other in their respective cells on Lindisfarne and on Derwentwater. The slight remains of a small building on the island are not those of St Herbert's cell but of a chapel built probably soon after 1374 when an annual pilgrimage was inaugurated to commemorate the Saint on 13 April, the date of his death in 687AD.

Rampsholme Island has no significant history. It is thought that Fountains Abbey may have had an iron-smelting furnace or bloomery here but otherwise it seems to have been largely undisturbed.

Three of the lakes have witnessed the unusual phenomenon known as a floating island. Those on Coniston Water and Esthwaite Water have long ceased to 'float' and have attracted little attention. These were smaller but much more substantial than the one on Derwentwater. Both Coleridge and Wordsworth observed the Esthwaite island and agreed that it had trees growing on it, a fact confirmed by Jonathan Otley some years later when he identified them as 'alder and willow of considerable size', adding that the island was 24 yards long and five or six yards wide. By the 1880s it had become stranded, blown by a gale on to the bank of Priest Pot, and despite the efforts of the 'old natives of Hawkshead' to pull it free with ropes, there it has remained.

Little is known of Coniston's floating island but in 1864 the observant Eliza Lynn Linton saw the spot where it 'got stranded among the reeds at Nibthwaite during a high wind and heavy flood, and has never been able to get off again.'

Derwentwater's floating island is rather different. This does not move about the lake; it just appears and disappears at irregular intervals in roughly the same spot – about 100 metres from the shore north of the point where Watendlath Beck enters the lake and almost opposite Cat Gill. It rises from the bed of the lake, in July or August, usually (but not always) after a period of warm, sunny weather. It made more than twenty appearances in the nineteenth century and became an object of fascination alike for tourists and serious scientists. Baddeley's famous Guide of 1886 wrote it off as 'hardly worth mentioning', but scientists of the calibre of John Dalton, William Russell and G. J. Symonds carried out detailed studies of the botany, geology, chemistry and structure of the island.

All came to similar conclusions: the island consisted mainly of peat moss with various aquatic plants such as quill wort and water lobelia. This vegetation normally rested on the soft clay bed of the lake but as the vegetable matter decayed it created quantities of marsh gas which became rarefied in hot weather and caused the mass (greatly variable in size) to rise to the surface. As Harriet Martineau commented this phenomenon acquired 'more celebrity than it deserves'.

Symonds' study appeared just in time for, as the scientists predicted, the island now appears much less frequently. In the 1930s so uncertain did its status and its future seem that a party of Keswick Girl Guides, perhaps suspecting that even the sovereignty of the elusive island might be in doubt, landed on its soggy surface, planted a flag and claimed it for England.

In the hot August days of the summer of 2003 this transitory part of the Queen's realm made a brief re-appearance but was largely unnoticed, its moment of fame long departed.

The small, beautiful lake of Rydal Water has two islands. Little Isle and Heron Island. The former was referred to by Coleridge as 'Rocky Island… like the fragment of some huge bridge, now overgrown with moss and trees.' Heron Island seems to have acquired its name in the early nineteenth century following the arrival of a heronry which Parsons and Whites *Directory* of 1829 refers to as 'recently established': the Wordsworths do not use this name but a little later Christopher North described a heron 'perched upon a tree near its home or fishing in the shallows of its island home.' As with most of the heronries in Lakeland this one disappeared in modem times and Heron Island is now the haunt of wild ducks and a flock of Canada geese.

Ullswater has four tiny islands: Norfolk Island, formerly known as Householme probably in reference to the nearby manor house of Glencoyne acquired by a Duke of Norfolk in the eighteenth century; Lingy Holm, a tiny heather-clad islet; Wall Holm, so-called, according to Nicolson and Burn, 'from its having been anciently walled about'; and Cherry Holm, again according to Nicolson and Bum, 'so-called from a cherry tree anciently growing there'. If only all Lakeland place-names were so easily explained…

Thirlmere lost its only island when the reservoir was created. (The present islands of Deergarth How and Hawes How were formerly outcrops beyond the shoreline of the original lake). Near the eastern edge of the northern reach, then known as Leathes Water, was the small island of Box Holme, notable only for its name: the Box Tree is rarely found in the north with very few specimens in Cumbria (except at Levens Hall). It seems probable that these originated as plantings, mainly for decorative purposes, and Box Holme may have acquired its trees through the horticultural aspirations of the Jackson family of Armboth House, on the opposite shore, who owned the Thirlmere Estate.

Wordsworth did not have a high opinion of most of the islands: they were 'not so beautiful as might be expected' nor was their shape or situation especially 'pleasing'. He also regretted that they were 'not ornamented (as are several of the lakes in Scotland and Ireland) by the remains of castles… or religious edifices.' He saw little to praise in the islands of Derwentwater but his opinions may well have been influenced by the activities of Joseph Pocklington and by the felling of ancient oaks on St Herbert's Island and their replacement by conifers. The 'beautiful cluster' of islands on 'Winandermere' earned his approval as did 'a pair pleasingly contrasted upon Rydal; nor must the solitary green island of Grasmere be forgotten.'

Wordsworth was unlikely to 'forget' this island for it was here that he and Dorothy and Coleridge spent many hours of light-hearted relaxation. Equipped with simple fishing gear, a supply of food and basic cooking utensils, they rowed out to the island to enjoy the newly fashionable pastime, popular on the Continent and known by the French as a 'pique-nique'.

17

Kendal Brown:
'A Gracious and Sociable Custom'

On his return from his voyages to the Indies Christopher Columbus reported to his patron, Queen Isabella of Castile, that the people there had a strange custom of sniffing a powder ground from the leaves of a plant they called 'tabaco'. Thus did Europe learn to take snuff. Within a few years the custom had spread to almost all the Royal and aristocratic courts, and within a century, to most other levels of society too. Snuff was widely believed to be a remedy against many ills including the plague which so often afflicted every country in Europe in the sixteenth and seventeenth centuries. Be that as it may, by the early 1700s snuff-taking had become a mark of civilised society and in 1724 Jonathan Swift claimed that in Britain 'the makers of snuff employ by far the greatest number of hands of any manufacture in the kingdom.'

The Lake District counties were well placed to take advantage of this new industry: Whitehaven and Maryport were two of the main ports for the import of tobacco leaf from Maryland and Virginia and the fast-flowing rivers of Westmorland had already proved to be eminently suited to dozens of successful watermills. Between 1740 and the mid-nineteenth century snuff mills were established at Eamont Bridge, at Penrith and at Pooley Bridge by the foot of Ullswater, but Kendal became the undisputed centre of snuff manufacture in the north with mills at Natland Beck (1740), Mealbank (1792), Low Mills (1805), Helsington (1851) and Aynam (1867).

Snuff is still manufactured in Kendal supplying a surprisingly large home market and also exporting to most parts of the world. Among the many varieties of snuff produced are those for which Kendal became famous in the heyday of snuff-taking – the rich, dark 'Kendal Brown', the medicinal 'Camphorated Menthol' and the popular 'Dr Rumney', first prescribed by the eponymous physician for his patients at Brough and launched as a commercial enterprise by his grandson who established Illingworth's snuff mill at Aynam in Kendal.

This was gutted by fire in 1983 but the two branches of the family of Samuel Gawith continued the 200 years old tradition of snuff manufacture in Kendal: Samuel Gawith & Company founded in 1792 and Gawith, Hoggarth & Company founded in 1807 (after the brothers Gawith had parted following 'a difference of opinion'). This partnership was renewed in 2015 and the snuff-making operation in Kendal is now based at Mint Bridge.

The Gawith mill at Helsington is of particular interest in the story of snuff grinding. This was the last water-powered snuff mill in Britain and survived until 1st March 1991 when Alan Powley, miller there for 51 years, brought his water wheel to a final halt. This ended not only the long history of water-mill snuff-grinding in Kendal but it also wrote the last sentence in a story which began before the Norman Conquest.

The first reference to a mill at Helsington appears in a Charter of 1297 when the Manor and its mill were granted to Marmaduke de Thweng, later Baron Thweng, a prominent figure in King Edward I's wars against the Scots. We may safely assume that a cornmill had stood here long before this, possibly as early as the tenth century, and a cornmill it remained until the eighteenth century when, in common with so many other mills it was converted to the manufacture of the products of the industrial revolution. For a while Helsington's water-powered machinery was used to polish Italian marble and the fossil-rich limestone quarried on Kendal Fell. From the mid-nineteenth century until its closure 140 years later its water wheel, itself a piece of fine craftsmanship and engineering housed in a narrow mill-race, ground the fine, velvety snuff which made Kendal snuff so famous and which no modern machinery has yet matched.

Tobacco leaf, at first from North America and more recently from Zimbabwe and Malawi, was carefully dried in special drying kilns and then ground in three pestle and mortar devices rotating with awe-inspiring force. The coarse powder was then placed in grinding barrels charged with steel ball-bearings to produce a velvety powder which was transferred to noisy vibrating sieves to be separated into fine, medium and coarse mixtures, with a rough residue returned to be ground again.

A skilfully controlled addition of various salts and sodas was the next part of the process and this served to enhance the flavour and to sweeten the mixture before further fine sieving prepared the powder for the final

Snuff making in the Gawith Mill at Helsingham, image courtesy of the Westmorland Gazette.

delicate operation – the selection and sprinkling of the aromatic essences and oils to produce the wide range of snuffs from which the connoisseur makes his choice. From his Aladdin's cave of bottled fragrances the miller conjured up fine snuffs redolent of bergamot, citrus, camphor, menthol, eucalyptus, sandalwood and attar of roses. In Helsington mill, beguiled by the aromas of so many sweet-smelling snuffs, it was quite possible to concur with Samuel Taylor Coleridge who declared that snuff was, perhaps, 'the final cause of the human nose'.

Although there are no known health or moral hazards associated with the sniffing of snuff there were those who looked upon the habit as a form of corrupting vice, such as one would expect to find in the dubious sensual depravities popularly associated with the Court of the Sultan of the Ottoman Empire. The colourful sign of a Turk which adorns the Lowther Street offices of Gawith, Hoggarth and Company in Kendal reflects the whiff of luxury and self-indulgence which accompanies the social history of snuff. This is deeply ironical since in the Islamic world the taking of snuff was regarded as a perversion and a crime punishable by execution!

By contrast, in western Europe the custom had developed among the gentry of exchanging snuff boxes finely crafted in gold, silver, enamel and jewels as a social courtesy and as a mark of respect and friendship. At the ball described by Dickens in the early pages of *The Pickwick Papers* 'Colonel Bulder and Sir Thomas Clubber exchanged snuff boxes while in Walter Scott's *Heart of Midlothian* a reference is made to the Scottish 'mull' or elaborately decorated snuff-box which formed the centre-piece of the table at dinner parties. Indeed, Dr Samuel Johnson considered the taking of snuff to be 'a gracious and sociable custom' infinitely to be preferred to the smoking of tobacco which he described as a shocking habit – 'blowing smoke out of our mouths into other people's mouths, eyes and noses' – and in 1773 he pronounced that 'smoking has gone out'.

So long as smoking remained out of fashion the snuff industry flourished and for about 100 years the snuff mills of Kendal prospered unchallenged by a rival tobacco industry. The almost uninterrupted succession of military campaigns in far-flung corners of Victoria's vast British Empire, where regiments lived for long periods in isolation and boredom or in nervous tension, created just the conditions for the return of smoking and by the end of the century the cigarette case was rapidly replacing the snuffbox as a necessary part of a gentleman's social effects and Oscar Wilde could confidently proclaim that, 'A cigarette is the perfect type of the perfect pleasure.'

This turn in the whimsical wheel of fashion plunged the snuff industry into a steady decline which two world wars only helped to accelerate. Yet there is, even today, a viable market with some half million customers in Britain and many more overseas. It was inevitable, however, that economic pressures and changes in technology should, sooner or later, cast a shadow over Helsington's water-driven operation and, like the Roman fort in the meadows on the opposite bank of the nearby River Kent, the ancient snuff-grinding watermill is now silent, a thousand years of service at an end.

18

Ill Met by Moonlight: The Kaber Rigg Plot

At 10pm on the night of 12 October 1663, a small group of armed men converged on Smardale Bridge, a remote spot hidden in a lonely gill a few miles south-west of Kirkby Stephen. Shortly afterwards, others emerged stealthily from the darkness, whispered the password 'God be with us' and soon a party of ten or a dozen was assembled. This was the somewhat theatrical beginning of a rebellion which was planned to strike such fear into the newly-restored monarchy of Charles Stuart that it would agree to the conspirators' demands for fundamental changes in government policies involving a return to Cromwellian ideals.

Between Smardale Bridge and Whitehall the Westmorland rebels would be joined by volunteer militiamen from Kendal, Durham and Yorkshire, and by a growing army of spontaneous sympathisers on the way. Carlisle and Appleby Castles would be immediately seized and Durham and the port of Hull would follow; a large Yorkshire contingent was waiting for the Westmorland force to join it; 'Parliamentary' aristocrats would give their support; the southern counties were ready to rise; wholesale desertions from all ranks of the army were confidently foreseen.

Such confident optimism proved to be totally unrealistic but all rebels must wear rose-coloured spectacles. The Restoration of the Stuarts in 1660 after eighteen years of violent political, constitutional, religious and social revolution may have seemed to many folk, especially in London, like a return to 'the old good days', but in the counties there was a bitter legacy of feuding between those who had 'won' and those who had 'lost', and there was a smouldering desire for revenge for past humiliations and present dispossessions. Plots, conspiracies and minor uprisings were numerous in the 1660s in many parts of the country; and in Westmorland, too, the knives were out, and the Kaber Rigg Plot was just one manifestation of the tensions which follow such an upheaval in the fabric of society.

The leader of the Westmorland rebels was Robert Atkinson who in 1663 lived at Blue Grass (now Dale Foot) in Mallerstang. He had been a Captain of Horse in Cromwell's Parliamentary Army and had been appointed Governor of Appleby Castle, with a reputation for hunting down and 'securing the King's friends'. In particular, he had harassed such influential Westmorland Royalists as Sir Philip Musgrave, Sir Daniel Fleming and Lady Anne Clifford – an animosity which was soon to cost him dearly.

Atkinson had attended 'secret' meetings held by the principal plotters in Yorkshire and had been persuaded to raise a posse of more than a hundred rebels in Westmorland, most of them from Kendal under the leadership of Captain French, another former officer of the Parliamentary Army. The Kendal contingent was to rendezvous with Atkinson's tiny force at a desolate spot known as Kaber Rigg, a few lonely miles west of Kirkby Stephen.

Moving off from Smardale Bridge Atkinson was met by a number of local gentry homeward bound from Kirkby Stephen who, on being told that Scotland, Cumberland and indeed 'all Englande' would be 'up in armes that night', agreed to join the enterprise, and Atkinson arrived at Kaber Rigg with a force of some 'thirty or above' armed followers.

Unfortunately, no-one else put in an appearance there. The Kendal force failed to arrive; and soon after midnight, at Duckintree under Kaber Rigg, Atkinson decided to dismiss his disconsolate little army. The Kaber Rigg Rebellion was over.

This sudden change of heart by Atkinson probably reflected his own more rational assessment of the futility of this naive enterprise. He already knew that government ministers were aware of the 'secret' meetings which had been taking place: Philip Musgrave, Daniel Fleming and Alan Bellingham, Lieutenants of Westmorland, had been informed of a 'fanatical design in hand of which the scene will first appear in the northern parts', and all suspects should be placed under surveillance. As a result Atkinson had been put under house arrest, but he had escaped and gone into hiding.

After the collapse of the plot Atkinson became a wanted man. He was eventually captured and imprisoned in Appleby Castle – where he had once been Governor and had hoped to be so again. Musgrave reported to the Secretary of State that 30 of 'the most suspicious persons

Appleby Castle in the eighteenth century, engraving by Thornton, image courtesy of Cumbria Library Service.

in Cumberland' had been secured: these included Quakers and non-conforming clergy who had been ejected from their livings as well as former Army Officers such as Captain French, 'a most dangerous pack of knaves' according to Musgrave who alleged that they were still hatching rebellion and planning to massacre the gentry of Westmorland. Atkinson had eluded his captors at Appleby and was preparing to turn King's evidence in return for a pardon. He was not, however, willing to give himself up to his Westmorland enemies but sought the protection of the Braithwaites of Burneside Hall (near Kendal) for safe escort to London.

This was achieved and Atkinson duly gave his evidence to the King's Ministers, and then, much to Musgrave's annoyance, he was allowed to return to Westmorland while the Braithwaites brought his pardon from London. This was done, according to Fleming with 'only the King and the Duke of Buckingham and his two real friends that went with him being privy thereto.'

The trials of those accused of complicity in the Kaber Rigg Plot opened at Appleby on 19 March 1664: three were found guilty and hanged. Musgrave's efforts to bring Atkinson to trial were frustrated by Sir Thomas Braithwaite who had been ordered to deliver him to London for further examination by the Lord Chancellor and the Lord Chief Justice who wished to extract evidence relating to several others involved in the conspiracy. In return for this information Atkinson was granted a provisional pardon before being sent to courts in York, Durham and Carlisle to provide evidence which would lead to the conviction of the eighteen men he had betrayed. Of these five were hanged, seven were acquitted, five escaped from prison, and the fate of the last is not known.

Musgrave eventually succeeded in bringing Atkinson to trial in August 1664 and, inevitably, he was found guilty and sentenced to death, his provisional pardon remaining unconfirmed. On 31 August this confirmation was signed and despatched from London to the High Sheriff at Durham instead of to Appleby where Atkinson awaited execution, much to the satisfaction of Sir Philip Musgrave and Lady Anne Clifford, Countess of Pembroke, both of whom had personal scores to settle with him. Lady Anne wrote in her Diary: 'Robt Atkinson, one of my tenants in Mallerstang, that had been my great enemy, was condemned to be hanged, drawn and quartered as a traitor to the King for having a hand in the late plot and conspiracy, so he was executed accordingly.'

Atkinson was unlucky. *The History of Mallerstang Forest* tells the following story: 'On the morning of the execution a King's Officer arrived at Stainmore (en route for Appleby) and asked at the inn whether there was any particular news. Whereupon they informed him that Captain Atkinson had been executed that morning. "Why", he replied, "I have his reprieve in my pocket."'

The Kaber Rigg Plot was an absurd conspiracy, almost juvenile in its naivety, inept in its planning, unworldly in its political innocence and bungling in its execution. However much we may disapprove of their treachery and their willingness to inform against one another to try to save their own necks, the punishment meted out to those involved was quite out of proportion and, one must suspect, was determined as much by personal animosity as by any danger to the State.

19

Breaking the Bridecake

A wedding is always a festive occasion and never more so than in the Cumbrian dales two centuries ago. A dales wedding then was much more than just a family celebration: it was a convivial, sportive carnival in which the entire community took part and each one was anticipated with much inquisitive excitement. A young couple seen sauntering along the moonlit lanes or furtively kissing among the haycocks did not pass unnoticed and news of an impending wedding was soon in circulation.

In his *Sketch of Cumberland Manners,* published in 1811, Francis Jollie describes a customary ruse to enable courtship to proceed in a positive and practical way by helping young lovers to get to know each other more intimately before the date of the wedding was finally arranged:

> Visits to the sweethearts at home are most commonly made on Saturday evenings, that the next day's work may not be incommoded. After the family have gone to bed, the fire darkened and the candle extinguished, he cautiously enters the house. In this murky situation they remain for a few hours, till the increasing cold of a winter's night or the light of a summer's morning announces the time of departure. This dark method of courting is economical; here is no loss of worktime, nor of those expensive articles, fire and candle. This, however, is its only advantage, and the misfortunes attending it are weighty – as may be imagined.

The question now on everyone's lips was, 'Would it be a bidden wedding or a bridewain?' For the former, guests were individually invited to the home of the bride's parents, but by custom the whole valley was invited; but for a bridewain, posters were printed and displayed in neighbouring dales inviting all who could to attend: one such poster has survived in a rather timeworn condition and is now in Keswick Museum. It gives notice of the forthcoming marriage, on 21 May 1807, of Joseph Rawlings and Mary Dixon of High Lorton – 'All Friends and Acquaintances and others' are invited with an assurance that every effort would be made 'to accommodate the company and render the day agreeable.'

An impression of what this involved has been vividly portrayed for us by the blind eighteenth century 'Cumberland Minstrel', John Stagg, in his lively dialect poem *The Bridewain,* and by Robert Anderson in his *Cumberland Ballads.* Anderson tells us that to the wedding he describes 'Thear were tweescore and Seebern inveyted' and, for these 47 lucky individuals, in the days before the wedding there was:

'Sec patchin', and weshin', and bleachin'.
And starchin', and darnin' auld duds;'

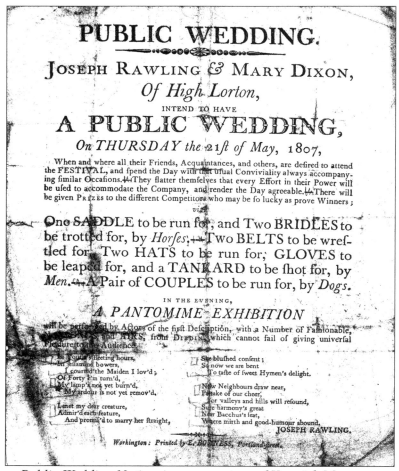

Public Wedding Notice, image courtesy of Keswick Museum.

and while:

> 'Some lasses thought lang to the weddin'.
> Unax'd others sat i' the suds.'

John Stagg's bridewain was a much grander affair for he informs us that:

> 'Frae ae nuik and anither
> Twa thousand war free far and near
> Assembl'd here together'

An improbably large number from which one might, perhaps unkindly, infer that the poet was among those who on their way to the gathering 'gat sae mislear'd wi' drink' that even approximate calculation was beyond them. Be that as it may, the first formal part of the day's proceedings was, of course, the solemnisation of the marriage in the valley church.

The wedding guests formed a procession to the church led by the bridal couple often seated in the 'bridewain' or bridal wagon and preceded by one of the well-known local fiddlers, a custom once common and still occasionally seen in country weddings in Norway where the 'wain' is often a boat rowed to church along the fjord.

Neither Stagg nor Anderson waste many poetic lines on the ceremony in church. Stagg portrays a bumbling priest searching to find his service book until at last:

> 'His lesson found, and a' set reeght.
> To wark they get wi' speed'.

The bride faltered ominously in her promise 'to honour and obey'; 'We'll see some day' the poet comments. Robert Anderson describes how:

> 'The breyde hung her head and luiked sheepish.
> The breydegruim as whyte as a clout.
> The bairns aw gleym'd thro' the kurk windows.
> The parson was verra devout'.

As they left the church the newly-wed couple faced the first obstacle in their married life: the church gate was fastened against them. The children who had been peeping through the church windows had been busy 'sneckin' up t' yat' – tying up the latch on the gate – and were prepared to open it only when the bridegroom 'shelled out', that is, threw a generous handful of coins for them to scramble for, coins known appropriately as 'hen silver'.

Honour satisfied and tradition observed, the real excitement could begin. There now took place the daredevil, pell-mell race, from the church gate to the bridal home, a fiercely contested competition, not for the fainthearted:

> 'Lyke wyld-fire off they flee.
> And nowther puol, nor peat-stack flinch.
> They gang wi' sic a bree;
> The lasses up hint their lads,
> Some stridlings and some sideways.'

Some riders took a fall 'wida whang' but, as Stagg reassuringly adds, 'a neck-break, it's uncommon'. The winner was rewarded with a blue riband presented by the bride herself.

The reception was usually held in a large barn where the fiddlers were 'rozling up their bows to stryke up *Cuddy's Wedding*' as the bridal pair arrived. A feast of Cumbrian country fare awaited their guests who were by now thirsty and hungry after their exertions and the many hours since their early breakfast.

Free and almost unlimited supplies of food and ale ensured a hearty meal for all, but many, as Stagg graphically relates, indulged to excess as they gorged themselves on great 'shives o' cheese and bread' and drank so much ale that 'they suin could hardly stand'. There were, however, a few, to Stagg's obvious disapproval:

> 'That luik'd to be ow'r nice.
> That nobut nibbling, pick'd and eat
> Just like as many myce'.

An idea of the stunning array of food on offer on these occasions is given by Robert Anderson in his account of *The Colbeck Wedding*:

> 'For dinner we'd stew'd geuse and haggish.
> Cow'd leady, and het bacon pye.
> Boil'd fluiks, tatey-hash, beastin' puddin',
> Saut salmon, and cabbish, forby
> Pork, pancakes, black puddin's, sheep trotters,
> And custert, and mustert, and veal,
> Grey-pez keale, and lang apple dumplin's;
> I wish every yan far'd as weel'.'

For some the end of the feast signalled the start of serious drinking:

> 'Whyle yele (ale) in jugs and cans was brought.
> And hail'd down ev'ry muzzle;
> They drank in piggins, pynts and pots.
> Or ought that came to hand…'

When supplies of the free wedding liquor were exhausted plenty more was to be had at the booths which local ale-house keepers had set up on the fringes of the wedding scene. Other enterprising hucksters sold sweetmeats, souvenirs and trinkets of all kinds.

For those who were young and still capable the afternoon was occupied with various sporting activities. Wrestling featured prominently as one would expect in Cumberland, the winners receiving a decorated belt. Jumping and running competitions for all ages were organised and both children and adults played 'hitch, step and loup' (hop, step and jump) and 'penny-stones' (pitch and toss). More frenzied horse-racing kept the excitement at a high pitch and 'the ladies not infrequently entered the lists and contended in speed for a piece of fine holland'. The older folk just enjoyed the opportunity to exchange local gossip and recall memories of bridewains of the past. Everyone laughed hilariously at the antics of those taking part in the 'gurning' contests, an old Cumbrian pastime known as 'gumin' thro' a braffin', making grotesque faces through a horse collar, the prize being awarded to the grimace judged to be the most convoluted facial contortion: 'a daft diversion' according to John Stagg.

More serious but equally daft and entertaining were the fights which inevitably broke out among 'rustics weel plied wi' drink'. It only needed some inebriated dunderhead to leap up and shout 'I'll box wi' onny here that dare' to earn a fluet under th' lug', and 'sae battle began'. John Stagg provides us with a ringside seat for one such encounter:

> 'Then off theer duds, their dobbies doft.
> And tirl'd to their bare buffs,
> Baith tyke-lyke tuolying round the bam.
> And dealing clumsy duffs;
> But Sir John Barleycorn sac sway'd
> Their slaps they a' flew slant.
> Till a… ow'r head they cowp'd at last,
> Lang streek'd i' th' midden pant,
> Weel sows'd that neeght'.

Meanwhile, less belligerent souls were preparing to enjoy the barn dance, a noisy, rumbustious revelry of traditional country dances – reels, square dances, and the Circassian Circle – to music played by fiddlers who dressed for the occasion like Johnny Shoestring in Hugh Walpole's *Rogue Herries*: 'in bright blue breeches and with silver buckles to his shoes, perched on a high stool fiddling for his life, the brass gleaming, the faces shining, the stamp of the shoon, the screaming of the fiddles, the clap-clap of the hands as the turns were made in the dance.' Famous among Cumbrian fiddlers on these occasions were Ben Wells, Jimmy Dyer and John Stagg himself.

An important and traditional part of the proceedings was that the bride should take her place on a stool or chair with a pewter dish – known as a dibbler – in her lap to receive gifts of money from her guests to assist her to set up her new home. This fund in later days became known as the bridewain and often amounted to a very useful sum. As John Stagg records:

'...crowns and half-crowns thick as hail
Are in the dibler jingling,
Reeght fast that day.'

The pewter dish could eventually be weighed down with coins worth £100 – a truly generous sum at a time when a farm worker could be hired for less than £15 a year.

One more ritual remained before the bride and groom could be put to bed. Seated on her chair the bride had a cloth cover placed over her hair. The bridegroom then had to break the bridecake on her head and the pieces were distributed among the guests. The bride's head suffered no ill effects from this experience: this wedding cake bore no resemblance to the weighty sugarladen creation of modern times – it was a thin, flat currant pastry requiring little effort to shatter into small pieces. The theory was that the more pieces there were, the more children the couple were likely to have.

The bridesmaids prepared the bride for bed and when she was safely (and decorously) settled there with her husband by her side, a final hilarious ritual ensued. A few close friends embarked on the curious custom of 'throwing the stocking'. Taking turns at the foot of the bed, the young men and women threw the bride's stockings over their shoulders, the men trying to hit the groom and the women the bride. Those who

Breaking the Bridecake, illustration by H. W. Reading.

were successful could be sure that this was a sign that their own marriage would soon take place.

At this point the older and more staid guests set off homewards but for the young the merry-making continued until the fiddlers became too fuddled to play. Much whispering and squealing could be heard among the haystacks:

> 'The lasses skirling clamb up the mews.
> And some slee hanniels follow'd...
> And mony a lad their sweethearts had,
> I'nuiks and corners huddled
> Unseen that neeght'

It was not until dawn was breaking that the party finally came to an end and the last revellers made their way home. Among them was our poet himself:

> 'Whyte tir'd at last wi' drink and noise.
> Half waken and half sleeping,
> I hamewards fettle'd off mysel',
> Just as the sun was peeping'

20

This Way to the Station

By a gap in a stone wall not far from Windermere's Ferry Nab is a footpath sign pointing into the woods and indicating that this is the way to 'Claife Station', a direction which has mystified many a visitor. Windermere train station is three miles away on the other side of the lake, Lakeside station is five miles away at the southern end of the lake, and to the north and west is a rail-free zone of many square miles. The incurious and the unbelievers shrug a shoulder and press on to the more certain goal of Hill Top; those of a more inquiring mind soon set foot on a gently-graded causeway which leads eventually to a rocky platform high above the lake, and on it stand the ruins of what has obviously been an impressive structure of fairly aristocratic origins. Equally obviously it has never had any association with a railway. What the visitor finds here is, indeed, a 'station', but this is an historic 'viewing station', one of the many described by Thomas West in his *Guide to the Lakes* first published in 1778.

West wrote that his *Guide* was compiled for persons 'of genius, taste and observation' and 'the curious of all ranks' who 'have caught the spirit of visiting the Lakes'. 'Here', he declared, 'are collected and laid out... all the select stations and points of view... exciting at once rapture and reverence.' Not only tourists would experience at these stations that 'agreeable surprise that attends the first sight of scenes that surpass all description' but 'artists in landscape studies' would also find them invaluable and 'more accessible than the Alps'.

So, conveyed by coach or wagonette along the rough tracks of Lakeland, the genteel tourists proceeded from station to station following West's prescribed itinerary, their emotions no doubt quickened by his warning that some of the scenes could be of frightening aspect — perpendicular crags of 'terrible grandeur', 'beauty in the lap of horror'. To soften the impact on sensitive natures West advised that the scenes should be viewed with the aid of a landscape mirror or Claude glass which, 'where the objects are great or near, it removes them to a due distance.' Viewers should turn their backs on the view and the mirror offered them a reduced image of the precipitous scenes which might otherwise cause them to swoon. Small coloured filters could be used to enhance the romance and perfect the sublime.

It is difficult to believe that the view from Claife Station could cause fear and trepidation in the most delicate Victorian lady for here there are no terrifying scenes of mountain horror but to the north and south lie 'noble expanses of water gloriously environed, spotted with islands more beautiful than would have issued from the happiest painter' while 'the eastern view is… adorned with all that is beautiful, grand and sublime.' The whole forms 'the most romantic landscape that nature can exhibit… a more beautiful variety is nowhere to be seen.'

When West visited this evidently beguiling spot in 1778 it must have been a small open plateau on the steep rocky flanks of what is now known as Station Scar. This, said West 'was embellished with growing trees, shrubs and coarse vegetation, interrupted with grey rocks that group finely with the deep green of yews and hollies.' Twenty years later the Reverend William Braithwaite, described by Wordsworth as a local recluse, had acquired Claife Heights, planted some 40,000 trees and conceived the romantic idea that Thomas West's station would be the perfect site for a summer house. So, as Joseph Budworth reported, he 'erected an elegant and commodious building thereon for the entertainment of his friends, called Belle View'. This was an octagonal structure parts of which may still be seen within the ruins of a larger and grander castellated edifice built a few years later by the Curwens of Belle Isle. Wordsworth made clear his disapproval of 'the new erections and objects about Windermere' but almost every guidebook in subsequent years directed tourists to the 'Station House' and employed every romantic adjective to describe the view. In Robert Southey's *Letters from England* Don Espriella visited Claife Station and considered it to be 'a castellated building in a style so foolish, that, if anything could mar the beauty of so beautiful a scene, it would be this ridiculous edifice.'

William Green informs us that in 1819 the house was 'two stories high, the lower story consists of a dining and other rooms, but the upper is a tasteful drawing-room.' Mary Higginson recalls a dance she attended there in a room 'well-suited for a dance, being large and a good springy floor.' Jonathan Otley reported that some of the windows had

*Claife Station, 1820, by R. Ackermann, image courtesy of
Cumbria Library Service.*

coloured glass 'to give a good representation of the manner in which the
landscape would be affected in different seasons', blue for winter, yellow
for autumn, green for spring and purple for a summer thunder storm.
Kitchens, a wine-cellar and storerooms were built into the thickness of
the walls on the ground floor.

Wordsworth was not alone in his disapproval of erecting such a building on this site. Joseph Wilkinson, in his 1810 guide to *Select Views in
Cumberland, Westmorland and Lancashire*, informs his readers that they
may visit the Station House by 'attending at a little lodge' where 'a person' will escort them on a guided tour. He then adds a forthright comment which would win the approval of many conservationists today:

The Pleasure House is happily situated, and is well in its kind, but without intending any harsh reflections on its contriver… it may be said that
he who remembers the spot less than thirty years ago will sigh for the
coming of the day when Art, through every rank of society, shall be
taught to have more reverence for Nature. This scene is, in its natural
constitution, far too beautiful to require any exotic or obtrusive

embellishment, either of planting or of architecture.

In 1820 when Ralph Ackermann came to sketch the scene he was guided by 'an aged female who inhabits a pretty cottage within the enclosure which surrounds the Station.' Today the cottage is no longer 'pretty' and visitors will find no guide of either sex or any age but are free to wander through the ruins and imagine the gatherings of the rich and genteel who came here to meet friends, to gossip, to party, to feast, to dance, to gamble at cards or backgammon, to plot family or business intrigues, or to keep lovers' trysts.

Regrettably, the view of the lake that all came to admire is largely denied to the modem visitor as too many trees have been allowed to grow unchecked thus obscuring a prospect described by Ackermann as 'one of the finest on the lakes, having every essential of a beautiful landscape.' The station itself (but not the trees) is now owned by the National Trust.

21

Change here for Ennerdale

There has been much wishful and wistful thinking in recent years about the revival of Lakeland's now dismantled railways. Enthusiastic groups have drawn up optimistic plans to re-open the Penrith to Keswick line and the abandoned section of the Eden Valley Railway. Voices have been heard regretting the demise of the scenic Foxfield to Coniston line, and even offending the ghost of William Wordsworth by lamenting that the railway engineers halted their work at Windermere and did not complete their original plan to continue to Ambleside, Grasmere and Keswick. What a relief, we are asked to believe, all this would have been to the traffic-congested roads of today; and what wonderful tourist attractions these lines would now be; what immense benefits would be brought to the local economy. The scars of construction, we are told, would long ago have blended into the natural landscape; most visitors today would be fascinated rather than appalled by Wordsworth's horrified cry 'Heard Ye that Whistle?' and the mass tourism which the poet together with John Ruskin and Canon Rawnsley so deeply dreaded has been with us for many years.

No voice has yet been raised to promote the resurrection of a number of railway schemes in Lakeland which never left the drawing board. The powerful opposition they encountered more than a century ago would almost certainly be redoubled today. Plans for a Borrowdale and Buttermere Railway and for a tramway over Styhead from Wasdale to Seathwaite have continued to gather undisturbed dust in the archives together with those for a Light Railway from Kendal to Arkholme. These schemes were all designed, as were almost all Cumbrian rail constructions, to benefit local industries. It was commercial interest, also, which inspired plans for the construction of a railway into the remote valley of Ennerdale.

Mrs Eliza Lynn Linton, a knowledgeable and intrepid Victorian traveller, visited Ennerdale and observed that 'the whole land hereabouts being more or less impregnated with iron ore, even Revelin (a formidable crag on the south shore of the lake) has had its secret chambers rifled with the rest and been forced to give up its treasures'. Less than twenty years later the ironmasters mining the Cumberland iron-fields decided to exploit the Ennerdale deposits more fully and efficiently by constructing a railway near the northern shore of the lake and along the River Liza to transport the ore to the furnaces near the coast. A rail link between Rowrah and the Kelton Fell Mines, a few miles north of Ennerdale, was soon to show the economic value of such an investment.

The ground was surveyed, the route planned and the Ennerdale Railway Bill came before Parliament in 1883/84. It seemed that the whole character of Ennerdale would soon be transformed. Wordsworth described the lake as having 'bold and somewhat savage shores' and as the scene unfolds beyond the lake it becomes yet bolder and more 'savage', an austere panorama of high and lonely peaks – a sight to thrill the hearts of modern tourists and fell-walkers but terrifyingly awesome to an earlier generation which preferred only that which was seductively picturesque. Ennerdale's geographical remoteness ensured that it had few tourists in those days. Mrs Linton commented that it was 'the least known and… the least likely to be visited of all the lakes… Until Ennerdale has the benefit of a carriage way along its banks, it will remain comparatively a terra incognita to the tourist world.'

It was to ensure that such a 'carriage way' in the form of the proposed railway should never be built that in 1883 the Lake District Defence Society, formed immediately after the campaign to prevent the construction of the Borrowdale railway, now sprang into action to thwart the ironmasters of Cleator Moor. Battle was joined to ensure that the banks of the Liza were not disfigured with heaps of iron ore, industrial clutter and a rail-head at Gillerthwaite.

The case against railways in the Lake District had been put in a forthright and succinct article a few years earlier by Robert Somervell. The alleged necessity to exploit the nation's mineral wealth was critically examined: 'Is material prosperity so pre-eminently desirable as to outweigh all other considerations?'; 'it is not true economy but selfish waste to destroy, without pressing cause, the beauty of the mountains that breathe of freedom'; 'the question is whether the interests of those who wish to make money out of the Lake Country ought to be treated as paramount'. Like John Ruskin who wrote a preface to his 'Protest against the expansion of Railways in the Lake District', Somervell feared the consequences of an invasion by the uneducated masses but he was more discreet in his expression. Ruskin shuddered at the prospect of a demand for more 'taverns and skittle grounds' and of lake shores littered with 'broken, ginger-beer bottles' and speculated that the minds of these intruders from 'our manufacturing towns' would 'be no more improved by contemplating the scenery of the Lake District than of Blackpool'.

Canon Rawnsley, representing the newly-formed Lake District Defence Society before a Parliamentary Select Committee appointed to consider the Ennerdale Railway Bill, had a more elevated brief: 'To protect the Lake District from those injurious encroachments upon its scenery which are, from time to time, attempted from purely commercial or speculative motives, without regard to its claims as a national recreation ground.'

The Select Committee reported against the proposed railway and after a close debate in the Commons, notable for a brilliant intervention by Sir James Bryce which probably determined the outcome, the Bill was narrowly defeated. Ennerdale would never hear that whistle.

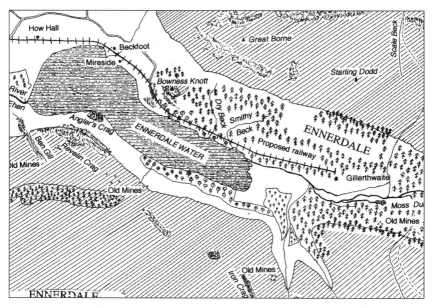

Route of proposed Ennerdale railway, map by the author.

The Ennerdale Railway aroused so much national interest that the magazine *Punch*, then in its heyday, published a cartoon under the caption 'The Ladies of the Lakes' with the accompanying commentary: 'The three lovely damsels, Ennerdale, Borrowdale and Derwentwater, rescued by the doughty knight of St Stephen's from the Railway Roughs and the Mineral Miscreants who would have done her injury.' And the *Pall Mall Gazette* amused its readers with a satirical poem entitled:'A Poetical Lamentation on the Insufficiency of Steam Locomotion in the Lake District'

> *Wake, England, wake! 'tis now the hour*
> *To sweep away this black disgrace –*
> *The want of locomotive power*
> *In so enjoyable a place.*
> *Nature has done her part, and why*
> *Is mightier man in his to fail?*
> *I want to hear the porter's cry.*
> *Change here for Ennerdale!*

Ennerdale still has no 'carriage way'; it is still the valley 'least known and the least likely to be visited'; it is still the wildest and most remote of all the Lakeland dales; it surpasses all others in dramatic grandeur. The railway would have disappeared long ago: the scars would remain.

In 2003 Ennerdale became the centre of an interesting environmental initiative which will transform the valley. The Forestry Commission, the National Trust, English Nature and United Utilities formed the Wild Ennerdale Partnership to promote the re-wilding of the valley in order 'to allow the evolution of Ennerdale as a wild valley relying on natural processes to shape its landscape and ecology.' Human intervention will be kept to a minimum but trails will be established for walkers, horse-riders and cyclists. Ennerdale will be a unique Lakeland environment.

22

The Packhorse Bridges of Cumbria

There has been no comprehensive, definitive study of the packhorse bridges of Cumbria and it seems unlikely that such a study will ever be possible; the historical and documentary evidence is much too sparse. Occasionally, a newly discovered document sheds a little light on the history of a particular bridge, but for the most part, there is no record of who built these bridges, when they were built, who paid for their construction, or who was responsible for their repair and maintenance. Nor is it always easy to identify with certainty many of the routes they served. We know little about the packhorse men who led these trains of sturdy ponies over long and lonely distances across the fells and mountain passes to remote valley farms and on to busy market towns.

A few surviving inn-signs tell us where they sought refreshment and found rest both for themselves and their weary beasts – The Woolpack, The Fleece and The Packhorse – but we have no portrayal of the lives they led such as Sir Walter Scott described so vividly for the cattle drovers. Yet for almost two hundred years the tracks and bridle-ways of the Lakeland fells, now largely the province of walkers and cyclists, were thronging, night and day, with strings of laden packhorses, the crags echoing the jingle of the leader-bells, the shouts and curses of the men who drove them.

The wealth of a whole region was carried in their panniers: primarily woollen fleeces but also woven or knitted textiles (including an annual cargo of nearly half a million socks); slate from the quarries; tons of ore from mines deep in the fells – iron from Furness and Eskdale, copper from Coniston and Newlands, lead from Glenridding and the Caldbeck Fells, plumbago (wad) from Borrowdale; charcoal from almost every woodland, peat from every moorland, to meet the insatiable demands of the smelting sites or bloomeries; tobacco and spices from Whitehaven for the Kendal snuff industry; the annual harvest of hazel nuts from the woods of Furness to be shipped from Broughton-in-Fumess; almost any moveable and saleable commodity could be found in a packhorse pannier – not

Smaithwaite Bridge, photograph by author.

least, quantities of rum and brandy, not all of it known to the excisemen. Daniel Defoe tells us that even salmon, freshly caught in the Derwent and Eden in Cumberland, were dispatched to London by packhorses 'which, changing often, go night and day without intermission, and, as they say, very much out-go the post; so that the fish come very sweet and good to London...' – perhaps not a judgement we would pass today on pannier-packed salmon after more than a week on the road.

There were a number of 'trunk' routes through the fell country, some of which can still be traced, with many feeder routes to villages and farm hamlets or to industrial sites. Cattle drovers could drive their animals through the many becks and rivers that had to be crossed along their routes but a train of 25 to 30 packhorses, each horse laden with 200 hundredweights (c100kg) of valuable trading goods, could not be put at unnecessary risk. So, at every crossing point a packhorse bridge had to be built – and in the well-watered fell country this demanded a great many such bridges.

Today approximately one quarter of all the known packhorse bridges in England are to be found in the county of Cumbria: they are indisputably a treasured feature of the Lakeland landscape, graceful and aesthetically pleasing in their architecture, their natural weathered stone blending perfectly into the scenery. Some have been lost to the needs of modern road construction, some have been rebuilt and changed beyond recognition, some have been widened to accommodate wheeled traffic but still retain much of their original design; a small number, usually in remote places now visited only by walkers or grazing sheep, have survived almost exactly as they were built, and it is these which are especially deserving of care and maintenance for they are truly part of our landscape and cultural heritage.

There is no simple definition of a genuine packhorse bridge beyond the obvious fact that it should be situated on a known packhorse route. As a general guide these bridges are not wide enough to take any wheeled vehicle and almost always measure less than six feet wide overall and often no more than half that width at the top of the arch. To allow for the easy passage of the bulky, tightly-packed panniers attached to each side of the horse's body, these bridges had very low parapets or often no parapets at all, but many have acquired kerbs, parapets or iron railings in modern times, additions which can usually be easily identified.

It is not possible in a short article to describe, however briefly, all the bridges in Cumbria which appear to have some association with packhorse routes and possess the characteristics of the authentic pack-horse bridge. Almost every visitor to the Lake District is familiar with the much- photographed bridges at Watendlath, or Stockley Bridge on the much-trodden track to Styhead, or Pasture Beck Bridge at Hartsop, or Birks Bridge across the River Duddon – all at one time 'authentic' packhorse bridges, as nineteenth century prints clearly show, but now adorned with parapets or railings, or widened to accommodate wheeled traffic. Some have been rebuilt almost entirely and are now recognisable only by the original arch, as at Sadgill, Hartsop and Walna Scar.

There are, fortunately, bridges in places now removed from modern traffic routes which have escaped such transformation and still remain very much as they were built. Most, it is generally believed, were con-structed between 1660 and 1760 at the height of the packhorse era, but a few may date from the days of the medieval monasteries. Many of these 'survivors' now provide a useful service on walkers' paths, while some appear to go nowhere in particular as the routes they once served have fallen out of use, but often a perusal of old maps and a study of local topography can indicate why these bridges were once important links on a busy packhorse track.

Fine examples of such bridges exist throughout Cumbria but most are little known and rarely visited. One beautiful small bridge stands a few metres away from the shore of Haweswater on the old road from the drowned hamlet of Mardale to Shap at the point where it crosses Rowantreethwaite Beck. This is usually known as the Corpse Road along which the dead were conveyed for burial at Shap but it was once busy with packhorses carrying butter, cheese and eggs to the ancient but-ter-market, also at Shap. The bridge is almost hidden from view but it is a gem of its kind, appreciated now only by the occasional walker on the lake-shore path.

Another hidden gem may be seen at Fawcett Mill, a short distance south of Orton: this has long been bypassed by a modern road-bridge just 100m upstream and is now quite isolated. It obviously served the mill but it seems highly likely that it was situated on a long-distance route from Kirkby Stephen and Ravenstonedale which joined the main trade route down the Lune Valley. Further north, bridging St John's Beck

Pasture Beck Bridge, photograph courtesy of University of Lancaster.

near the foot of Thirlmere, stands Smaithwaite Bridge. Its proximity to the engineering operations consequent on the construction of the Thirlmere reservoir dam had only the slightly unfortunate result of leaving it marooned in the middle of the beck, with less than handsome wooden walkways to restore its link to the banks and maintain the right of way. Its main purpose now is to enable sheep to pass over the beck to pastures on the other side but at one time two important packhorse routes converged here: one from the south to Keswick via the eastern side of what was then Leathes Water and, from the east, lead ore was carried from the Glenridding mines, via the Sticks Pass and over Smaithwaite Bridge to the smelting works at Brigham.

Two other bridges on a long abandoned 'ore' route stand forlorn and unfrequented in the pastoral country of the West Cumbrian Plain. The now heavily forested fells south of Lamplugh in the north-west corner of the Lake District National Park were once the scene of early iron-mining and the ore was transported by packhorse to the bloomery at Furnace, some ten miles to the north. At Ullock the route crossed Black Beck by a seemingly fragile bridge which now stands in a pleasant setting and in a state of beautiful preservation. Further north, at Calva Hall, the packhorses carried their burden across the River Marron by a much more substantial bridge, structurally in excellent condition but its road surface very overgrown. At some time the bridge acquired parapets, only eleven inches high at the top of the arch, and on one side is inscribed 'HEAF 1684' whatever that may signify.

In the west, near the once flourishing port and market town of Ravenglass, from which important packhorse trails fanned out in several directions, we find Holme Bridge crossing the River Irt on the route to Drigg and the north carrying merchandise of all kinds but notably imported rum, tea, tobacco and sugar – much of it smuggled goods. The cobbled surface of this bridge is almost certainly original but the parapets are later additions. This must have been one of the more exciting routes with revenue sloops likely to ambush the convoy at any time in search of contraband. A little more than two miles north of this bridge a cache capable of storing a considerable quantity of illicit goods was discovered near the home of one Mary Largs who met her end on Gallows Hill nearby. Much of this route has now vanished under pasture land.

In the south there are several ancient bridges probably built by the monks of Furness Abbey and so among the oldest packhorse bridges in Cumbria. The Cistercians were very active traders and businessmen and on their extensive land-holdings in Furness and the central Lake District they exploited all the resources available including wool from their great flocks of Herdwick sheep, dairy produce from their vaccaries, iron from the haematite deposits in Furness and Eskdale, and a great variety of articles manufactured from the vast areas of woodland they controlled. Several bridges are often said to have links with these monastic activities, perhaps the most well-known being the remote and graceful Lingcove Bridge (also known as Throstle Garth Bridge) in Upper Eskdale. This bridge was almost totally rebuilt after destruction by flood in 1966 but it was an 'authentic' reconstruction (except for the concrete roadway) of the original which was probably a medieval monastic structure. It is often stated that this was used by packhorse trains carrying iron ore from Eskdale via Ore Gap to the Furness Abbey bloomery in Langstrath, but this route does not necessitate a crossing of Lingcove Beck. If it was part of a long-distance route it is more likely to have been to the abbey's properties in Borrowdale via Styhead. The name 'Throstlegarth' translates as 'Frosthildr's enclosure' suggesting that the original bridge gave access to a Viking lady's sheepfold. During the period of mild 'climatic

High Sweden Bridge, photograph by the author.

optimum' of Viking and early medieval times these now barren or boggy heights would have been rich summer pastures – a grant made in 1290 allowed the Furness monks to 'enclose the pastures of Lingcove' as part of their great sheepfarm of Butterilket.

Another monastic bridge linked to iron mining activities is Horrace Bridge near Ulverston. The modern road has, fortunately, by-passed this almost perfect example of a genuine packhorse bridge which was on the route from the Furness Abbey iron-ore mines near Marton and Lindal to the smelting bloomeries near Lowick and Coniston Water where there were abundant quantities of charcoal.

A curious bridge crossing a narrow gorge of the River Calder is also thought to have monastic associations. This is the diminutive bridge at High Wath with its asymmetrical pointed arch usually referred to as Monk's Bridge or Matty Benn's Bridge. Its original purpose is not clear.

An almost unknown example of an 'authentic' packhorse bridge may be seen just a few feet away from the busy Lyth Valley road near the

Stanegarth Bridge, photograph courtesy of D. Woodhead.

village of Winster. It spans the infant River Winster with a small eight-foot arch and its narrow overgrown roadway has no parapets. This neglected bridge once stood on the main road from Kendal to Ambleside via Underbarrow and Crosthwaite, and was used by several hundred packhorses every week.

Occasionally one finds a bridge having all the characteristics of an authentic packhorse bridge but apparently remote from any of the major packhorse routes and serving no obvious purpose. Fine examples of such bridges may be seen at Barbon, Stainton, Fawcett Mill, Burnbanks, and (now seen only with binoculars) Willy Goodwaller's Bridge in Far Easedale which is believed to have served a long vanished fulling mill. Other bridges, too, may have provided access to isolated mills and farms no longer in existence, and all the principal trade routes had a network of linking routes which also required bridges to cross rivers and becks: some may still be traced as footpaths or bridleways. Nor should we forget the many chapmen or pedlars who travelled the country selling their wares to every farmstead and cottage where they were sure of a market for the simple but essential household goods they carried. (Observant fell-walkers will know of the simple cross of stones which marks the grave of a woman pedlar who met her end more than 200 years ago by Rossett Gill as she made her weary way over the high fells after completing her round of the farms in Langdale).

Many of these bridges are found in picturesque settings now remote from any modern trade route. Noteworthy examples are at Wasdale Head, once on a main packhorse route to Ennerdale via a lost bridge over Gatherstone Beck; at Lind End in the Lickle Valley which carried charcoal to the iron bloomeries further down the valley; at Rosgill (Parish Bridge) once an important link on routes to Shap Abbey and the markets of Shap itself; Bleabeck Bridge served first a packhorse track and later a coach road out of the Duddon Valley; Cawdale Bridge was probably on the route from Penrith to the south along the west shore of Haweswater; High Sweden Bridge was most probably on a link route to the main packhorse trail through Scandale; the much photographed Slater's Bridge in Little Langdale may have had associations with the slate quarries nearby but probably received its name from John Sleyther who lived in the fourteenth century, thus establishing a claim to be one of the few surviving medieval bridges. Other famous bridges have links

Winster Bridge, photograph courtesy of Ann James.

with Furness Abbey: Bow Bridge, a red sandstone three-arched bridge in a woodland setting, and Souterhouse Bridge, referred to in a document of 1433 and the oldest recorded bridge in Cumbria, but now buried in modern industrial development and far from picturesque.

Many bridges were once genuine packhorse structures but have been widened to accommodate wheeled vehicles or have undergone major reconstruction. Notable examples are Doctor Bridge in Eskdale, Water Yeat Bridge over the River Lickle, Ashness Bridge in Borrowdale, Laverock Bridge across the River Mint, Stockley Bridge, Walna Scar Bridge and the re-sited bridge at Wet Sleddale.

The well-known bridge by the mill at Boot in Eskdale does not conform in its measurements to an 'authentic' packhorse bridge – its 6'6" width seems to disqualify it but the mill exhibition illustrates a padded wooden packhorse saddle laden with two sacks of corn and the archives record that each week a train of twenty packhorses passed over the bridge travelling on the route from the west to Eskdale and on to Ambleside via Hardknott Pass.

All these bridges are an integral part of our historical and landscape heritage and we should aim to ensure that they are protected and maintained against the ravages of time and the hand of man.

In recent years the National Park Authority has embarked on two ventures to reconstruct packhorse bridges. The first, New Bridge in Easedale, can best be described as an attempt to combine authenticity with a tractor-friendly roadway. The second was a worthy project to replace a long-lost bridge over Hollow Gill near Wasdale Head on the old Corpse Road over Burnmoor. This has a double arch and low kerbs and looks 'authentic' as well as being eminently useful to walkers and to any passing packhorse.

Packhorse routes in Cumbria

Packhorse bridges are associated with packhorse routes. Many of these routes are known from reliable historical evidence; some may be inferred from the needs of industry and from the presence of packhorse bridges to serve them; a few are largely speculative and derive from local needs which may now have disappeared. Here are just a few:

Kendal to Ambleside: Kendal was an important trading centre and numerous packhorse trains left the town every week for various destinations, even as far as Southampton and London. It was a focal point in the network of routes in Lakeland. The route to Ambleside via Underbarrow, Crosthwaite and Winster was especially busy; much of it is now overlaid by modern roads.

Duddon Valley to Coniston: This linked the Duddon with the markets at Coniston and at Hawkshead. Generally known as the Walna Scar Road it left Seathwaite to follow Tarn Beck to Hollin House where it continued directly to Coniston skirting Walna Scar and Coniston Old Man before descending to Coniston and Hawkshead.

Ravenglass to Grayrigg: From Ravenglass this route followed the Roman road via Eskdale, Hardknott, Wrynose and Little Langdale to Ambleside where it joined the busy route to Kentmere, Sadgill, Longsleddale and on to Grayrigg and Kirkby Lonsdale.

Borrowdale to Ravenglass: This important route left Seathwaite by the path to Styhead and descended via Spouthead Gill and Lingmell Beck to Burnthwaite at Wasdale Head. From here there were two routes to Ravenglass – to Miterdale via Tongue Moor or via Strands and Drigg.

Cockermouth to Grasmere: This route went directly through the Vale of Lorton to the busy packhorse 'station' at Lanthwaite Green and proceeded via the old road over Honister to Rosthwaite and then by Stonethwaite Beck and Greenup to Grasmere.

Langdale to Broughton-in-Furness: This linked the farms of the Langdales with the busy market at Broughton. The route followed the main packhorse trail over Wrynose to Cockley Beck where it turned off along the River Duddon to Birks Bridge to take the track to Grassguards, Stonythwaite, Wallowbarrow and on to Duddon Bridge and Broughton.

Patterdale to Keswick: This route was mainly to transport lead ore from the mines at Glenridding to the smelting works at Brigham near Keswick. It crossed Sticks Pass to Stanah and then passed via Smaithwaite Bridge to Shoulthwaite and on to Brigham or Keswick.

Mardale Green to Shap: Known as the corpse road this route was also busy with goods traffic to and from the market at Shap. It followed the Swindale valley direct to Shap with a link route at Truss Gap to Rosgill Bridge and Bampton.

23

Lakeland Echoes

Sydney Smith, Canon of St Paul's and almost exact contemporary of Wordsworth, declared that his idea of Heaven was eating pâté de foie gras to the sound of trumpets. If he had ever ventured to join the throng of genteel early tourists in the Lake District he would have discovered his Heaven on Earth. For among the various 'tourist attractions' on offer at that time was a stylish picnic on Ullswater, Derwentwater or Windermere comfortably seated in a colourful aristocratic barge, rowed sedately by liveried retainers while trumpets, horns, bassoons and clarinets created music which echoed pleasingly among the surrounding rocks and fells. Dreams of Heaven may well have been shattered by a subsequent part of the entertainment which consisted of a succession of bursts of cannon-fire which reverberated up to seven or eight times and could be heard many miles away.

Such was commercialised tourism in the age of the Romantic Poets. Many of the early guidebooks inform us that the Duke of Norfolk, the Duke of Portland, the Earl of Surrey and the Curwens of Belle Isle on Windermere all provided barges with brass cannon and resplendent oarsmen, and with strategically positioned musicians, to enable visitors to savour this 'Lakeland experience'.

Never one to shun an opportunity to indulge in a spectacle, however bizarre, the raffish Mr Pocklington of Derwent Island erected a mock fortress equipped with a battery of cannon which could create an echo lasting 'upwards of thirty seconds' – 'a dreadful discharge of musketry' which could, it is said, be heard as far away as Appleby. A visiting Irishman who had been boasting of the unrivalled echoes of Killarney was compelled to exclaim that 'By Jasus, I never heard anything like it in all my life.'

It was not long before enterprising landlords of several lakeside inns began to hire out boats with small cannon on board while at the Lodore Falls in Borrowdale visitors were invited to enjoy the discharge from either a small cannon at a cost of half a crown or from a larger cannon for four shillings (approximately £10 in today's money) – a fee which led Robert Southey, who had met similar tourist entertainments abroad, to comment that 'English echoes appear to be the most expensive luxuries in which a traveller can indulge.'

Guidebook authors found the sound of gunfire among the fells a fascinating experience but there was occasionally a degree of circumspection in their description of its effects. William Hutchinson was quite carried away by the 'wondrous tumult and uproar' and William Gilpin believed that the 'awful sounds' had 'a wonderful effect on the mind', but both were agreed that the overwhelming impression was 'as if the very foundations of every rock on the lake were giving way; as if by some internal combustion they were rent in pieces and hurled into the lake'; the noise, they thought, was 'appalling' but the echoes were 'wondrous'.

However, Gilpin goes on to say that 'there is another species of echoes… which recommend themselves to those feelings which depend on the gentler movements of the mind.' These were the echoes produced by musical instruments alone, without bursts of cannon fire, and such lyrical accounts of these were penned that one wonders why the custom ever fell out of favour. In a famous passage in his *Excursion to the Lakes* Hutchinson relates how they were relieved from the 'wondrous tumult' of cannon-fire 'by the music of two French horns whose harmony was repeated from every recess which echo haunted on the borders of the lake.' Bassoons, clarinets and comets joined in and soon 'all this vast theatre seemed to be possessed by innumerable aerial beings who breathed celestial harmony.' For his part William Gilpin was so overwhelmed by it all that he declared his belief that 'Mountain guides from their infancy ought to be taught the clarinet, the bassoon and the flute and even the horn, in order to gratify the refined in musical feeling.'

Today cannon-fire and musical echoes would be by many frowned upon as a form of tourist entertainment. By no artifice of the spin-doctors could such activities be brought within the National Park definition of 'quiet enjoyment'; with the greatest of ease they could be classified as 'noise pollution'. Even so, although the guns, the trumpets and their echoes are no longer part of the tourist scene, can we claim that Lakeland is now a haven of peace and quiet?

We, at the beginning of the twenty-first century, are in no position to

The falls at Lodore, by T. Allom, courtesy of Cumbria Library Service.

point a disapproving finger at those who, at the end of the eighteenth century, found pleasure in the extraordinary, and obviously not entirely displeasing, echoes conjured up by the occasional discharge of small cannon or the purposeful playing of musical instruments.

In the same exuberant Regency years when tourists to the Lake District were thrilling to the echo experience Ralph Ackermann described some of the sounds of the natural world which could be heard 'half-way up Skiddaw':

> The voice of the distant waterfalls is heard perfectly distinct and not one confusing with another. The loud-crowing cock at every cottage, joined to the warbling of the smaller feathered choir, comes with an almost magical sweetness to the ear, whilst the bellowing of bulls and cows forms a rural bass to the concert.

The world of Nature does not operate in silence; William Cowper knew this well: 'Not rural sights alone, but rural sounds, Exhilarate the spirit, and restore The tone of languid Nature.'

And among those many rural sounds are often the sounds from the world of Man. How many of us recall, perhaps with nostalgia, the ring of the blacksmith's anvil, the clonk of the woodsman's axe, the whistle of a steam train, or the wind-blown peal of church bells, – according to the poet, 'a happy noise to hear'.

24

Changing the Landscape

William Pearson was bom in 1780 and for most of his 76 years he lived in or close to the Lyth Valley. In those years he witnessed the most dramatic change in the landscape seen in any Lakeland valley since the clearance of the primeval forests. In his *Papers, Letters and Journals* he has left us a remarkable portrait of the valley as it was at that time and of the transformation which took place in his lifetime. With the prospects for farming in the Lake District now so uncertain we must prepare for future changes to familiar landscapes and we may have much to learn from Pearson's account of an earlier revolution in the pattern of agriculture.

The precipitous limestone edge of Underbarrow Scar offers a grand-stand view over the Lyth Valley as it is today, a neat tapestry of fields, hedges, woods and water-filled dykes. Small herds of cattle and scattered groups of sheep graze peacefully on the geometric pastures; a roe deer feeds alertly at the edge of a plantation; the river, channelled and con-fined, is a dull, metallic ribbon leading the eye towards the distant sea and the vast expanse of golden, treacherous sands; the only sounds are the mewing of a buzzard and the bark of a farmyard dog. A few rocky knolls punctuate the flatlands emphasising that most of this valley is no more than a few feet above sea-level, its green pastures kept free from flooding only by an expensively maintained system of drainage chan-nels, dykes, sluices, pumps and embankments.

It is not difficult to imagine this narrow strip of land leading directly from the sea towards the high fells, as a kind of fjord, an arm of the sea, and in the distant ages following the last Ice Age this is exactly what it may have been. Even in historic times high tides regularly flooded the valley, with storm waves beating against the cliffs of Whitbarrow, Un-derbarrow and 'Leofa's Ness', the headland we now know as Levens. But for much of the past 2,000 years this low-lying land has been a vast peat bog with scattered pools of open water; but even so until modern times it was still subject to not infrequent inundations. Thomas Jeffrey's 1770 map clearly shows that towards the end of the eighteenth century

Lyth Moss, courtesy of C. Isherwood.

the Lyth Mosses extended from the Kent Estuary to the higher ground some five miles inland, with only one passage for man and horse across it – and that a less than reassuring causeway made of bound birch logs resting on the water-logged peat. Those who travelled between Lancaster and Furness with valuable merchandise preferred the long detour via Kendal and Crosthwaite along old and well-trodden trackways.

The Lyth Valley we see today has been created within the past 200 years by human hands. William Pearson describes it as it was in the early 1800s and how, within his lifetime, 'instead of a wide expanse of marsh and bog... there appeared wide fields of golden grain and glistening crops.' 'No event', he wrote, 'has produced a greater change in the appearance of our district than the enclosure of the commons.' It was the Agricultural Revolution which brought about this man-made transformation of the landscape of Lyth.

In the Lake District, as in every other part of the country, common lands were seized, measured, partitioned and enclosed; and then subjected to 'agricultural improvement' by enterprising and opportunist landowners who made a great deal of money from their acquisitions but also helped to provide food for a population which had doubled in the eighteenth century and would soon double again. Enclosure Commissions visited Lyth in 1803, the common lands were apportioned to several landowners, and within a generation the moss had been reclaimed – drained, channelled, cleared, fenced, marled, limed, ploughed and exhibited as a fine example of the new agriculture.

Where once the bittern had boomed, the wild cat prowled and the Westmorland peasant dug and stacked his peat, there were now crops of oats, wheat, turnips, mangolds, potatoes, ryegrass and clover. And on the high ground, too, the landscape had changed; where once the uplands had been open pastures they were now enclosed with 'stone walls thrown like chains across the front of these noble mountains – as if to subdue and bind down their natural freedom.'

Pearson relates that before the enclosures the Lyth Mosses were always busy with families of local peat-diggers who each had an appointed 'pot' where they dug out the two distinct types of peat: an upper layer of some two feet of fibrous peat the best of which was used as kindling while the dust was collected for baking bread as it generated great heat; and below this was a layer of several feet of deep black peat used (and sold in Kendal market) as fuel. A well-known feature in the landscape of the moss was the innumerable stacks of cut peat left to dry in the sun and the wind. A few small pots were still dug after the enclosures but peat-digging went into steady decline and a 1906 Directory listed only one remaining peat dealer in the area. Also hit by the draining of the mosses were the 'poor people' whom the *Lonsdale Magazine* reported as making 'a tolerable living by peeling rushes for candles and making besoms and bears [mats] of the peelings.'

Pearson was always deeply interested in the wildlife which frequented the mosses and his journals recount in detail the many species and their habitats and how they were affected by the disappearance of the mosses. He tells us that by 1839 the wild cat was extinct, the badger had become an 'extreme rarity', the otter 'not extinct but very scarce', and the hedgehog greatly reduced in numbers as they succumbed to the hostility of farmers who believed they milked cows in the fields. The foulmart (polecat) could still be found and the dormouse had managed to survive but rabbits and weasels had become a pest. The red squirrel was 'plentiful' but, to Pearson's obvious disgust, the true Lakeland grey fox had been almost supplanted by the red 'interlopers from Yorkshire… with no more honesty then a buccaneer.' These noticeable changes in the animal world were possibly less the result of loss of mossland habitat than the consequence of relentless shooting and hunting, or probably a combination of the two.

The decline in the numbers of many bird species concerned Pearson even more. On the Lyth marshes, he said, 'there may be found at one time or other almost every variety of bird common to the North of England.' The splendid kite had become extinct in Lyth in 1800: 'we have nothing left like him; the buzzard is a mere barndoor fowl compared to him… a sluggish, indolent bird.' The wild ducks which flocked to and bred on the rushy pools on the moss 'are become scarce and you may look in vain for those large flocks in the autumn.' Bittern, red grouse, and snipe used to breed on the moss 'but the progress of cultivation is narrowing [their] domain every year, as it is that of the lapwing or peewit which was formerly found there in great plenty.' The herons which came from the heronries at Rydal Water and Dallam Tower to fish on the moss 'are now rarely seen'; the partridge is 'not so plentiful as it used to be'; the sandpiper was formerly found 'in great numbers but now we have few or none'; woodcock are 'getting scarcer every year' while the numbers of many other species – curlew, plover, waterhen, jay – are 'diminishing as more land is brought into arable cultivation.' Even the geese which used to graze on the mosses in great numbers – 'never was there a pasture so incessantly nibbled as this' – were being ousted by grain, root crops, sheep and cows.

The only birds which seem to have gained advantage from the conversion of the mosses to arable land were the rooks. They had increased in numbers by some eight to ten times within Pearson's memory, feeding happily on the grain and potato crops and raiding the newly planted orchards of cherries and pears. These 'sable-coated plunderers' were 'no favourite with anyone' particularly as they showed total contempt for the snares set to catch them, used the 'scarecrows' as convenient perches, and 'placed sentinels in the trees' to give warning of any approaching guns. Their partiality for the grubs which attacked the crops was, apparently, not balanced by their own depredations.

Pearson was a keen botanist and he mourned the loss of the many marsh plants which had been so abundant on the mosses before drainage began. As the plough advanced across the newly created fields so the cranberry, crowberry, cloudberry and bogbean disappeared; and with them went the bilberry, cowberry and butterwort, the sundew, the sedges, the reedmace and the bog rosemary. In a few short years almost all the

Lyth Valley flooded, 2015, photograph courtesy of Janet Riley

marshland flora of the mosses had been lost.

In these years, too, Pearson saw the construction of the new turnpike roads across the former moss. The old causeway from Levens was replaced in 1818 by a new straight turnpike which involved straightening out the natural bends of the River Gilpin and by 1825 a contemporary recorded that 'carriages and the heaviest wagons now pass safely over four or five miles of morass where, a few years ago, except in very dry weather, the human foot could not tread with security.' Pearson was less put out by this road than by the 'improvement' of the old Lyth Lane running along the higher ground on the western side of the moss. This was formerly used only by farmers but two 'sagacious innkeepers' living at each end had developed it into a new tourist route. But it was unseemly for 'an elegant chaise... to come into grievous contact with the massy wheels of a vile and vulgar dung-cart' so 'the tall luxuriant hedgerows are to be swept away' to make way for 'a common turnpike road... for lakers and gentlemen's carriages.' With heartfelt anguish Pearson exclaimed 'Lyth Lane: thou art changed – metamorphosed – vanished – extinguished!'

Within a few generations this new landscape of Lyth was once again to be changed by the works of man – but this time less dramatically. The construction of the canals and then the railways brought cheap food into the area and put an end to the profitability of arable farming in the valley, while the arrival of cheap coal soon displaced peat as the main fuel for both industrial and domestic use. Peat digging on what remained of the moss soon disappeared for good and the fields of root crops and waving corn were replaced by the grazing pastures we see today.

Nothing could be further from the truth than to imagine, as many still do, that the landscape can for ever be preserved without change. As William Rollinson so concisely put it some years ago: 'This is a largely artificial environment, constantly changing under the influence of man and his activities.' In no other valley has this been so vividly demonstrated as in the modern story of the Lyth Mosses. The twenty-first century will almost certainly bring changes to the Lakeland landscape which may cause as much heartache as that felt by William Pearson as he watched the ancient landscape of Lyth disappear before his eyes.

The National Trust, the Royal Society for the Protection of Birds and the Cumbria Wildlife Trust are now implementing plans to restore areas of wetland in the Lyth Valley and several species of wildlife are already returning.

25

Cumbria's Icy Heritage

In 1645 John Evelyn, diarist and traveller, discovered in the heat of an Italian summer the delights of iced drinks, cool wine, chilled fruit and icecream, luxuries then unknown in his own country. When he was informed that these pleasurable indulgences were made possible by the simple device of an ice-house he returned to England filled with enthusiasm to introduce his countrymen to these 'conservatories of ice and snow'. However, it was not until Charles II was restored to the throne a few years later that any useful progress in this direction was made: he, too, during his long exile in France, had enjoyed all the gastronomic pleasures which summer ice could bring, and within a short time he had had an ice-house built in what is now Green Park and was persuading Robert Boyle to deliver a lecture to the newly-founded Royal Society describing the advantages of ice-houses and outlining the method of their construction.

Thus were Englishmen made familiar with one of the joys of life which inhabitants of Eastern and Mediterranean lands had known for 4,000 years and in parts of Europe since the days of the Roman Empire. Twelfth-century English crusaders, sweltering in the Palestinian summer, had stared in disbelief when Saladin the Saracen sent iced pears and peaches to their king, Richard Lionheart, and a consignment of snow to cool his fevered brow; medieval pilgrims were astonished to see ice on sale in the stifling streets of Italy and Spain; Tudor diplomats relished the iced desserts and cooled wine at Paris banquets; but no-one, it seems, had considered that such delicacies might also be possible in England. Royal example and the eighteenth century vogue for the Grand Tour were to change this insularity and within a few generations almost every stately home and manor house had its ice-house, and the tables of the English gentry were furnished with chilled wines, iced fruits, icecream and elaborate ice-confections. Gracious hospitality in Ancient Athens decreed that 'it was not seemly to drink a friend's health in lukewarm drink'; nor, henceforth, would it be seemly in England.

By 1720 recipes were already in print for the making of ice-cream, water-ices, neiges (whipped cream in a mould) and sculptured ice-desserts but it was only the wealthy upper classes who could afford them. Ice-houses were costly to build and many labourers were needed to fill them and if a supply of ice was not readily available the cost of purchasing it from an ice-retailer was significant even for a gentleman's household: Hartley's, the ice-retailers in Windermere, supplied ice to the county's country houses at a price which could be as high as £28 per ton and most ice-houses required up to 20 tons of ice to fill them (in modern values this would amount to approximately £50,000).

Almost all Cumbria's ice-houses date from the nineteenth century but the oldest ice-house in the county is at Holker Hall which is referred to in the Steward's Account Book for 1720. This ice-house is constructed to a design most commonly used: a deep, cylindrical, brick-lined pit, 5.5 metres in diameter, tapering towards the base, and covered by a domed chamber. At the bottom of the pit is a drain and at the apex of the dome is a ventilation pipe. The brick dome is roofed with Burlington slates covered with a thick layer of turf. The entrance tunnel is fitted with three heavy slate doors, the spaces between them packed with bales of straw.

According to the gardener's record book in the 1880s fourteen or fifteen men were employed for a fortnight each winter for the task of filling the ice-pit with ice from a nearby pond, labour for which they received a special bonus of bread, cheese and ale. Just as there were certain basic features in the construction of ice-houses so there were certain necessary procedures in filling them. These were demonstrated in an experiment conducted in recent times at the well-preserved ice-house built for Levens Hall. The purpose was to test, as scientifically as possible, the efficiency of ice-houses to conserve ice using the method of storage practised since the first millennium BC and as used for the ice-pits constructed for Alexander the Great at Petra.

The 4.25 metre deep, cone-shaped pit was cleaned out and the drain filled with loose stones and covered with an iron grating and 20cms of compressed straw. The walls of the pit were lined with 10cms of straw, a traditional insulation material. Seventeen tons of ice were tightly packed into the pit by ramming and trampling and finally covered with a thick layer of straw. The spaces between the slate doors were packed with bales of straw as historic custom required. The workforce consisted of twelve boys from a Kendal school and eight adults and the operation took just over eight hours spread over two days.

Thermistors were placed between the ice and the straw in the pit, on the top of the ice and on the dome. All temperatures were recorded weekly including the air temperature outside the ice-house. The temperature on the surface of the ice remained constant at 3°C even when the air temperature reached 21°C and that in the dome touched 15°C. The last of the ice melted at the end of thirteen months and would probably have lasted longer if the humidity in the chamber had not been greatly increased by a blocked ventilation pipe. This experiment clearly demonstrated that ice-houses of this type would ensure a supply of ice for at least a year.

Hundreds of ice-houses were built in all parts of Britain and in 1867 the *National Encyclopaedia* commented that 'most of the country houses of England of the better class are furnished with ice-houses for storage'. A survey carried out in 1990 identified 1,954 ice-houses in England, Scotland and Wales, 53 of which were said to be in good condition. Thirty-eight have been located in Cumbria and of these about half are in fairly good condition and help to illustrate various types of ice-house.

Most, like those at Holker and Levens, have circular pits covered by a domed chamber. Hassness, by Buttermere, is distinguished by its multi-coloured bricks; Old Hall, Endmoor, adopted the then new double-cavity wall construction for its ice-pit; Patterdale Hall hid its ice-house in the dam of Lanty's Tarn; Barrock Park has the only ice-house in Cumbria built with a tunnel shaped chamber; Muncaster Castle's ice-house has been transformed into an electricity substation. At Armathwaite Castle and at Brougham are two good examples of ice-caves hewn out of sandstone bluffs. The ice-house at Duddon Hall, built into a rocky outcrop, although in poor condition, is of interest as it is one of the few which incorporated a larder for the preservation of food. Icehouses with rectangular chambers were constructed at Crofton Hall, Edenhall, Flass Hall and Staveley Park Farm.

Ruskin's ill-fated ice-house at Brantwood is referred to in W. G. Collingwood's *Life of Ruskin*: it was 'tunnelled at vast expense into the rock and filled at more expense with the best ice; opened at last with great expectations and the most charitable intent, for it was planned to supply invalids in the neighbourhood with ice, as the hothouse supplied them with grapes; and revealing, after all, nothing but a puddle of dirty water.' Why this structure failed is unexplained.

In the mid-Victorian period it became fashionable among the wealthy to make their ice-houses an ornate architectural feature in the grounds of their mansions. Flass Hall's ice-house masquerades as an ornamental grotto and at Lowther Castle the Earl of Lonsdale adopted a neo-classical design for his ice-house which was to form part of an elaborate rock garden (now long vanished); at Whitehall (near Mealsgate) the distinguished architect, Anthony Salvin, was engaged to design what is, in fact, a very modest structure.

Until supplies of pure crystal ice from Norway began to arrive in the latter half of the nineteenth century British ice-houses were filled with ice from any source nearby – pond, lake, river, reservoir or canal – and this was far from pure. Louis Pasteur's revelations in the 1860s on the subject of bacteria caused some alarm and gradually more houses were purchasing Norwegian ice which soon began to be shipped into Britain in great quantities. This added to the expense of course and many clung to the belief that bacteria died when the water was frozen; even in the early years of the twentieth century the ice-houses at Helme Lodge and Sedgwick House were still filled with ice cut from the Kendal Canal. It was fortunate that the ice rarely came into contact with food but was usually packed into special ice-chests in which food and drinks were placed in separate containers to chill or in elaborately designed silver wine-coolers, but the risk of bacterial infection must always have been present.

By the 1940s the new electric domestic refrigerator was being installed in many homes and the ice-houses were rapidly being abandoned and demolished or even forgotten – that at Netherby Hall, near Longtown, was re-discovered in 1978 during woodland clearance. A few have been restored but they are obviously dangerous places and only a small number are open to the public by special request.

Many of the hundreds of thousands of visitors who every year travel to the stately homes and country houses of Britain hope to discover something of what life was like in these splendid mansions of a rich and privileged upper class. A tour of the kitchen quarters usually reveals details of the lavish and abundant dishes which furnished the daily dining table but rarely is reference made to the special gastronomic pleasures

Holker Hall ice-house, photograph courtesy of B. Stephenson.

of cooled wine, iced drinks, icecream confections and ice-cream itself – all made possible in the heat of summer by the store of ice hidden away in the ice-house in the woods. Such delights were quite unknown to the rest of the population and so should figure more prominently in the picture presented to those who, as the National Trust Handbook puts it, 'want to experience the drama of the past'.

26

The Floating Island of Derwent Water

In the hot August days of the memorable summer of 2003 an eighteenth century tourist attraction made a brief reappearance in the Lake District. For three sunny days it basked on the surface of Derwent Water, unnoticed by the tourist throngs, seen only by the passing ferrymen, its moment of fame long departed. It is an oddity, a strange natural phenomenon which for most of the time is invisible beneath the water but rises to the surface at irregular and unpredictable intervals, with a constantly changing size and shape, before sinking once more to rest on the bed of the lake. Scientists have long predicted that it may never appear again.

This is Derwent Water's floating island, which has its base in the bay where the Watendlath Beck pours its waters into the lake. As a curiosity it attracted the attention of the first guidebook writers, whose readers were as fascinated by the exotic, the eccentric and the mysterious in these wild, outlandish places as they were bewildered by the 'horror' of the mountain scenery. Unfortunately, its appearance could never be guaranteed from one year to the next and its very existence was often called into question. William Hutchinson, having been fortunate enough to see it in 1773, informed the readers of his *Excursion to the Lakes* that it was 'a very extraordinary phenomenon'. But on a subsequent visit he failed to find it and declared the whole thing to be a hoax. 'The tale of a floating island appears, on strict examination, to be fabulous,' he wrote. In this he was mistaken.

The island made 20 appearances in the first half of the nineteenth century and it became an object of speculation and investigation by both amateur theorists and serious scientists for many years. No-one any longer doubted its existence. Joseph Budworth sailed a boat through it in 1792 when it split into two halves; the *Philosophical Magazine* gave details of its measurements in 1801, and John Postlethwaite, the geologist, had a picnic on it.

As a tourist attraction it has its limitations, for it is little more than a soggy mass of decaying vegetation covered with an assortment of small

Floating Island on Derwentwater by W. Westall, image courtesy of Tullie House Museum, Carlisle.

water plants. Harriet Martineau considered it to have ' more celebrity than it deserves', while Wordsworth's *Guide to the Lakes* merely commented that, 'It might be worthwhile to mention… a considerable tract of spongy ground… which is called the Floating Island.' By 1886 Baddeley's famous guide dismissed it as 'hardly worth mentioning'.

The scientists thought otherwise. Jonathan Otley studied it for almost twenty years: he measured it, probed it, walked all over it and described its every detail, from the nature of the lake bed on which it usually rested to the names of the aquatic plants growing on its surface. His conclusions were that the island consisted of 'a congeries of decayed vegetable matter forming a stratum of loose peat earth about six feet in thickness which rises from a bed of very fine soft clay.'

He noted that the island appeared only during the summer months and only during a period of very warm weather. This led him to believe that the gases produced by the decomposition of the vegetable matter became rarefied in the heat, thus rendering the whole mass of less weight than an equal volume of water and so it rose to the surface.

Once the gases had dispersed the island sank once more to the bottom of the lake where it remained until the cycle was repeated. He found that the most interesting plants growing on the island were quillwort, shoreweed and water lobelia, all of which flourished whether they were above or below water. Otley predicted that since the decay of the body of the vegetation was not accompanied by equivalent amounts of new deposits there would be a steadily decreasing volume of gas produced and therefore the island would rise less frequently as the years passed and would also be gradually smaller in size – a prediction which has been fully borne out in the past 50 years. In 2003 it was very small and rose only some 15-20cm above the surface of the lake.

Otley's studies encouraged several eminent scientists to investigate the island. John Dalton analysed the gases given off by the vegetation and concluded that there were 'equal parts of carburetted hydrogen and azotic (nitric) gases'; Dr W. J. Russell, some years later, found that as much as 80% of the gas was marsh gas (methane); and Dr A. Knight's observations indicated that 'the vegetable matter brought down by the Lodore stream formed a delta of a spongy character forming peaty earth with little to anchor it.' In the 1880s the first systematic and comprehensive scientific study of the island was undertaken by G. J. Symonds, the eminent meteorologist.

He published his findings in 1888 under the title *The History and Mystery of the Floating Island*. In a detailed analysis of every occasion on which the island had appeared, Symonds calculated that there were about 40 appearances between 1753 and 1888. The size of the island varied considerably, the smallest, in 1876, being 320 sq.ft. (30 sq.m.), and the largest, in 1798, 250 times greater at 81,000 sq.ft. (7,525sq.m.). The earliest recorded date of the island's surfacing in any year was 5 June 1883, and the latest date of its disappearance in any year was at the end of October 1813.

The longest period during which it remained on the surface was from 10 June to 24 September 1831. In most other respects Symonds largely confirmed the conclusions of other studies, adding only that the 'soft clay' on the bed of the lake referred to by Otley was diatomite and it was this which allowed the peaty mass to lift cleanly from its resting place. With characteristic thoroughness Symonds also conducted experiments to ascertain the weight-bearing qualities of the island's surface. This varied greatly: sometimes it was too soggy to bear one person's weight for more than a few minutes; often, several people could stand on a plank quite safely; and on one memorable occasion it is said that the Keswick Town Band gave a concert on the island.

Today little interest is taken in this curious phenomenon and nothing of significance has been added to Symonds' researches. It now appears only very rarely. Its diminished size makes it an undistinguished feature on the lake, it has no merit as a scenic attraction, its strange behaviour is no longer a mystery, it has ceased to find a place in the guidebooks, and few visitors know of its existence. Indeed, so uncertain had its status become in the 1930s that a posse of enterprising and patriotic Girl Guides, suspecting perhaps that even the sovereignty of the island was in doubt, organised a landing party to set up a flag to claim it for England.

Esthwaite Water and Coniston Water also had floating islands but they differed from Derwent Water's in that they were always floating on the surface and were frequently blown about the lake by strong winds. Little is known of Coniston's floating island but in 1864 Eliza Lynn Linton visited the site where it 'got stranded among the reeds at Nibthwaite during a high wind and heavy flood, and has never been able to get off again.' Esthwaite's island was seen by both Wordsworth and Coleridge who particularly noted that it had trees growing on it, a fact confirmed by Jonathan Otley who identified them as 'alder and willow of considerable size', adding that the island was 24 yards long and five or six yards wide. An interesting description of this island appeared in a book entitled *The Diversions of Purley* by John Home Tooke, the eighteenth century philologist and maverick politician:

> Adjoining Esthwaite Water, near Hawkshead, there is a lake or small tarn called Priest Pot, upon which there is an island containing a rood of land and mostly covered by willows, one of them 18 or 20 feet high, and known by the name of 'carr'.

At the breaking up of the severe frost of 1795, a boy ran into the house of the proprietor of the island and told him that his carr was coming up the tarn. The owner and his family looked and beheld with astonishment as their woody isle approached them with slow and majestic motion. It rested before it reached the edge of the tarn and afterwards frequently changed its place as the wind shifted. Esthwaite's island continued to be blown about Priest Pot until the 1880s when a violent storm blew it hard ashore and, despite the efforts of the natives of Hawkshead to pull it free with ropes, there it remained.

27

Journey's End

The Countryside and Rights of Way Act, passed by Parliament in the year 2000, marked the end of a long and at times bitterly contested campaign to secure freedom of access to large tracts of the countryside previously closed to the public. The Act also paved the way for a clarification of the legal status of rights of way and for an improvement to the network to facilitate a wider recreational enjoyment of the countryside. In many respects, this brought to a successful conclusion a journey which began in the nineteenth century when exploring the open spaces and walking in the countryside became a popular form of exercise and relaxation.

In modern times most of the interest in rights of way has been in the context of recreational activity. This was not always so. Historically, most of the lanes and paths which form the rights of way network had a distinctly practical, utilitarian origin: in the days when most people travelled on foot or on horseback almost all journeys were 'necessary' journeys – from home to work or to the local markets, to neighbouring farmsteads or to isolated barns or a remote shepherd's bothy – or, eventually, the final journey to church.

In Cumbria, the corpse roads along which bodies were taken for burial, either strapped to the back of a sturdy fell pony or drawn on a sled, are probably our most ancient rights of way and they were vigilantly protected down the centuries against obstruction or encroachment. To appreciate their importance we must try to visualise the pattern of human settlement as it was in the early Middle Ages eight or nine hundred years ago. Within the central area of Lakeland the population was very sparse and scattered in remote farmsteads where folk lived a rough life based on subsistence farming and self-sufficiency. Much of the land in the dales was still covered in ancient woodland or with the debris and swamps left by the long-vanished glaciers. There were no towns or villages as we have them today – a few cottages clustered round a homestead formed the only community settlements and these could hardly be

Funeral party on the Swindale corpse road, image courtesy of the British Horse Society.

described as hamlets.

They had no church they could call their own. The parishes to which they were formally attached were large and the church itself could be many demanding miles away: thus Holy Trinity, Kendal, served most of the valleys of the south and east as far as Grasmere, Langdale, Windermere and Longsleddale; St Kentigern's at Crosthwaite extended its parochial care as far south as Dunmail Raise and over the vast area around Derwentwater, Borrowdale and Bassenthwaite; Buttermere, Lorton and Wythop formed part of the parish of Brigham, near Cockermouth; for Loweswater, Ennerdale, and, (until about 1445 when St Catherine's in Eskdale was consecrated), Wasdale and part of Eskdale, the parish church was at St Bees; Furness, the Duddon Valley, Hawkshead and Upper Eskdale looked to Millom and Dalton; the boundary of Barton Parish extended over Patterdale and Martindale and all the land round Ullswater, and reached to the summits of Helvellyn, High Street and Fairfield; the well-settled land of Cartmel had its own Priory Church but the dead from Mardale had to be carried seven miles across bleak moorland to Shap.

The medieval folk of the Lakeland dales did not normally go to church, except for baptisms, weddings or burials; eventually the church came to them. Local dales churches were founded as the centuries passed, but the process was slow – between 1291 and 1535 only Bowness and Grasmere obtained their own churches. Others followed rather more quickly but even then these dales churches rarely had consecrated burial grounds and the ancient corpse roads to the 'Mother Church' remained in use, a few of them until the eighteenth century.

Before this last journey was undertaken folk custom and superstition demanded that certain rituals be observed. As soon as someone died, for example, it was of the utmost importance 'to tell the bees' and to adorn the hives with a black ribbon. Bees were regarded as part of the community and would take offence – and were even likely to die or fail to produce honey – if they were not treated with due consideration. It was important, too, that they were given a share of the funeral repast. This strange communion with 'the sacred bee' has been traced to the traditions of classical Greece and Rome and was practised among folk of Scandinavian origin until the nineteenth century.

It was customary to invite two guests from each farmstead in the neighbourhood to the funeral repast and all those 'bidden' were under a strict social obligation to attend as a mark of respect to the dead. All visitors were expected to 'touch the body' not only as a sign of respect but as symbolic proof that they were innocent of the death of the deceased, a superstition founded in the violence and rough justice of the times when personal quarrels often ended in murder.

For the funeral repast special 'arvel ale' was brewed, 'arvel cheese' prepared and 'arvel bread' baked – again a custom of Scandinavian origin, *arvel* being related to the Norse word for inheritance, in this case probably suggesting a parting gift. This modest feast was usually held when guests returned after the interment, but it is not difficult to surmise that some of it would be consumed at rest-points on the long journey to and from the church, a journey which in winter (when many people died) could be hard and not without hazard.

A brief account of one such journey has survived in the ecclesiastical archives but we may be sure that there must have been many others like it. One of the few corpse roads in Cumbria still recorded on the map is that once used by the inhabitants of the hamlet of Garrigill, near Alston, to convey their dead for burial at Kirkland in the Eden Valley. This ancient track, part of which is now a section of the Pennine Way, is ten miles long and rises to a height of almost 2,600 ft (800m) near the summit of Cross Fell.

Today the hazards of the route are the numerous deserted pit shafts, but in earlier times when winters were more severe, the coffin bearers were almost certain to face bitter cold, heavy snowfall and blizzards. On one such day the deceased never arrived at Kirkland: a snowstorm forced the procession to abandon the journey and the body was quickly buried on the open moor. This sacrilegious treatment of the dead soon reached the ears of the Bishop of Durham who travelled to the scene to consecrate the site and ordered a wall to be built round it. On Meg Moffat's Hill, the nineteenth century Ordnance Survey maps show a small round enclosure, the only man-made feature on this vast expanse of cold, bleak moorland. Is it too fanciful to imagine that Meg Moffat was the name of the abandoned lady and that this desolate enclosure was her final resting place? To try to avoid a repetition of such impromptu interments the bishop ordered that a note of all future births and deaths in the area

'Coffin Rest' stone between Grasmere and Rydal, photograph by the author.

should be placed in a box deposited at the Fox Inn in Garrigill.

Another corpse road, still marked on the map, was used for many centuries to take the dead from Mardale for burial at Shap. Crossing the Rowantreethwaite Beck by a diminutive packhorse bridge the route climbs steeply towards Selside Pike before descending into remote and secluded Swindale. It then traverses the empty wilderness of Ralfland Forest by a track still known as the Kirkgate, to Keld and so to the burial ground at Shap – a distance of seven desolate miles. A successful petition in 1728 by the inhabitants of Mardale for their own consecrated burial ground pleaded that it was not only the dead who had to travel these long journeys but 'the souls as well as the bodies of infants taken to be baptised'. Their request was granted in 1736 but the corpse road did not fall into disuse. Mardale's dairy produce was taken this way to the butter market at Shap and when the mainline railway came to Shap in the mid-nineteenth century over 3,000lbs (1,360kg) of butter were sent each week to market at Manchester.

The Norse hamlet at Wasdale Head was even more isolated than Mardale. For several centuries its infants and its dead had to be taken to St Bees for baptism and burial. By what route is unrecorded, but it could not have been less than sixteen miles. This changed in the mid-fifteenth century when St Catherine's in Eskdale was consecrated and a corpse route of less than half the distance came into use. This negotiated the wetlands at the head of Wastwater fording several becks on the way, and then climbed to the high moorland of Burnmoor. Passing Burnmoor Tarn it then descended to Boot and to the church by the River Esk. As any walker knows these moorlands can be eerie places in thick mist, as perfect a setting as any for ghostly tales and macabre legends. The Burnmoor corpse road is said to be haunted by the ghost of a horse which bolted into the mist while bearing a coffin to Eskdale – neither horse nor coffin nor the body it contained was ever seen again – in their worldly manifestation at least.

Other corpse roads are known to have existed but their precise routes are lost. A number of them appear to have been extinguished during the great changes to the landscape brought about by the enclosures of the eighteenth and early nineteenth centuries: such a route is believed to have existed from the scattered settlements of Kershope Forest to the church at Bewcastle. A few were 'green lanes', which were later absorbed into the modern highway system and were tarmaced. This was the fate of one of the most poignant of all the old corpse roads. In the graveyard of Cartmel Priory are gravestone memorials to many people who drowned while travelling on the then much used 'road' across the shifting sands and channels of Morecambe Bay. These victims of the tides were taken to Flookburgh from where they were borne to Cartmel along the local corpse road, then a green lane, but now a minor motor road via The Green and Birkby.

The routes followed by the corpse roads from Coniston to Ulverston, from Hawkshead to Dalton and from Grasmere to Kendal are now largely a matter for speculation, but they were in jealously guarded use until these remote and tiny hamlets acquired their own burial grounds. There are very few relics to remind us of these long-forgotten tracks: on the popular footpath which runs from Rydal Hall to Grasmere, once part of an ancient corpse road, many a weary walker has rested on a large boulder near How Top which, according to tradition, was a Coffin Stone, or Corpse Rest, where the funeral cortege would pause for a while for rest and refreshment – and, it was believed, to give the soul of the deceased a moment of repose. A few similar resting points still survive.

These are visible artifacts, unlike the legend of Jenkins Syke, a small beck a short distance from Coniston Church along the former corpse road to the old Norman Church at Ulverston. The story goes that the coffin bearing the body of a Mr Jenkins slipped, unnoticed apparently, from the sled on which it was being drawn and fell into the beck. Its loss was eventually noticed, and after safe recovery from the beck, it was finally delivered to its more permanent place of rest. As the origin of a place-name Jenkins's hapless, if posthumous, plunge into the syke must surely be unique. Is it possible that the family of the dead man had neglected to 'tell the bees'?

28

By Road and Rail in Borrowdale

William Wordsworth famously fumed in poetry and in letters to the press against the construction of the railway into the Lake District in the 1840s.

> *Is then no nook of English ground secure*
> *From rash assault?*

We may not readily agree with some of the reasons he gave for his protest, but we have now learned the full implications of his concern that ease of access would result in an explosion of tourism which would inflict injury on the peace and quiet of the district. In the wake of the tourists, he warned, would come 'entertainments' and 'excitements and recreations', 'most of which might easily be had elsewhere.' He pleaded that 'the beauty be undisfigured and the character of retirement unviolated.'

Wordsworth was realist enough to see that 'the railway power… will not admit of being materially counteracted by sentiment' and he lived just long enough to witness the arrival of the first trains into Windermere. He was shrewd enough also to appreciate that it was commercial calculation rather than his public protests which caused the abandonment of the plan to extend the line to Grasmere. Even so, he would, no doubt, have been foremost among those who vigorously campaigned, 50 years later, against the threatened violation of the tranquillity of Borrowdale and of the wilderness solitude of the old pack-horse route over the Sty Head Pass.

In the 1880s the green-slate quarries at Honister were in trouble. Unlike many other Lakeland quarries the Buttermere Green Slate Company had not yet acquired easy access to a railhead. The Furness Railway had reached the Kirkby blue-slate quarries by 1850 and the Coniston quarries by 1859; the green-slate operations in the Langdales had also benefited from the Coniston link and the branch-line to Lakeside; the great stone quarries at Shap, Threlkeld and Stainton-in-Furness had their own railhead. Slate from Honister was no longer laboriously hauled by pack-horse fifteen miles to Ravenglass along the flanks of Grey Knotts, Brandreth and Great Gable, but in the 1880s it still had to be taken by pack-horse down to Grange-in-Borrowdale and then by horse and cart to the new railhead at Keswick, a slow and expensive procedure at a time when customers were plentiful and annual production had increased from just under 2,000 tons in 1880 to almost 3,000 tons in 1888. A report to the managers in 1884 stated that the future viability of the company depended on cheaper and quicker transport.

It was, therefore, proposed to construct a railway from the quarry to link up with the Penrith to Cockermouth line at Braithwaite near Keswick. The estimated cost was £14,000 – about £1.5 million in modern values. The plans drawn up for this line show that from Braithwaite the route was intended to follow the Newlands Beck to the west of Swinside before swinging over to the shore of Derwent Water near Hawes End. From here it ran along the slopes of Cat Bells to Manesty and then on to Hollows Farm near Grange. Slate wagons – and in time, no doubt, passenger trains – would then travel under Castle Crag and along the lower contours of High Scawdel, a fine scenic route with splendid views over the Derwent and the Borrowdale valley. But transporting slate rather than enjoying scenic beauty was the purpose of this enterprise. Just above Seatoller the line would turn to follow the contour round to Honister Hause where it would link up with the tramway which already carried the slate down to this point.

Many tons of slate could be transported in minutes along this eight mile journey compared to the small loads which took a whole day to complete the same distance by pack-horse and by cart along sometimes steep and narrow roads which were little more than rough tracks. An annual production of 10,000 tons of slate was (optimistically) envisaged, securing a prosperous future for the company.

The Borrowdale and Buttermere Railway (it was planned to extend the line to Buttermere later) would have had a great impact not only on the fortunes of the Honister slate quarries but also on the Borrowdale Valley itself. The very prospect of its early completion led to considerable investment in improving production at the quarry and by 1891 annual output exceeded 3,000 tons for the first time. By this time, however, it was beginning to be apparent that the line might never be built. Land along the route was owned by a Mr Marshall who stubbornly refused to consider negotiating a sale to enable the work to begin. He appeared to be as a frustrated company official put it, 'completely obsessed with preserving the beauty of the Lake District', but one must suspect that it was not so much the beauty of the landscape which concerned him as the price offered for the land, since at the same time he was trying to promote the construction of a rail line along Ullswater to Pooley Bridge.

Marshall's refusal to negotiate was finally set in stone when he was further antagonised by one of the directors of the Honister Slate Company who provoked a petty quarrel with him over the operation of the Borrowdale Wad Mines. In 1894 negotiations came to an end. In 1907 a road was built between Honister and Seatoller and slate was transported to the railhead at Keswick by a traction engine pulling loads of sixteen tons. No more was heard of the railway.

Attention now turned to another extraordinary scheme to relieve Borrowdale from its 'isolation'. In 1896 George Bell, then Surveyor and Bridgemaster of the Highways of Cumberland, and John Musgrave of Wasdale Hall, a Whitehaven solicitor and owner of estates in Wasdale and in Borrowdale, came to the conclusion that the old packhorse track over the Sty Head Pass was an anachronism in late Victorian England and an obstacle to developing the prosperity of the two valleys. Their influence was brought to bear on members of the Whitehaven Rural District Council who in the same year solemnly pronounced that such a highway would be an appropriate way to commemorate the Queen's Diamond Jubilee, adding that 'The time may come when this Empire will need all its resources in battle... Of great importance is the free communication between all parts of the country. The making of roads was one of Rome's chief glories... A needful proposal for developing our county's resources is a carriage road over Sty Head Pass.' Musgrave was at pains to point out that if this road were constructed the distance between Keswick and Wasdale Head would be reduced from forty to seventeen miles – a blessing which would certainly benefit the interests of John Musgrave and might even prove to be the salvation of the British Empire.

George Bell had estimated the cost at £10,000 but quickly discovered that the Cumberland County Council Highways Committee was far from enthusiastic about his plans, while Eskdale Parish Council made their approval conditional on the road's extension over Burnmoor to Boot.

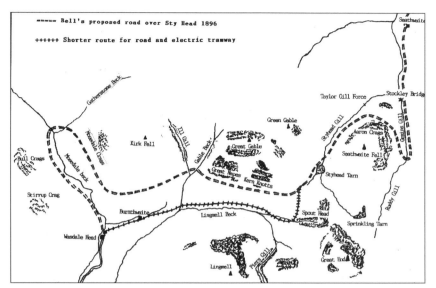

Proposed rail route Sty Head, map by the author.

Only the *Whitehaven News* expressed a keen interest in the scheme, pointing out that the new carriage road would offer 'increased access to Wasdale for the thousands of tourists who are at present confined to the beaten tracks of the coach roads about Keswick, Ambleside, Windermere and the Langdales.' But not everyone shared this concern for the tourists – an Eskdale parish councillor commented that they 'always forgot to close gates and were quite a nuisance to the farmers.'

In his report to the Highways and Bridges Committee in 1896 Bell outlined the route he had surveyed for a carriage road eighteen feet wide to link Wasdale Head and Seathwaite Farm in Borrowdale, thus reducing the distance by road between these two places from 66 miles to just under eight miles. For most of this distance the gradients would be between 1 in 12 and 1 in 20.

From Wasdale Head Bell's route went up the Mosedale Valley passing under Stirrup Crag and Bull Crags before swinging round to cross Gatherstone Beck. It then followed the contour under Mosedale Crags and across the face of Kirk Fell before crossing Gable Beck and passing under the towering crags of Great Napes and Kern Knotts to arrive at the summit of the pass near Styhead Tarn, 'the whole being on sound ground and well above all moving screes'.

For the descent to Seathwaite the route followed the well-travelled pack-horse track (and present bridleway) to just above Taylor Gill Force where it turned along the contours under Aaron Crags to descend on a 1 in 12 gradient to Grains Gill and Ruddy Gill and straight down to Seathwaite. Bell confidently informed the committee that there were no engineering difficulties involved and the construction of this road could be achieved 'with the ordinary pick, shovel and crowbar, except in a few isolated places, and at the summit, where explosives will be needed.'

Bell's optimism and Musgrave's enthusiasm were not shared either by the county council who were uneasy about the financial commitment involved or by the public who subscribed only £1,000 of the £5,000 they were asked for. At a meeting in Keswick in the summer of 1896 a stormy session ended when the chairman asked members 'to do nothing more to the Borrowdale road to the end of time.'

Musgrave was undeterred and in 1901 commissioned Bell to survey an alternative route which would be both shorter and less costly. This would follow the ancient pack-horse and sheep track from Wasdale Head along the course of Lingmell Beck, crossing Spouthead Gill under Great End and swinging round to the head of the pass near Styhead Tarn. This also failed to arouse public or financial interest but, undaunted, Musgrave now turned his attention to the newest form of transport which was about to enter its golden age: the electric tram. He drew up a plan to build such a tramway from Seascale to Keswick via Wastwater, Sty Head and Borrowdale. Electric power would be generated by turbines sited by the waterfalls along the way. These plans were boosted when in 1909 Parliament passed the Development Funds Act which Musgrave hoped to exploit to raise the necessary financial resources.

Once more the *Whitehaven News* joined the fray and in 1910 enlisted the new pastime of cycling in its campaign in support of the road:

> To cyclists a carriage road over the Sty Head Pass would be an inestimable boon. People have been known to take cycles over the pass (for the greater part of the way on their shoulders) but for the cyclists making radial excursions from Keswick it has been usual to leave their machines at Seathwaite when bound for Wastwater and spend the rest and better part of the day on foot.

Again the county council adhered to the resolution of 1896 that nothing more should be done about the road, this time expressing its belief that the local valley roads would be unable to cope with the increase in traffic which the Sty Head road would bring. It was the threat from the motor-car which dominated the council's final debate on the issue in 1919 and the proposal was soundly defeated by 39 votes to 9. It was significant that on this occasion environmental considerations played a part in the controversy: *The Times*, *The Manchester Guardian* and even *The Whitehaven News* published letters deploring the prospect of the 'stenchy motor car' intruding into this mountain wilderness, one correspondent exhorting the authorities 'to keep motors away, and with a flaming sword guard the sacred Paradise of Styhead Pass.'

A formidable letter from Canon Hardwicke Rawnsley to the *Carlisle Patriot* did much to destroy any illusions about the enterprise. He wrote that most arguments in favour of the road were a threadbare cover for commercial scheming. It was not a wish to foster relations between farmers or to enhance the nation's strategic defences or 'an amicable desire to allow the aged and infirm to see the wonders of Great End and Mickledore' which was the inspiration, but a plan 'to exploit private property at Wasdale and the Sty' and 'to promote the construction of a sanatorium and a hotel at Sty Head... with future possibilities for development for commercial enterprise in the Scawfell solitudes.'

With withering sarcasm Rawnsley commented that:

> the Sty Head sun-cure establishment, at an elevation of 1,600 feet, with a rainfall of 156 inches and a cloud blanket for days, nay weeks, together, above it, is, we are seriously told, to prove a counter attraction to the hotels at elevations of 3,000 feet in their sunny cloudlessness upon the mountains of Italy and Switzerland. The Sanatorium will indeed be a first-class hydro; no better place for the complete water cure could probably be found.

Furthermore, Rawnsley pointed out, the county council had made it clear that this would be a district council road and so the ratepayers of the parish and district councils through whose areas the road would pass would bear 'all the responsibility of maintaining this costly coach-way'.

Even so the project did not die. In 1927 Barber and Atkinson wrote in their book *Lakeland Passes* of the 'spasmodic attempts... made to re-open the question of making roads over Wrynose and Hard Knott and Sty Head,' adding uncompromisingly that 'to drive roads through them would be an act of sheer vandalism.' The wartime surfacing of Wrynose and Hard Knott caused much concern but in 1951 the establishment of the Lake District National Park and a wider public appreciation of the concept of conservation probably gave the final coup de grace to any scheme to desecrate the landscape over Sty Head.

You will rarely find yourself alone on the Sty Head Pass, for this is one of the great crossroads of Lakeland where paths meet from many points of the compass. But here neither sight nor sound of modern traffic will disturb that tranquillity which is the joy of walking in the quiet wilderness and the misty solitudes.

29

The Natland Treacle Mine

Cumbria is rich in legend and tales of the mysterious and the supernatural; and fortunately much of this traditional folklore has now been preserved in various compilations. It is not difficult to discover the story of the Orton Dobbie, the fairies of Mallerstang, the Devil at work in Kirkby Lonsdale, the giants of Penrith, the ghosts of Martindale or Levens Hall, or the phantom army of Souther Fell. It is, however, almost impossible to get to the bottom of the Natland Treacle Mine: this has long been a legend wrapped in whimsical evasion, lapse of memory, and obscurantist protection of a village secret.

Any attempt to piece together the miscellany of information the curious enquirer is able to glean about this unusual local phenomenon is, therefore, fraught with difficulty; but one version of the story might go like this:

Once upon a time – in the year 1211 to be precise – a man wandering in the woods near the village came across the entrance to a cave. Inside, on a flat rock by an underground stream, he saw a small pot which, with eager hands, he seized upon, believing it to be the treasure which, according to a local tradition, had been discovered in the ruins of the nearby Roman fort and then secretly hidden to save it from marauding Vikings. In his excitement he failed to see a dangerous serpent lying under the rock and it suddenly attacked him, biting him on the hand which held the pot. The poisonous venom worked quickly; the pot fell to the ground and shattered and the unfortunate man sank to the floor of the cave, apparently lifeless.

After a while he recovered consciousness and when he realised where he was he looked round frantically for the serpent; but it had vanished. To his surprise he felt no pain and seemed none the worse for his close encounter with death. His hand was covered with a golden, sticky liquid which had leaked from the broken pot and, eventually, he realised that the 'treasure' he had found was not gold but a miraculous cure for poisonous bites. And, flowing through the cave was a river of this healing liquid: he could soon be a rich man – if only he could keep the secret of the magic treacle mine.

Tales of hoards of gold, usually in a pot, in remote caves guarded by serpents or dragons, appear frequently in the mythology of Ancient Greece and Rome and also in medieval folk literature throughout Europe. The north of England has its share of such legends and it is not surprising that Cumbria has its own version with its own original twist to the story.

But why a treacle mine? Myths and folk-tales often demand that we suspend reality for a while and indulge in flights of fantasy, but to ask for belief in a river of golden syrup forever flowing beneath the green fields of Westmorland is a step too far. It is no wonder that curious visitors to Natland have moved on, baffled and amused, or, like Arthur Mee in the 1950s, have impatiently declared that 'There are no treacle mines'. This will not do! A closer examination of the word 'treacle' soon reveals that in its original meaning it had nothing to do with molasses or golden syrup. This is a comparatively modern meaning dating only from the development of the West Indian sugar trade in the eighteenth century. Before that 'treacle' meant something entirely different.

The Greek word *theriake*, (Latin *theriaca*) meaning an antidote against poisonous bites, passed into medieval French as *triacle* and this passed directly into medieval English. In time the word acquired a wider meaning as a remedy not only for poisonous bites but for almost any poisonous infection or bodily ailment. In the *Introduction to the Pardoner's Tale* in Chaucer's *Canterbury Tales* the love-smitten Host tells of the violent palpitations of his heart which, he says, will surely fail unless he is given a *triacle* or a draught of good ale; and in the fifteenth century the Paston family sent an urgent request that 'the first man that comyth from London' should bring 'two pottes of tryacle of Jenne.'

This Genoa treacle was only one of the various treacles which were available. Treacles were also made in London, Rome and Flanders, but most prized of all was Venice Treacle used by emperors and kings of ancient times and by others throughout history; it was a standard prescription recommended by physicians of nineteenth century Europe and Victorian England. All these treacles were salves or ointments made from a compound of numerous herbs mixed with honey. Venice treacle contained as many as 64 different herbs and the flesh of a viper or scorpion.

Such 'pottes of tryacle' were very expensive and only the wealthy could afford them. The Pastons paid eight pence a pot for their Genoa treacle, the equivalent of two days wages for most ordinary folk at that time. But every housewife in the Middle Ages had an intimate knowledge of the special virtues of all the herbs which grew in the neighbourhood and many local 'treacles' were concocted, using honey or resin and the pure spring waters which were found everywhere. Thus in the famous books of Herbal Medicine garlic and rue and germander speedwell are referred to as 'the poor man's treacle'.

From this it was but a short step to the widespread belief that the 'healing' waters of mineral springs and Holy Wells could act as a kind of treacle to cure or alleviate almost any ailment known to the human frame. This is dramatically illustrated in the stained glass window by Burne-Jones in Christ Church Cathedral, Oxford, showing a crowd of sick and maimed pilgrims at St Margaret's Treacle Well near Oxford.

Cumbria is especially well-endowed with these healing mineral springs, some of them known to the Celts and the Romans, some of them modestly famous as holy wells and even as spas. Some may at one time have been known as treacle wells but today that description survives in only one location – and that, by virtue of its subterranean nature, is known as a Treacle Mine.

It is now impossible to determine when the legend of the Natland Treacle Mine originated but we can plausibly deduce from the version given above that the author was aware not only of the historical meaning of the word treacle but was also acquainted with the golden syrup of modern usage. He must also have been well-read in classical mythology, familiar with the use of herbal medicines and with the cult of 'healing waters'. The date he gives – 1211 – is too precise for ready acceptance: perhaps he was keen on cricket since in Roman numerals 1211 becomes MCC XI. In any event to combine all this into a simple legend is a lively feat of imagination.

We have, therefore, established that treacle wells did actually exist and that, once upon a time, the word 'treacle' was in common usage to mean a healing medicine, either a genuine treacle as a balm or ointment or, more popularly, as herbal medicine made with the waters from a mineral spring.

The healing properties of the treacle well at Binsey, near Oxford, were first noted by St. Frideswide in the seventh century and it became a famous place of medieval pilgrimage, and it is this well which appears in Lewis Carroll's *Alice's Adventures in Wonderland*, a book which achieved enormous success in the later years of the nineteenth century. It is not impossible that this may have been the inspiration for the legend of the Natland Treacle Mine. Was this as truly a genuine topographical feature as Alice's treacle well near Oxford? Or is the whole story pure fantasy?

In 1983 a remarkable discovery was made which puts the whole story in a new perspective. In that year contractors for the North West Water Authority were excavating a trench for a new water pipe across a field near the village when they broke through into a subterranean cavern. Two experienced cavers investigated and discovered a totally unexpected cave system several thousand feet long with a subterranean stream flowing rapidly through it. A full exploration was not possible in the time available but in the 2,000 feet which were explored the cave rose in places to a height of 30 feet with the width varying from several feet to a narrow passage. Most of the usual features of limestone caves were found but of especial interest were several clusters of helictites, a pocket of cave pearls and several cascades. Regrettably, North West Water Authority did not permit a complete survey of the whole length of the cave and permanently sealed the only known entrance with many tons of concrete. Further investigation has since been denied.

This discovery raises the question whether this natural feature was known to earlier generations. It is only a few feet below the level of the fields, the watercourse must have an outlet not too far away, there is evidence of sink-holes in the vicinity, and in former times local folk had an extraordinarily detailed knowledge of their neighbourhood. Earth movement or some other activity may have blocked an entrance once well-known in the locality. The underground waters were clean and pure and often rise to flood the fields above,* ideally suited for the concoction of home-made 'treacle' with the herbs which grew abundantly in the surrounding woods.

Perhaps the best-known reference to 'treacle' in its original meaning appears in the so-called 'Treacle Bible', the 1535 translation of the Bible into English by Miles Coverdale. In the Book of Jeremiah the prophet

---

* Elderly correspondents write to say that as children they were sent to drink this water when they complained of stomach upsets.

cries out in despair 'Is there no treacle in Gilead?', a translation which in 1611 the Authorised Version changed to 'Is there no balm in Gilead?', an indication that even by that date not everyone would have understood the original meaning of treacle. By 1865 when *Alice in Wonderland* was published the idea of a treacle well clearly belonged to the world of fantasy – even if Lewis Carroll himself knew precisely what it meant.

He, one may surmise, would have been content for the Dormouse to tell his story under a tree in our Westmorland village:

Once upon a time there were three little sisters… and they lived at the bottom of a well –
'Why did they live at the bottom of a well?'
'It was a treacle well'.
'There's no such thing,' Alice was beginning very angrily… and the Dormouse sulkily remarked, 'If you can't be civil, you'd better finish the story yourself.'
'No, please go on,' Alice said very humbly… 'I dare say there might be one.'

30

The Eruption of Solway Moss

Solway Moss lies between the Rivers Esk and Sark in the north west corner of Cumbria where England and Scotland merge. It is a flat and desolate landscape with few if any of the conventional scenic attractions, but it has vast skies, artistic cloudscapes and fiery sunsets spreading shimmering colours across the distant sands of the Solway Firth. It is the most northerly of the five raised bogs which collectively are often referred to as the Solway Mosses; the other four are situated south of the Firth, all are protected as Sites of Special Scientific Interest, and two, Glasson Moss and Drumburgh Moss are National Nature Reserves. Much damage has been inflicted on these mosses – in the nineteenth century by peat-digging by local householders exercising their rights to cut peat for fuel on common land and, far more destructively, by mechanised commercial operations in more recent decades.

Reclamation of land for agricultural use has also, over the years, eroded much of the original moss. Environmental protection arrived just in time to save just a few hundred hectares of this once vast area of rare landscape together with its specialised plants and the varied wildlife which flourish there: bog rosemary, bog asphodel, great sundew and a variety of sphagnum mosses; the rare large heath butterfly and the adder, the redshank, reed-bunting and curlew, and the red grouse which feeds on the abundant heather.

Geographically, Solway Moss is as remote from the centre of government as it is possible to be in England and on only one occasion has it made a dramatic appearance on the stage of national history. Roman soldiers stationed in the forts on Hadrian's Wall, which skirted the mosses would probably have viewed these empty tracts of marshy wilderness with some apprehension but one imagines that their watch here was fairly uneventful. Throughout the Middle Ages the Solway Mosses were at the western edge of the long border conflict between the English and the Scots, much of it not political or territorial, but family feuding, systematic robbery, indiscriminate plundering and cattle-stealing, all accompanied

Solway Moss, photograph courtesy of Cumbria Wildlife Trust.

by wanton destruction, brutality and blackmail. The mosses provided places of sanctuary where pursuit could be thwarted. This was a lawless and ungovernable no mans land where the Border Reivers held sway for 400 years.

With the end of the Wars of the Roses and the establishment of the Tudor monarchy the ancient rivalry between the Kings of England and Scotland took on a more aggressive form. It was a time-honoured tradition that when the English embarked on yet another pretentious military expedition against the French, the Scots promptly invaded the north of England. In accordance with this custom, and with a burning desire to avenge their catastrophic defeat at the Battle of Flodden in 1513, on 23 November 1542 a Scottish force of up to 20,000 men entered the 'Debateable Lands' near Solway Moss to challenge a posse of several hundred Cumberland Borderers, famed as The Northern Horse and reputed to be 'the finest light cavalry in the world'.

In the resulting skirmish, known to history as The Battle of Solway Moss, the Scots were put to flight leaving behind several hundred prominent prisoners and 20 guns. Solway Moss was no Flodden but it was a disgrace to Scottish arms and when it was followed shortly afterwards by the death of the distraught Scottish king, leaving the throne to a daughter who was only one week old, it assumed far greater significance in the story of Anglo-Scottish relations. Life for those who lived on and around the moss resumed as before, governed only by the turning seasons and only disturbed from time to time by the unpredictable moods of Nature.

Such a disturbance came on the night of 16 November 1771 when Nature struck with sudden and unprecedented fury, in a cataclysm, which a foreign envoy in London compared to an eruption of Mount Vesuvius – Solway Moss had exploded.

Thomas Pennant writing in 1772, described Solway Moss as 'sixteen hundred acres (c650 hectares) of thin peaty mud… even in the driest summer', held together by a fragile crust which had been weakened on one side by local peat-diggers who found here their only source of fuel. An unusually heavy November downpour had deposited a prodigious weight of water into this morass thus adding to the huge volume of water already held in such a great bog.

The surface crust came under enormous pressure and in the stormy darkness a local farmer was alarmed by a thunderous roar, 'a rumbling noise like a number of mill-races.' By the light of his lantern he eventually discerned a wave of liquid mud flowing from the moss towards him, spreading round, into and over cottages, barns and byres. He roused his neighbours but as William Gilpin tells us: 'one house after another was filled and crushed to ruin, just giving the terrified occupants time to make their escape. Scarcely anything was saved, except their lives: nothing of their furniture, few of their cattle. Some people were even surprised in their beds and had the additional distress of flying naked from the ruin.' Others had to be rescued by being hauled up their chimneys. Some 500-600 acres (c240 hectares) of fertile, cultivated land were inundated to a depth of 40-50 feet (12-15 metres). Contemporary reports state that 28 families lost everything; as Gilpin put it, they 'had the whole world totally to begin again.'

There seems to have been no loss of human life in this catastrophe, but deaths among farm animals and wildlife were severe as the suffocating mud invaded cowsheds, sheepfolds, barns and every place of shelter and refuge. Those animals which survived often suffered greatly from the terror of their ordeal. Thomas Pennant relates that one poor cow 'the only one of eight in the same cowhouse that was saved after having stood 60 hours up to the neck in mud and water... would not taste water nor even look without showing manifest signs of horror.'

Six weeks later the *Bristol Gazette* reported that the roofs and chimneys of some of the submerged houses were beginning to emerge from the mud but the inundation continued to spread covering an acre every day until it reached the waters of the River Esk where, as William Gilpin remarked, 'its quantities were such as to annoy the fish; no salmon during that season venturing into the river.' Thomas Pennant describes how it 'flowed like a tide charged with pieces of wreck... and great fragments of peat with their heathy surface... leaving upon the shore tremendous heaps of turf, memorials of the height this dark torrent arrived at.'

The spectacular nature of this bog-burst attracted wide attention at the time but eruptions on a much smaller scale were not uncommon in the days before extensive draining for agriculture resulted in the diminution of so many of the raised bogs which were a feature of many wetland areas. The central mound of Solway Moss subsided by 25 feet (7.5 metres) as a result of this eruption and the ecological damage must have been devastating. No observations were kept of the natural renewal of Solway Moss in the years following this upheaval but studies of later bursts on similar peat mosses suggest that the surface peat layer would have been left in a shattered condition, which would facilitate the fairly rapid regrowth of new vegetation characteristic of such habitats. Birds, butterflies and other wildlife would return soon afterwards. It seems reasonable to assume that within a few years the scars of Solway Moss would have healed and, although much reduced in size, it would once again have become a fine example of a raised bogland. Regrettably, commercial peat extraction denies it that description today, but across the Firth at the Cumbria Wildlife Trust's Drumburgh Moss we can appreciate much of what disappeared on that dark November night in 1771 – and what we have lost today.

31

Millom's Forgotten Castle

Red sandstone glows warmly in the sunshine and golden wallflowers cling to every cranny in the ruined walls. Sheep now graze where ladies strolled in terraced gardens and birds nest on crumbling window seats; a wire fence runs where once a handsome stone balustrade looked out to the wide Duddon marshes, a cow byre casually leans against the four-teenth century kitchen walls and the moat is a tangle of unkempt shrubs. Millom Castle today is a quiet place in which to reflect on the transience of the works of humans.

Yet amid these long-neglected ruins there still looms, huge, gaunt and menacing, the great tower-house, 44 feet high, 50 feet square and with walls seven feet thick, a farmer's residence now but built as a mighty fortress to deter Scottish raiders and to guard the ford across the Duddon. It serves to remind us of the power wielded in these parts by the Lords of Millom who held sway for almost 500 years over lands which covered all of south-west Cumbria, Eskdale, Duddon and most of Low Furness. Another grim reminder of this power may be seen on the edge of the marsh less than half a mile from the castle where the Gallows Stone marks the spot where the Lords of Millom meted out justice in the King's name.

In the redistribution of land which followed the Norman Conquest these lands fell into the hands of Ranulf le Meschin, Earl of Chester, who also controlled the baronies of Kendal, Appleby and Copeland. In 1120, Ranulf, now too powerful for the King's comfort, surrendered his northern territories and Copeland was given to his brother, William, who in turn granted this part of his Barony to the Boyvilles who changed their name to de Millom. Their newly built castle passed by marriage in the mid-thirteenth century to the Hudlestons who rebuilt it and held it until its final days 500 years later.

Much of what remains today appears to date from an extensive re-building which followed the damaging raids on Cumbria carried out by Robert Bruce in the 1320s. John de Hudleston received a licence to

Millom Castle, 1739, by Samuel Buck,
courtesy of Cumbria Library Services.

crenellate his 'Manor House at Millum' in 1335 and he probably built the first pele- tower. Millom thus became part of the chain of fourteenth century fortified houses which guarded the southern coast of Cumbria: Irton, Muncaster, Millom, Broughton, Dalton, Piel, Levens, Sizergh, Dallam, Arnside and Beetham.

Little is known of the detailed history of Millom Castle but a glimpse of life in the household there is revealed by two surviving records of accounts of the daily expenditure for the household and for the castle farm. The first is from the early years of the reign of Henry VIII and the second from Queen Anne's reign 200 years later.

So we learn that in the early sixteenth century the castle figured largely in the economy of the local community. Employment was provided for household servants, shepherds, stockmen, day labourers, seasonal labourers, and the suppliers of essential commodities: malted barley for ale, peat and sea coal for the fires and ovens, linen and woollen cloth for clothing, many items of food, and innumerable articles for the house and the farm – livery for the resident servants, new ropes for the louvres in the hall and kitchen, horseshoes, spades and wagon wheels.

Farm crops were mainly oats and bigg (barley) with a small quantity of wheat for the family's own wheaten bread. Most of the other grains went to make ale, dog bran and fodder for the horses. Fish formed a regular part of the diet – turbot, salmon, herrings, eels and 'salted porpas' appear frequently in the accounts – while they seem to have had a special taste for butter, eggs, beef and 'old crokes' or mature Herdwick sheep which produce a flavoursome mutton. The purchase of large quantities of salt suggests that both fish and meat were laid down for preservation.

The local cottage textile industry also benefited from Hudleston patronage. The liveried servants wore woollen jackets, white woollen hose, linen shirts and smocks, and gloves and doublets made of sheepskin. Local spinners and weavers also supplied the family's clothing and from these dry-as-dust household account books we can even conjure up a picture of 'Little Anne' in her woollen kirtle, linen neckband and kerchief and secondhand gown.

Two centuries later the cash books and day books of Humphrey Senhouse, the agent for Madam Bridget Hudleston in the early 1700s, reveal what has changed and what has remained very much the same. The general pattern of farming changed little but a reference to the purchase of potatoes is of special interest as this vegetable first reached Cumbria in the years just before 1700 and was not widely grown until 30-40 years later.

Other new items in the castle diet seem to indicate that Bridget was very much the post-Restoration lady, for we read that in 1708 she bought anchovies, coffee and 'chockellet' and managed to acquire a consignment of French claret even though at that time there was a government embargo on trade with France – an evasion of the law perhaps not unconnected with the fact that her agent held shares in a Whitehaven shipping company. Bridget was also more demanding in the provision of her wardrobe than her Tudor predecessors: she now had a resident seamstress, 'Irish Jane', who was paid 1½ pence per day; and finer garments were purchased in London, Manchester and Penrith, while her workaday clogs were made in Whitehaven. She was carried about her seignory in a fashionable sedan chair and she enjoyed entertaining her guests at card parties and at convivial Christmas gatherings when the 'Gordon Pipers' were hired to provide music for dancing. Sixty cart loads of peat were ordered to keep them warm and thousands of tapers, candles and rushlights shed light on the festive scene.

This was a modest life-style for the gentry of Queen Anne's time but was not based on the capital resources, thrusting enterprise in trade and the economic exploitation of their estate lands which raised so many eighteenth century landed families to affluence and prosperity. The Hudlestons continued to rely on rents from their tenants and on sales of surplus crops and livestock; and these brought Madam Bridget an annual income of no more than £350 – less than the country parson, James Woodforde.

At the same time the self-sufficiency of her estate was clearly neglected as much food produce was regularly purchased which could have been grown on the home farm. We read that apples, bullaces, eggs and scores of chickens are bought in as are quantities of wheat, beans and rye. Only oats and barley are now grown for household needs. Perhaps Bridget was deterred from capitalist ventures by the recent experience of her predecessor, John Hudleston, who, in a bid to pay off the huge debts left by his predecessor, Ferdinand, partially destroyed the Castle Park by selling off £4,000 worth of its timber to make charcoal for the smelting furnaces of the local iron industry – 'and was little profited thereby'.

This ineptitude in economic management was not the first serious misjudgment of the Hudlestons of Millom. They had over the years made several political miscalculations. They had joined the Earl of Lancaster's ill-fated rebellion against Edward II and were lucky to be among those who received a royal pardon.

They had supported the Yorkists in the Wars of the Roses at a time of Lancastrian ascendancy and the castle was severely damaged as a consequence. In the Civil War they had adopted the Royalist cause – Ferdinand and all his nine sons fought for King Charles – and in 1644 Millom Castle was besieged by Parliamentary forces after the Royalist defeat in a skirmish at Lindal-in-Furness where Colonel Hudleston was taken prisoner. The castle fell after a brief siege and was then extensively 'slighted', while the Hudlestons lost a large part of their lands and received a crippling fine. There was to be no lasting recovery from this disaster.

Ferdinand, however, was an audacious, swashbuckling character and, plunging the family even further into debt, he made the castle habitable once more and gave its battle-scarred walls a brave new face to the world by creating an elegant new entrance with a broad flight of steps to replace the destroyed drawbridge. On the filled-in moat he created lawns and gardens fronted by a long stone balustrade. All this is clearly seen in Samuel Buck's fine engraving of 1739.

Soon after this date the male line of the Hudlestons failed and in 1774 the castle and estates were sold for £20,000 to Sir James Lowther who bought it, as he bought so many other properties, solely as a commercial proposition. The castle consequently fell rapidly into dereliction and, except for the tower house, has been almost totally neglected since. Few would now recognise it as the seat of the Lords of Millom who held power of life and death over all who dwelt in Furness, Eskdale and Dunnerdale. Indeed, few have ever heard of the Lords of Millom or their castle; Millom today is best known as the lifelong home of the poet Norman Nicholson who in all his poems made no mention of either.

(The author acknowledges the assistance of Dr Angus Winchester of the University of Lancaster, and the Earl of Lonsdale for permission to use material which is in their copyright.)

32

Men and Mountains

John Ruskin famously pronounced that 'Mountains are the beginning and the end of all natural scenery', a sentiment which would have seemed absurd, even incomprehensible to an earlier generation. For more than a thousand years until the eighteenth century mountains had been looked upon with distaste: they were repulsive, dangerous, useless disfigurements in the landscape. They were described as 'Nature's shames', 'warts', 'wens', 'monstrous excrescences', 'barren deformities', 'impostumes', 'the rubbish of the Earth'. In his *Guide to the Lakes* Wordsworth wrote 'There is not, I believe, a single English traveller whose published writings would disprove the assertion that where precipitous rocks and mountains are mentioned at all, they are spoken of as objects of dislike and fear, and not of admiration.'

Celia Fiennes passed through the Lake District on her tour of England in 1698 and considered the mountains 'very terrible' and the entire scene 'desert and barren'. Ralph Thoresby, the topographer, visiting the year before, found the area 'full of horrors, dreadful fells, hideous wastes, horrid waterfalls, terrible rocks and ghastly precipices'; Chief Justice Roger North, journeying south from Carlisle to Appleby, cast a disapproving eye on all 'the hideous mountains' on the way; John Morton, the Northamptonshire naturalist greatly preferred the gentle fertile landscape of his own county where there 'are no naked craggy rocks, no rugged and unsightly mountains.'

Daniel Defoe, on tour in the 1720s, considered Westmorland 'eminent only for being the wildest, most barren and frightful' of any county he had passed through, and he turned away from the 'high and formidable' mountains which 'had a kind of unhospitable terror in them'; William Gilpin, 'the apostle of the picturesque', believed that mountains needed to be seen in a selected framework, as in a landscape painting, in order to soften their 'disgusting deformities' and 'grotesque shapes'. As late as 1701 Joseph Addison could still write that 'The Alps… fill the mind with an agreeable kind of horror, and form one of the most irregular mis-shapen scenes in the world'; and even later in the 1770s Dr Samuel Johnson considered the Scottish mountains to be nothing more than 'a wide extent of hopeless sterility'.

Throughout the Middle Ages and until about 1600, centuries when the Church's teaching dominated attitudes to the Creation of the Universe, people's relationship to the natural world was based on the book of Genesis and the Church's interpretation of it. Mountains were not regarded as part of God's original design for the Earth which, it was believed, was created with an entirely smooth surface and oval in shape like an egg, with no sea and no irregularity in the landscape – its beauty lay in its symmetry, fertility and freedom from danger to mankind from natural hazards such as chasms, ravines, precipices or mountains. All this changed when God sent earthquakes and the Flood to punish mankind for its sins. The original smooth surface of the Earth was destroyed; even Luther subscribed to this theology when he wrote: 'Since the Flood mountains exist where fields and fruitful plains flourished before… the whole face of Nature was changed by that mighty convulsion'.

The seventeenth century theologian, Thomas Burnet, in his widely read *Sacred Theory of the Earth* still clung to the idea that 'The face of the Earth before the Deluge was smooth, regular, and uniform; after the Flood there stood the mountains – the Ruins of a Broken World.' But Burnet, however appalled he was by the chaotic 'ruins of the Earth' he saw on his journey to the Alps, he was a man of his time, well aware of the recent scientific advances made in geology, microscopic biology and astronomy – Isaac Newton's discovery of mountains on the moon made a deep impression on him, as did Edmund Halley's theory that the Deluge was caused by the famous comet – and he reflected the seismic shift in attitudes towards mountains when he admitted that 'There is nothing that I look upon with more pleasure than the wide Sea and the Mountains of the Earth. There is something august and stately in the Air of these things, that inspires the Mind with great Thoughts and Passions.' Like many of his contemporaries he was awed by the vast grandeur of the mountains but he did not consider them to possess any special beauty.

Awe, horror and fear were part of the 'sublime'; a sense of beauty came with an appreciation of the pleasure and spiritual uplift a mountain scene can convey. Even in the early nineteenth century William Cobbett declared that he had 'no idea of picturesque beauty separate from the fertility of the soil' and Wordsworth regretted that 'In the eyes of thousands and tens of thousands a rich meadow, with fat cattle grazing upon it, or the sight of what they would call a heavy crop of corn, is worth all that the Alps and Pyrenees in their utmost grandeur and beauty could show to them.' Yet, as Wordsworth knew when he wrote his *Guide to the Lakes*, there were also many others who were visiting the Lake District in order to experience the beauty of the mountains: enthused by the torrent of paintings and engravings of the Lakeland scene which poured from the brushes and pens of almost every artist in the land, and by the guidebooks of Gray, West, Gilpin, and others, they came, like Charlotte Bronte, hoping to drink in 'the full power of the glorious scenery of these grand hills and sweet dales.'

Out of the early eighteenth century attempts to reconcile the theological with the new scientific explanations for the existence of mountains, there emerged the idea that they were part of God's plan to create variety and diversity on Earth. It was noted that there was such diversity among animals, birds and plants and even among rocks – 'He who created the stones made them not all diamonds' – and so people had 'no less reason to bless God for the less fruitful mountains than for the fat and fruitful valleys.' The Earth adorned with mountains was surely aesthetically better than 'a languid flat thing'.

The debate on the origin of mountains continued for many years, but by the mid-eighteenth century talk of 'monstrous excrescences' and 'rubbish of the Earth' had been replaced by the vocabulary of beauty and the sublime. Mountains were no longer to be shunned but embraced with an almost religious fervour; they were not only beautiful, they were spiritually healing. The poet, Thomas Gray, who is often mocked for his apparent fear of the 'horrors' of the Lakeland mountains, was among the first to see the beauty of mountain scenery.

On Gray's tour to the Alps 40 years before he visited the Lake District, he noted the 'Cascades pouring down from an immense height… and the solemn sound of the stream that roars below, all concur to form one of the most poetical scenes imaginable', and he considered that the Highlands of Scotland 'ought to be visited in pilgrimage once a year. None but those monstrous creatures of God know how to join so much beauty with so much horror.' 'Horror' at the time implied a pleasurable feeling of awe rather than revulsion and fear: as the poet put it: 'Horrors like these at first alarm, But soon with savage grandeur charm. And raise to noblest thoughts the mind.'

Many explanations have been suggested for this fundamental change in attitudes to mountain scenery and to all wild and uncultivated landscape. An important, but not the most important, factor was the greater accessibility to such areas – the moors of the West Country, the Highlands of Scotland, the mountains of Wales and the Lake District – all remote from the southern and eastern counties where the great majority of the educated gentry, professional, ecclesiastical and academic classes of society had their homes.

Following the shock of the 1745 Jacobite Rebellion, which revealed the disastrous inadequacy of the nation's roads, a frenzy of road construction began. Within thirty years 15,000 miles of turnpike roads had been built, including almost 400 miles in and around the Lake District. This prepared the way for the era of the stage-coach and gradually the time taken to travel from London to Kendal was reduced, from nine days in 1734 to three days in 1773, and by 1825, given fine weather and no breakdowns, the journey could be made in 24-36 hours. Travel was also made less arduous by great improvements in the construction of coaches, which by 1800 were comfortably upholstered and equipped with steel springs to cushion passengers against the ruts and potholes encountered even on the new turnpikes.

The development of a chain of coaching inns along the routes also made travel more relaxed with their assurance of hospitality and overnight accommodation. But improved travel by itself would not explain the eighteenth century rage for mountain scenery. Other radical changes were also taking place to disturb traditional ways of life. This was the age when, in a comparatively short period of time, the population doubled from 5.5 million to 11 million, more and more of whom lived in the towns. The growth of towns was not accompanied by provision for a supply of clean water or by improved sanitation. Conditions, particularly in London, became overcrowded, unhealthy, unhygienic and seriously polluted. Those who could, escaped in the summer months to the fresh air, clean water and open spaces of the countryside. But the countryside itself was being transformed. The open landscape was rapidly disappearing. Between 1750 and 1820 two million acres of heath-

land, common land and 'wasteland' hitherto uncultivated were enclosed, as were a further two and a half million acres already in agricultural use.

This totally changed the appearance of much of the English landscape
and, except for those who profited by it, the change was painful to be-
hold. John Clare's poetry lamented the destruction of the,

Moors loosing from the sight far smooth and blea,
Where swept the plover in its pleasure free

William Pearson, in the Lyth Valley, chronicled in detail the disappearance of almost all the varied wildlife there as the wetlands were drained,
hedged and fenced and brought under cultivation; William Wordsworth
noted that 'Wheresoe'er the traveller turns his steps. He sees the barren
wilderness erased. Or disappearing'; and John Stuart Mill declared that
there was not:

much satisfaction in contemplating a world… with every foot of land
brought into cultivation which is capable of growing food for human
beings; every flowery waste or natural pasture ploughed up, all
quadrupeds or birds which are not domesticated for man's use exterminated… every hedgerow or superfluous tree rooted out, and scarcely a
place where a wild shrub or flower could grow without being eradicated
as a weed in the name of improved agriculture.

These upheavals may have been necessary at the time to provide food
for the rapidly increasing population but to those who had no need to
concern themselves with the supply of their daily bread this profound
transformation in the English landscape would have been an unwelcome
shock. Some sought consolation in transforming their own estates by
abandoning the formal 'continental' style of garden for open landscape
gardens and parklands as promoted by such landscape artists as 'Capa-
bility' Brown and Humphrey Repton.

Many more found solace in visits to the wild, untamed, mountainous
regions of the country such as the Lake District which by 1800 had become the 'home' of the Romantics, those who believed, genuinely or
otherwise, that spiritual enrichment and physical and mental renewal
could be found in communion with Nature in the quiet tranquility of the
mountains, seeking 'the joy of elevated thoughts; a sense sublime of
something far more deeply interfused.'

It would be absurd to suggest that such exalted thoughts motivate the many millions of visitors who come to the Lake District each year in our own time. Many may be described as holiday-makers whose recreational needs could easily be provided elsewhere but many others come with a genuine appreciation of all that Lakeland has to offer and return again and again to discover new delights and to confirm the truth of William Camden's observation more than 400 years ago when he wrote of the Lakeland landscape that 'the variety thereof it smileth upon the beholders, and giveth contentment to all who travail it.'

And the mountains are the 'beginning and the end of it all'. Let Wordsworth have the last word:

> in the combinations which they make towering above each other, or lifting themselves in ridges like the waves of a tumultuous sea, and in the beauty and variety of their surfaces and colours, they are surpassed by none.

33

John Richardson

The 'Lake Poets' of the academic literary world flourished in the early years of the nineteenth century. The poets most closely associated with the group were William Wordsworth, Robert Southey and Samuel Taylor Coleridge, with several others, such as John Keats, Dorothy Wordsworth and Thomas de Quincey, also recognised as part of the 'Romantic Movement'. All these names have long been well-known in the annals of the literature of the period but less well-known is a poet whose roots were firmly in Lakeland and who wrote mainly in the local dialect of his native Cumberland. His poetry usually receives only a passing reference in most of the many books written on the literary history of the Lake District yet his work includes some of the classic poetic compositions in an English dialect.

John Richardson was born over 200 years ago, in 1817, at Stone Cottage in St John's-in-the-Vale, a few miles south of Keswick, a Lakeland dale described by Harriet Martineau as a 'valley of character and charm from end to end.' His father was a stonemason and, after John had attended the local school where he received a good basic knowledge, he then followed his father as a builder and mason. For the next 25 years he worked on many building projects in Keswick and at farms throughout the district, notably in his own parish where he was responsible for the construction or reconstruction of the parish Church of St John the Baptist in 1845, and a new school (now part of the Youth Centre) in 1849. He also built the first parish vicarage in 1856.

Throughout these years Richardson was acquiring a detailed knowledge of the Cumberland dialect which he was later to put to such masterly use in his poetry. In 1841, at the age of 24, he married Grace Birkett from City, a tiny hamlet at the southern end of Wythburn Water now drowned under the waters of Thirlmere. After their marriage the couple lived in the cottages (Stone Cottage and Piper Cottage) where John was born and where all their ten children were born. The story of their courtship and marriage is generally believed to be related in what is probably John's best-known poem – *It's Nobbut Me*. The story is told from Grace's point of view:

Ya winter neet, I mind it weel,
Oor lads 'ed been at t'fell,
An', bein' tir't went seun to bed,
An' I sat be mesel.
I hard a jike on t'window pane,   *(jike = to creak or squeak)*
An' deftly went to see;
But when I ax't 'Who's jiken theer?'
Says t'chap, 'It's nobbut me.'

'Who's me?' says I, 'What want ye here?
Oor fwok ur aw i'bed.' –
I dunnet want your fwok at aw,
It's thee I want,' he sed.
'What can 'e want wi me?' says I;
'An' who the deuce can't be?
Just tell me who it is, an' than –
Says he, 'Its nobbut me.'

'I want a sweetheart, an' I thowt
Thoo mebby wad an' aw;
I'd been a bit down t'deal to-neet,
An' thowt at I wad caw;
What, cant 'e like me, dust 'e think?
I think I wad like thee' –
'I dunnet know who 't is,' says I,
Says he, 'It's nobbut me.'

We pestit on a canny while,
I thowt his voice I kent
An' then I steal quite whisht away
An' oot at t'dooer I went.
I creapp, an' gat 'im be t'cwoat laps,
'Twas dark, he cuddent see;
He startit roond, an' said, 'Who's that?'
Says I, 'It's nobbut me.'

An' menny a time he come agean,
An' menny a time I went,
An' sed, 'Who's that 'at's jiken theer?'
When gaily weel I kent:
An' mainly what t'seeam answer com,
Fra back o' t' laylick tree;
He sed, 'I think thoo knows who 't is:
Thoo knows it's nobbut me.'

It's twenty year an' mair sen than,
An' ups an' doons we've hed;
An' six fine bairns hev blest us beath,
Sen Jim and me war wed.
An' menny a time I've known 'im steal,
When I'd yan on me knee,
To make me start, an' than wad laugh –
Ha! Ha! 'It's nobbut me.'

In 1858 Richardson was appointed schoolmaster of the school he himself had built and he and his large family moved to Bridge House which was just below the church and school by St John's Beck, a home he seems to recall fondly in a later poem – *What I'd Wish For*. And what he would wish for above all else was lots of *beuks, lang neets to cheer*, a loving wife and children, and sufficient money to get by, and:

Nut far away, a beck I'd hev,
'At twistit 't hills an' neuks aboot;
Where I wi' fishin' rod could gang
An' flog, an' watch for t' risen troot.

It was from his years as master of the school that he recounted the custom of 'barring out' the schoolmaster, an unruly occasion when the pupils barricaded themselves inside the school and refused to allow the schoolmaster in again unless he agreed to certain conditions:

It used to be than, when t' time com for brekkin' up
For t' Christmas or Midsummer hellidays, 'at when t'maister
went heam tull his dinner, we use to bar up aw t' dooers
an' windows, an' wuddent let 'im in agean.

The bargain was that if the master could not succeed in securing entrance to his school then the pupils would not have any tasks set for the holidays, but if he did manage to get in they received not only *a gay lang task* for the holidays but *mebby a good hiden to be gaan on wi'*.

Richardson had the poet's observant eye and compassionate understanding of the foibles of human nature combined with a whimsical sense of humour. This is seen in almost all his writings and never more clearly than in his poem Robin Redbreast where he also conveys his love of birds and animals:

> *When winter winds blow strand and keen,*
> *An' neets are lang an' cauld,*
> *An' flocks o' burds, wi' famine team 't,*   *(made tame)*
> *Come flutteren into 't fauld;*
> *I hev a casement, just ya pane,*
> *'At Robin kens reet weel,*
> *An' pops in menny a time i' t' day,*
> *A crumb or two to steal.*

> *At first he's shy an' easy flay't*   *(frightened)*
> *Bit seunn he bolder gits,*
> *An' picks aboot quite unconsarn't.*
> *Or here an' theer he flits.*
> *An' when he gits his belly full,*
> *An's tir't o' playin' pranks,*
> *He'll sit quite still, on t'auld chair back,*
> *An' sing his simple thanks.*

> *Bit when breet spring comes back ageann,*
> *An' fields ur growen green,*
> *He bids good day, an' flees away,*
> *An' than na mair he's seen;*
> *Til winter comes ageann wi' frost,*
> *An' driften snow, an' rain,*
> *An' than he venters back ageann,*
> *To leuk for t'oppen pane.*

Noo, burds an' fwok ur mickle t'seamm,   *(much the same)*
If they be i' hard need;
An' yan hes owt to give, they'll come,
An' be girt frinds indeed.
Bit when theer nowt they want to hev,
It's nut sa lang they'll stay,
Bit just as Robin does i' t' spring,
They'll seun aw flee away.

John Richardson, courtesy of Rev. G. Darrall, source unknown.

This was Richardson the realist who by the time, in the 1870s, when his two volumes of *Cummerland Talk* were published, had almost reached the age of 60 and had acquired a philosophy of life which combined an affectionate appreciation of the basic goodness of his fellow humans, with a pragmatic understanding of their eccentricities and occasional self-interest.

John Richardson may not be recognised as one of the Lake Poets who, with the exception of Wordsworth, had no roots in the Lake District but were visitors from London, university educated, only temporarily resident in the district and wrote little poetry reflecting the 'romantic' scenery and culture in which they allegedly found inspiration. Richardson, on the contrary, like Wordsworth, was born in Cumberland and spent all his life there, but, unlike Wordsworth, he was always 'a man of the people', whereas Wordsworth belonged to the elite few who were privileged to study at Cambridge University. Their perspectives on their environment and on poetic composition were thus very different, a disparity most obviously reflected in the language in which they wrote, but also in the themes which inspired them. This, it may be argued, ought not to influence their status as poets but, as Thomas Hardy so candidly put it: 'Dialect words – those terrible marks of the beast to the truly genteel.' Richardson did not always write in dialect – either in prose or verse. One of his most attractive poems describes the view from the summit of Blencathra:

> *I stood on the summit of lofty Blencathra,*
> *And gazed with rapture on mountain and vale;*
> *As far as the eye could reach endless variety*
> *Of hills intermixed with streams and dales.*

Richardson loved his native Cumberland and its slow, unchanging way of life. He had little time for the developments in urban life and the revolution in transport of the Victorian age. In one of his later poems – *T' Country For Me* – he comes close to Wordsworth:

> *They may talk o' the 'r wonderful cities,*
> *An' brag o' the 'r toons as they will;*
> *Bit moontains, an' valleys , an' rivers*
> *To me ur mair wonderful still.*
> *They may talk o' the 'r railways an' stashons,*
> *An' tell hoo the 'r trains swift can glide;*
> *Bit what's aw the 'r speed to yan storm-clood*
> *'At darts acros t' craggy fell side?*

John Richardson died on 30 April 1886. His grave is close to the east end of the church of St John's-in-the-Vale.

34

Outlaws of Inglewood

England's most famous and most popular legendary folk-hero is Robin Hood. From Somerset to Northumberland, from London to Cumbria, there are at least 150 places which bear his name and for more than six hundred years tales of his adventures in the great medieval forests have been told in songs, ballads, novels, plays, films, television series and pantomimes. Yet in earlier centuries Robin Hood's popularity was rivalled by others who are almost unknown today. Among these was a band of three renowned outlaws whose greenwood refuge from the law was the great forest of Inglewood in Cumberland which covered a vast area from Carlisle to Penrith. The tale of Adam Bell, Clym of the Clough and William of Cloudsley, was told in a ballad first registered with the title *Adam Bell* in 1557 but it was certainly well-known long before that. Together with Robin Hood and Little John, Adam Bell and his friends were familiar characters in English folklore from the fourteenth century; and by 1575 they were so much a part of the national culture that they featured in the entertainments provided for Queen Elizabeth's visit to Kenilworth Castle in that year.

The ballad tells us that Adam Bell, Clym of the Clough and William of Cloudsley were yeomen who had been 'outlawed for venyson', that is to say for poaching deer in Inglewood Forest, an offence which was severely punished according to the Laws of the Forest. Not even the Bishop of Carlisle escaped being fined for killing a hart but lesser men could expect more serious consequences if they were caught. Adam and his fellow outlaws, escaping from justice in Carlisle, had found a hidden glade where they felt secure and could continue to live off the king's venison.

One day, the ballad relates, 'as they sat in Englyhshe wood', William of Cloudsley decided to go to Carlisle to visit his wife, Alyce, and their children. Adam advised strongly against such a risky venture:

> *For if ye go to Carlel, brother,*
> *And from thys wylde wode wende,*
> *If justice mai you take,*
> *Your lyfe were at an ende.*

But William, lightly dismissing such dangers, made his way to Carlisle and was happily reunited with his wife and children. An old woman whom William had taken into his home as an act of charity some years previously chose to betray his presence in the town to the magistrate and the sheriff who promptly sent a posse of men to arrest him. William was a highly skilled archer and he and Alyce, 'with a poleaxe in her hande,' put up a stout resistance until the sheriff ordered that the house be set on fire. William was not willing to let his family die in this way so he opened a window and 'wyth shetes he let hys wife down, And hys children thre'. William himself then ran into the street and with his sword 'smote downe many a man'. He was eventually captured, bound hand and foot and thrown into a dungeon.

> *Now, Cloudsle,' sayd the hye justice,*
> *Thou shalt be hanged in haste.*

A boy who looked after Alyce's pigs saw the gallows being erected and, when he was told that William was to be hanged there, he squeezed through a gap in the town walls (the gates had been closed and locked) and ran off into the forest to tell Adam and Clym of the Clough that William's life was in danger and they set off at once to rescue him. They tricked their way through the gate by persuading the illiterate porter that they were King's Messengers with letters bearing the King's seal. They then 'wrange hys necke in two,' and took his keys.

Hurrying to the market place they found the magistrate and the sheriff by the gallows.

> *And Cloudesley hymselfe lay redy in a carte,*
> *Faste bounde both fote and hand,*
> *And a strong rop about hys necke,*
> *All readye for to be hanged.*

There was clearly no time to lose. Adam shot an arrow and killed the sheriff; Clym did the same for the magistrate. William was released from his bonds and a street battle ensued during which the outlaws laid low many of the men ordered to capture them. 'The batyle dyd longe endure'. Eventually, using the keys they had taken from the murdered porter, all three escaped from the city and returned to their sanctuary in the forest. It was not long before Alyce and the children also found their way to the forest glade and joined the outlaws. Soon Cloudsley announced that they were going to London to ask for the King's pardon for the crimes they had committed. The older son would go with them; and Alyce and the other two children would seek sanctuary in a nunnery.

Admission to the King's presence was achieved with bold audacity but to their dismay, as soon as they identified themselves and stated their request for pardon for stealing the King's venison, the immediate response was to order them to 'be hanged al thre'. Adam Bell pleaded for mercy and, although the King was unmoved, the Queen intervened on their behalf and persuaded her husband to pardon them. Soon afterwards messengers came from Carlisle with the news that the sheriff, the justice, the mayor and more than 300 others, not to mention some of the finest deer in Inglewood Forest, had been killed by the three outlaws who had just received the King's pardon. Perhaps suspecting that three archers alone would not be able to accomplish so much slaughter the King demanded that they demonstrate their shooting skills at the butts. Cloudsley was an unusually skilful archer and offered to split a hazel wand from 400 paces, a feat the King declared to be impossible. When Cloudsley then went on to perform this feat the King had to admit that he was 'the best archer… forsooth that ever I did see.'

Cloudsley, sensing the King's more favourable mood, now proposed a far more dramatic demonstration of his shooting prowess:

> *I have a sonne is seven yere olde,*
> *He is to me full dere,*
> *I wyl hym tye unto a stake,*
> *All shall see that be here.*
>
> *And lay an apple upon hys head,*
> *And go syxe score paces hym fro,*
> *And I myseld, with a brode arrow,*
> *Shall cleve the apple in two.*

Incredulous, the King warned that if 'thou touche his head or gowne… I shall hange you all thre.'

But this feat too was successfully performed and the astonished King confirmed his pardon, awarded the former outlaw a pension and made him his 'chefe ridere… over all the north countre.'

The Queen also gave Cloudsley a pension and appointed Adam Bell and Clym of the Clough to be Yeoman of her Chamber and Alyce was summoned to be her 'chefe gentelwoman to govern my nursery.'

There are several aspects of this story which feature in the tales of Robin Hood while the legend of shooting the apple later became familiar throughout Europe through the Swiss legend of William Tell. But this and similar tales were, by the early Middle Ages, already part of the travelling minstrel's repertoire since they had already appeared in the tenth and eleventh centuries in Denmark, Norway, Finland, Iceland and the Faroe Islands.* So many incidents in these stories demand a suspension of belief that it would be naive to readily accept them all as historical fact. The medieval ballads were primarily intended to tell a good story and to entertain. Audiences would have been disappointed if a minstrel failed to include such familiar legendary tales in his performance. Adam Bell, Clym of the Clough and William of Cloudsley, like Robin Hood, Little John and Much the Miller's son, may or may not have been real, living, historical characters, but a good story is always worth telling, retelling and embroidering on the way.

---

* The story of William Tell dates from 1307 when Albrecht Gessler, a tyrannical agent of the Austrian Habsburg Empire, ordered the citizens of Altdorf, in Switzerland, to salute his cap placed on top of a pole in the market square. William Tell refused to do this and he was arrested and ordered to shoot an apple placed on his son's head. Tell was a highly skilful archer and successfully performed this feat. Gessler noticed that Tell had a second arrow ready to use and asked what it was for. Tell bluntly replied: 'It was for you. Had I shot my child, know that it would not have missed you.' He was re-arrested but escaped and eventually inspired a rebellion which led to the freedom and independence of Switzerland.

35

Perfected by Music?

For almost 300 years the landscape of the Lake District has attracted artists, poets, novelists and guide-book writers: John Constable, J. M. W. Turner, Thomas Allom, William Westall, Alfred Heaton Cooper, William Wordsworth, Norman Nicholson, Mrs Humphry Ward, Richard Adams, Thomas West, Alfred Wainwright and innumerable other well-known names have found inspiration for their works in the incomparable landscape of this small corner of England. But where are the musicians? Where is Lakeland's equivalent of Beethoven's *Pastoral Symphony*? Or Rikard Strauss's *Alpine Symphony*? Or Edvard Grieg's *Morning*? Or Jean Sibelius's *Tapiola*? Or Gustav Mahler's *Third Symphony*? In Britain the Malvern Hills and the countryside of Worcestershire inspired Edward Elgar; the gentle undulations of the Sussex Downs inspired John Ireland's *Downland Suite*; and the familiar sounds of the English countryside were portrayed by Frederick Delius and Ralph Vaughan Williams; while the spectacular landscapes of Scotland brought inspiration to (among others) Felix Mendelssohn (*The Hebrides*), Max Bruch (*A Scottish Fantasy*), Peter Maxwell Davies (*Farewell to Stromness*) and Hamish MacCunn (*Land of the Mountain and the Flood*).

Norman Nicholson wrote in his book *The Lake District* that 'with Wordsworth the mountains of Cumberland... became, like the music of Beethoven and the paintings of Turner, symbols of the power, the vitality, the force of nature.' But, while we are fortunate to have the paintings of Turner and the poetry of Wordsworth, we do not have a Lakeland Beethoven to translate into grand symphonic music Wordsworth's vision of the mountains 'towering above each other, or lifting themselves in ridges like the waves of tumultuous seas' or of the lakes 'reflecting... the clouds, the light, and all the imagery of the sky and surrounding hills' or of 'the stream pushing its way among the rocks... its noisy and turbulent motion (contrasting) with the gentle playfulness of the breeze.'

This is not to say that there is no music in Lakeland. On the contrary, in almost every town or large village, from Carlisle to Cartmel, from

Keswick to Kendal, choral and music societies flourish and concerts by visiting national orchestras are regular features of local cultural life, while each summer a festival of music attracts artists of international repute and enthusiastic audiences to hear them. Of particular note is the Mary Wakefield Music Festival, founded in 1885 and now a nationally renowned event. Its purpose is to encourage local music-making, notably by young people and especially in the schools, with, hitherto, a strong emphasis on choral music. But, admirable as all this may be, there has been no obvious encouragement or motivation to compose or perform music inspired by the uniquely beautiful landscape which has inspired so many authors and artists. For that one has to dig deeply into the annals of music to discover a small number of unjustly neglected compositions, some by well-known composers, but few of which are now available on record, and even fewer appear on concert programmes, even in the Lake District.

Perhaps the most substantial 'Lakeland' composition was written by Armstrong Gibbs (1889-1960). His Symphony No. 3, the *Westmorland Symphony*, was composed in 1944 when his Essex home became a military hospital and the family was evacuated to Windermere. The symphony was described by a *Gramophone* review as music of 'great lyrical beauty', of 'sombre, elegiac demeanour' and of 'soothing, consoling serenity'. It was broadcast by BBC Radio in 1956 but only almost forty years later was it recorded by the National Orchestra of Ireland in 1995. The next 'live' performance seems to have been by the Essex Chamber Ensemble in 2006. His eight piano preludes bear the title *Lakeland Pictures* and capture the mood and the picture of Thirlmere, Rydal Beck, Watendlath, Langdale, Borrowdale, Winster, Wastwater and Tarn Hows in musical insights which have hints of Brahms and Rachmaninov. They were recorded by Alan Cuckston a few years ago. In 1999 the Guildhall Strings recorded a selection of Gibbs's light music with the title *Dale and Fell* of which an evocative piece, *Dusk*, became a popular favourite.

Arthur Butterworth (1923-2014), a northerner through and through, composed *Lakeland Summer Nights* while still a student in Manchester. They were also originally written for solo piano but may perhaps be more fully appreciated as they were incorporated in his later orchestrated version entitled *Northern Summer Nights: Three Nocturnes,* largely inspired by the Scottish Highlands, but perfectly reflecting his life-long fascination with the wide, empty spaces of Europe's northern landscapes, from the Lake District to Scandinavia. *Northern Lights* was recorded in 2010 by the Royal Scottish National Orchestra as part of a selection of Butterworth's music.

John Cameron's musical fame rests largely on his compositions for the realm of pop music, with notable successes for Cilla Black and ABBA, for many film and television productions, and for the theme music for the musical version of *Les Miserables*. His little-known composition, entitled *A Cumbria Suite*, is said to have many attractive passages inspired by A Grasmere Morning, Daffodils, Castlerigg and the Hawkshead Stage-coach.

Jan Hurst (1890?-1967) whose light music orchestra was renowned in the 1920s and 30s for entertaining the holiday-makers at most of the well-known British seaside resorts, composed a short orchestral piece entitled *A Windermere Idyll*. I have not traced any reference to the performance or recording of either of these compositions by Cameron or Hurst.

One of the most accomplished Lakeland compositions is by Maurice Johnstone who was at one time Secretary to Sir Thomas Beecham and for many years was Head of the BBC's Music Programmes in both Manchester and London. He played a significant part in the formation of the BBC Northern Orchestra which later became the BBC Philharmonic Orchestra. He composed very little but his *Cumbria Rhapsody* with its tranquil evocation of Tarn Hows is among the most exquisite of musical portrayals of a landscape: fifteen minutes of woodwind enchantment.

A more recent work which has won much acclaim was composed by John McCabe (1939-2015) for the final of the 1985 National Brass Band Contest. Its title, *Cloudcatcher Fells*, is taken from a line of a poem, *Cockermouth*, by David Wright. McCabe wrote that it was composed 'in response to my feelings about a landscape... that I love' and the four movements reflect the different moods and features of the Lakeland fells: 1. Great Gable, Grasmoor and Grisedale Tarn; 2. Haystacks and Catstycam; 3. Angle Tarn; 4. Striding Edge and Helvellyn. It is now regarded as one of the classic landscape compositions for brass bands. McCabe was described in a review of his life and work in the magazine *Gramophone* as 'one of Britain's finest composers of the past half-century.'

One of the most influential musicians of the early decades of the twentieth century was Cyril Rootham (1875-1938) who was a brilliant tutor at Cambridge University and an influential and innovative figure in the musical life of his day. He composed many works for orchestra, piano and chamber ensembles, among them his String Quintet in D major which had a slow movement for viola, violin, cello and piano with the title *In the Lake Country*. Although this Quintet has been highly acclaimed there appears to be, at present, no recording of this piece.

The only composer to have been born (and buried) in the Lake District is Sir Arthur Somervell (1863-1937) but although he achieved renown nationally, particularly for his song cycles such as *Maud, A Shropshire Lad,* and *Silent Worship*, his contributions to Lakeland music is notable, not for a native's response to the landscape in which he spent his youth, but for his once-popular *Grasmere Carol*, and for his setting for Wordsworth's poem, *Ode on Intimations of Immortality.* The Miscellany Singers have included the Grasmere Carol on a CD collection entitled *Christmas Miscellany*.

Finally, the Lakeland masterpiece that was lost. Sir Edward Elgar frequently spent time in the Lake District and on one occasion he stood on Orrest Head and was so deeply moved by the panorama of Lake Windermere and the high fells beyond, that, according to his wife, he afterwards wrote 'furiously' to compose *A Lakeland Overture*, a work he never finished but much of which he later incorporated into his famous tribute to medieval chivalry, the overture *Froissart*.

This brief review of the minimal corpus of musical response to the landscape of the Lake District is reflected in the 2017 UNESCO report which awarded the National Park the prestigious status of a World Heritage Site. Reference is made specifically only to 'the inspiration it has provided to artists and writers.' Most subsequent commentators have enthused about the 'stunning scenery', the landscape contribution of farming, the legacy of innumerable painters, poets, and writers such as Beatrix Potter and Arthur Ransome – but not a mention of music.

The Lake District is in urgent need of a musician who could do for Lakeland what Edvard Grieg did for Norway – to elevate the musical interpretation of the landscape from the level of romantic kitsch to a positive force in the formation of a national cultural identity,* from a mere

---

* See Daniel Grimley, *Grieg: Music, Landscape and Norwegian Identity* (2006)

pictorial representation to a cultural symbol of the spiritual and elemental forces of Nature, a medium towards solace, contemplation, reflective nostalgia, and personal fulfilment.

The distinguished Norwegian composer, Ola Geilo, is reported to have stated in a recent interview that to him 'the Lake District is just the most inspiring place.' Perhaps one day Geilo may present us with a Lakeland composition to complement Grieg's evocative musical interpretation of Norway's inspiring mountain landscape.

The Lake District landscape has inspired an impressive number of artistic and literary figures who have created works of universally acknowledged excellence. Only the jewel in the crown is missing – music on an epic scale or even a musical suite to complement the beauty and grandeur of the Lakeland landscape that people and nature have created. The Chinese philosopher, Confucius, asserted that man may be stimulated by poetry but he is perfected by music.

36

The Nine Standards:Fact and Fantasy

FACT: Three miles south west of Kirkby Stephen, at the head of the Eden Valley and on the watershed of the Pennines at a height of 660 metres (2,170 feet), there is a prominent group of tall cairns known as the Nine Standards. They command extensive views in all directions and one must assume that they were of some special significance to those who first constructed them. Their origin and purpose have long been the subject of speculation and scientific investigation but the mystery surrounding them still remains unsolved. A comprehensive attempt was made just a few years ago to discover evidence which might provide an answer to the engima. Every device of modern technology was enlisted, from ground-penetrating radar and electronic conductivity to close aerial photography; and much archaeological expertise was employed to interpret the results. The report on this operation stated that the cairns had probably been in existence for 800 years or more and that this 'is clearly a high status site, dominating a vast swathe of the upper Eden Valley and beyond, situated at the focus of the major rivers flowing east to the North Sea (Swale and Greta) and west to the Irish Sea (Eden and Lune), and close to the major routes across the north Pennines. The research is ongoing but there are no conclusive findings as yet.

The name itself is possibly derived from Old Icelandic or Old Norse. *Niun Standr* means nine standing stones. The number nine has always been a 'magic' mystical number, from the Nine Muses of Ancient Greek to the Biblical Nine Orders of Angels and the Nine Worlds of the Norse Niflheim; from the medieval game Nine Men's Morris to the:

> *Thrice to thine and thrice to mine,*
> *And thrice again to make up nine*

incantation of Shakespeare's witches and the innumerable centuries-old superstitions of folklore. It is possible that the nine cairns of the Nine Standards were originally related to this ancient belief in the mystique inherent in the number nine.

There is clearly much we do not know about the origin and purpose of the Nine Standards: to a large extent they remain, in Winston Churchill's famous phrase, 'a riddle wrapped in a mystery inside an enigma', and so they may fairly be regarded as one of those 'unknown regions' described by George Eliot as 'happy hunting grounds for the imagination.'

FANTASY: The Bronze Age in Norway was notable for its rock carvings rather than for its megalithic monuments: wonderful representations from this age of animals, ships and symbolic human figures may be seen in many parts of Scandinavia but there is nothing comparable to the stone circles, avenues or menhirs of western Europe. Our story therefore accepts the archeological estimate that the cairns of the Nine Standards are at least 800 years old and so it is set in the middle of the twelfth century and it begins in the Jotunheim mountains of Norway almost 900 years ago.

Sunset over Jotunheim - Sunrise over the Pennines

> *Prinsessen sad høit i sit Jomfru bur*
> *Smaagutten gik ned og blæste paa Lur.*
> *"Hvi blæser Du altid, ti stille,Du smaa,*
> *det hæfter min Tanke, som vide vill gaa,*
> *nu,naar Sol gaar ned."*
> Bjørnstjerne Bjørnson (1832-1910)
> (Nobel Prize for Literature, 1903)

❀❀❀❀❀❀❀❀❀❀❀❀❀❀❀❀❀❀❀❀❀

The young princess sat in the maiden's bower, lonely and forlorn.
A small boy strolling nearby blew loudly on a shepherd's horn.
"Why must you blow all the time, boy? Just be quiet," she said,
"My mind is far away as the sun sinks down to its bed,
And you're confusing the thoughts in my head."
> (Author's translation)

The late summer sun was setting over Norway's Jotunheim mountains and the maiden's thoughts were, indeed, very far away. She sat with her head bowed and she scarcely saw the last rays of the sun sparkling on the snow-capped summits of the high mountain peaks or casting long shadows across the glaciers. She did not reply when the boy pointed out a small herd of reindeer crossing a snow-field and a tiny fishing boat gliding silently over the waters of the lake in the valley far below. Puzzled by her silence he came to the foot of the shieling steps and saw that her long blonde hair had fallen over her face but not quite hiding the tears which rolled slowly down to fall in silent drops on to her folded hands. The boy felt he had upset her by noisily blowing the horn and he timidly placed his hand on hers and whispered "I'm sorry I made you sad. I was blowing to annoy the trolls in the mountains."

Astrid raised her head, gave a forgiving little smile and said, "It is not your fault that I am sad. I am glad that you want to annoy the trolls. They came two days ago and took my little sister, Solveig, and I miss her so much. I wonder all the time where she is and if she is safe and well. I am very worried about her – that is why I am sad. I wish there was some way to set her free. I just want her to come home again. So blow your horn as loud as you can – if it annoys the trolls that will make me feel better."

The boy said "Well, now is a good time. Now that the sun is setting they will soon be coming out of their caves. They should hear this!" And he gave several long loud blasts on his horn and then, turning to the princess with a secretive smile he announced confidently that he would think of a plan to rescue her sister and deal with the trolls. And off he ran, leaving the tearful princess to wonder what he was planning to do. Trolls could be dangerous.

Trolls were giants and lived in caves in the mountains. They were often ugly with grotesque features; they were very hairy and had huge, long noses and some of them had several heads. But they were very slow-witted and could usually be easily tricked. They could not tolerate the smell of Christians nor the sound of church bells. They were well-known to be thieves and especially to be obsessive hoarders of gold and silver. They were most feared for their habit of kidnapping 'princesses', the daughters of the more important farmsteads of the valleys. Many had troll-wives who were smaller but also had ugly features and had long tails which they hid beneath their skirts. The princesses they captured were, in contrast, beautiful, and, although usually well-treated, they were closely-guarded prisoners. It was not easy to release them from such captivity.

The boy, Knut, knew that his father was very angry with the trolls because a few nights ago they had deliberately driven some of his goats over the crags to a painful death. The neighbouring farm had lost ten sheep in the same way. He knew, too, that two other princesses from the next valley had been kidnapped and their parents had searched the mountains in vain to try to find them. He felt sure that there were enough farmers in the valleys nestling in the folds of the mountains who had suffered at the mischievous hands of the trolls and would be willing to teach them a lesson or even to get rid of them altogether. It ought not to be too difficult to outwit creatures as naïve and simple-minded as trolls. If only he could think of a clever plan!

As he ran home he realised how late in the evening it was and his mother would probably be wondering where he was and would begin to be worried. Sure enough, when he eventually arrived there was his grandfather, Olaf, waiting by the farmhouse door and, as Knut came to a breathless halt before him, he said "Look, young man, have you any idea what time it is? Your mother has been worrying about you for the past hour or more." But Knut hardly heard him: all his attention was on the shining gold torque his grandfather was wearing, a family heirloom brought out only on special occasions. He suddenly surprised the old man as he shouted, "Gold! That's how we can trick them!" He then ran indoors to make peace with his anxious parents and to find out what 'special occasion' was being celebrated. This, he soon learned, was the happy return of their neighbour's daughter who had outwitted her troll captors and escaped. Knut then told his parents about his meeting with Astrid up by the shieling.

A few days later Knut's father and others from neighbouring valleys, all of whom had scores to settle with the trolls, had drawn up an elaborate plan which, if it succeeded, would free the missing princesses and rid them of the trolls forever. And, as young Knut had realised, the trolls' obsessive craving for gold would be the fatal attraction to trap them. Knut and his grandfather would take the first steps.

They set off together into the mountains, Knut with his shepherd's horn, and Olaf with his newly polished gold torque and the great Viking sword he had inherited from his war-like ancestor. When they eventually stood under the crags by the snowfield where Knut had seen the reindeer, Knut blew several loud blasts on his horn to attract the trolls' attention. Soon, several of the giants, one of them with two heads, appeared from the crags and demanded to know why these smelly Christians were disturbing their mountains. Then the two-headed troll caught sight of the torque and, wielding his heavy club, demanded that it be handed over to him. Knut's grandfather drew his sword and threatened to remove at least one of the troll's two heads if he came any nearer. This subdued all the trolls and they listened in silence but with obvious interest as the old man in his quiet, persuasive voice explained the purpose of their visit.

The trolls, he said, had caused a great deal of damage and distress to local farmers and their families in recent times, including the kidnapping of their daughters and the loss of valuable crops and livestock. The time had come to agree to end such un-neighbourly activities. Everyone knew that the trolls disliked Christians; everyone also knew that the trolls had a great desire to possess gold and silver. If the trolls would attend a meeting at the shieling above the lake at sunset on the following day and bring with them the princesses they held captive, they would be guided to a buried hoard of gold and silver such as they had never seen before. This gold torque, the grandfather explained, was just one item from the great hoard buried by a Viking ancestor who did not live to recover all the rest. He saw that the trolls were excited at the idea of all that treasure and he concluded by saying "It is all there for you to take – if you bring the princesses to us and stop your raids on our farms."

With that he sheathed his sword, put his hand firmly on Knut's shoulder, and walked away.

At sunset the next day six trolls from the mountains lumbered up to the shieling with the captive princesses, tiny and helpless, in their midst. Six men from the valley farmsteads were there to meet them and immediately asked that the trolls lay down their clubs and that the princesses be set free before any talks could begin. When the two-headed troll refused and demanded to know where the gold was, Knut's grandfather once more drew his sword and with two swift strokes cut off both his heads. The five remaining trolls stood apart sullenly and silently but could not resist the lure of gold and eventually agreed to listen to what the valley folk had to say. They stubbornly refused, however, to release the princesses until they were told where the hoard of gold was to be found. Neither trolls nor valley folk were prepared to give way on this and as dusk descended it began to seem as if no progress would be made and the captive princesses became distressed and tearful.

As the angry dispute continued, at a secret signal from his grandfather the boy, Knut, slipped away from the shieling and ran as fast as he could down to the valley where he roused a surprised priest from his evening siesta, breathlessly explained the situation and asked him to ring the church bell.

Meanwhile the trolls had been told to go to Skjolden at the head of Sognefjord at midnight on the following day, bringing the princesses who were to be handed over to their parents. A boat would then take the trolls down the fjord and on to the spot where the treasure was buried.

This vague promise seemed to satisfy the slow-witted trolls and they were about to depart, taking the princesses with them, when the sound of the church bell rang out loudly in the still evening air. The trolls covered their great ears with their hands and fled into their mountain fastness, abandoning the girls to be happily free to join their delighted parents, several of whom now wished to forget all about the trolls and their gold. Others warned that trolls were vengeful and would not hesitate to inflict reprisals on the community.

These were not long in coming. That same night the trolls came to take away the body of their two-headed brother, unsettling the sheep and goats whose bleating wakened the two sisters in the shieling and, as they ran out to investigate the disturbance, they were seized by the angry trolls and carried off screaming into the night. When, soon after dawn, their disappearance was discovered the valley folk determined to proceed with their plan to send the trolls into permanent exile. Accordingly, accompanied by Olaf and by young Knut who pleaded not to be left behind, they set off through the mountains to Skjolden to await the arrival of the trolls and their two recent captives. A large Viking ship lay by the quayside manned by a muscular crew who were no strangers to arduous and challenging voyages and who had been given precise instructions as to their destination. Informed in advance of their unusual passengers, the ship's crew were wary but showed no great surprise when they appeared: five grotesque giant trolls and their smaller but equally ugly wives with their enormous noses and graceless bodies. The only evidence of human elegance and beauty in the group was revealed as the two sisters were released from their captivity and rushed into the arms of their joyful parents.

The trolls were excited and somewhat apprehensive as they climbed into the ship in anticipation of a short journey by water which for them would be a new experience. Eventually all ten trolls were on board and in the first faint light of dawn the journey began, the trolls protected from the sun and the wind and the sea-spray by a large awning which covered the centre of the ship. They sailed calmly and smoothly over the still waters of the fjord with their ever-changing reflection of the mountains, waterfalls and farmsteads on each side. All this proved endlessly fascinating to the trolls but they averted their eyes whenever they passed by the Christian churches then being built for the tiny settlements along the shore. They seemed to have forgotten about the object of their journey until the calm waters of the fjord came to an end, the land slowly passed out of sight and only the open sea lay ahead. The captain ordered the striped sail to be raised and the ship surged forward into the unsettling waves of the North Sea.

The trolls now became restless and remembered to demand to know where the ship was taking them. The captain sensed that this was the moment for Olaf to reveal that the gold they were anxious to find was across the sea, in Britannia, and in a few days' time the ship would arrive at Witeby and there they would be told precisely where the treasure was to be found. This news led to much heated argument, some of the trolls threatening the crew and demanding that the ship return to Sognefjord, others content to complete the voyage if there would be gold at the end of it.

The captain decided to restore calm and safety to his ship by providing every troll with a powerful sedative, disguised as an antidote for the sea-sickness which had begun to afflict most of the trolls. He had been forewarned of the purpose of the journey and that trolls were not aware of the long sea voyage which lay ahead. He had anticipated trouble and he had brought on board plentiful supplies of valerian. Each of the trolls was persuaded to take a dose of a concoction substantially more powerful than one would give to an ordinary human being. Before long the ship sailed on into the night accompanied only by the sound of the wind and the waves and the cacophony of snores from recumbent trolls, heavily asleep under the awning.

A few days later, valerian, a favourable wind and a calm sea brought the ship safely into Witeby Bay without further disturbance and the trolls were led ashore where the local people stared unbelievingly at these strange creatures as they made their unsteady way up the steep pathway to the moor above. There they were given food and drink, and Olaf, who had been to the north of Britannia many times before, explained that he would take them along the route they had to follow to discover the gold and silver hoard waiting for them at the end. They were to travel due west for five or six nights across heather moors and through forests and hills, and at the end Olaf would then show them a small stone pillar marking the site where the treasure was buried.

There were farmsteads and other settlements – mainly Norse – along the way where help could be found if necessary, but they should remember that their appearance could be frightening to many. No-one asked about arrangements for their return across the sea but one of the ship's crew muttered the question to the captain who bluntly replied that there was every possibility that that might not be necessary: the place Olaf had in mind was only a short distance from the newly-built castle of the Norman baron, Ranulf le Meschin, and the soldiers guarding it were highly unlikely to treat such alien intruders kindly.

And so for the next six moonlit nights Olaf and Knut led this strange, outlandish and restless band across long tracts of heather moors where numerous ancient burial mounds excited their curiosity, through dense forests and over bleak hills, past waterfalls and along narrow fertile valleys where Norse settlers had created small farmsteads in forest clearings. On the third night one of the troll-wives complained of stomach pains and soon she said that she could go no further. A local shepherd guarding his flock suggested that she should seek help from the nuns at the Priory which had just been built nearby. The trolls were unwilling to go to a Christian place but Olaf saw that the sick wife needed urgent attention, and she, too, was quite content to seek help from anyone, Christian or not, and so the troll-wife was escorted to the Priory by young Knut.

At first the nuns refused to admit such a monstrous creature who was clearly neither a real human being nor a Christian but Knut took the troll by the hand and explained that she had been a very gentle and beautiful girl whose features had been transformed by a wicked witch. The boy's innocent story changed everything and, while Knut could not be allowed into the Priory, the troll-wife was taken in and treated with all the skill and care the nuns could offer. Her distress, it was quickly discovered, was caused by a mildly poisonous mushroom casually eaten in the forest. A concoction of crushed fennel seeds, plenty of pure spring water and the prayers of the nuns soon brought relief and the troll responded warmly to the care and gentle comfort she received.

The following day Knut was sent to ask if the troll-wife had recovered and would be able to continue the journey. The Prioress replied that a wonderful miracle had taken place: the troll-woman had quickly responded to treatment and she had announced that she wished to become a Christian. She had been taken to the Priory Church to be baptised and during the ceremony her grotesque features were transformed to those of the beautiful girl the boy had described. Her troll's tail, which had been hidden beneath her skirts, had fallen to the ground. And, she had expressed her wish to join the community of nuns and to remain within the Priory.

Out of the shadows from behind the Prioress a figure suddenly appeared wearing the black habit of a Benedictine nun and whispered a few words to the Prioress. She then spoke directly to Knut: "Would you tell your mother that you met Ingrid, her childhood friend? One day, years ago, I threw a stone at a witch I met in the forest and she cast a spell over me. I became an ugly troll and only now have I been restored to my human form by these kind nuns who have baptised me as a Christian once again. And now I wish to remain here where I feel safe and cared for. But please tell your mother that I shall always remember her with love and for the happy childhood we spent together."

When Knut returned to the waiting trolls with this news they seemed unconcerned, shrugged their giant's shoulders and, muttering that nine was a special mystical number and would bring them good luck in their search for the gold, they continued on their way.

After an arduous crossing in the moonlight of many miles of high and hilly moorland they came down to a long pleasant valley where more Norse settlers had created fields and farmsteads and built barns, byres and cottages along the banks of a rushing river which Olaf said was called the Suala. The trolls were in good humour as they made their way high above the river and had been told that they were now approaching the end of their quest.

The next stage of their journey, however, was a long uphill plod, at first by many fine waterfalls and a deep ravine and finally once more on to high moorland with low flat-topped hills disappearing into vast distant moonlit horizons. As they approached the highest point of this long trudge, Olaf asked them all to halt and he pointed to a grassy hill just a short distance ahead, beyond a boggy area, with two quite small white rocks marking the summit. "That," he said, "is called White Mossy Hill, and beneath those stones is where you will find the treasure buried by my Viking ancestor to keep it safe until he could return to recover it. He kept this gold torque which I inherited but he died on a Viking expedition to Byzantium before he was able to return to Britannia. I suggest that you recover the treasure in the early hours of the morning and as quietly as possible in order not to alarm the soldiers who guard the castle in the valley below, for they will not deal gently with any suspicious intruders."

Olaf was well aware that the trolls were not at all intelligent so he was not surprised when they failed to act on his warning and rushed forward yelping with excitement at the prospect of getting their great hands on the gold they had come so far to find. It was only with difficulty and by drawing his Viking sword that he restored order and persuaded them that if they insisted on making so much noise they would be unlikely to escape a hostile visit from the castle guards. The trolls were clearly restive and Olaf feared a violent free-for-all, so he demanded that they stand away from the summit stones and he stood over them with his sword unsheathed. He pointed out that the treasure belonged to him, legally inherited from his ancestor, but he would share it with the trolls in return for their agreement to cease their kidnapping of the princesses and their destruction of farm crops and livestock. There were probably a large number of items buried here and they had to be uncovered in a quiet and orderly manner which he would supervise.

With the gold almost within their grasp the trolls readily agreed to Olaf's terms (although he was well aware that this would mean nothing to them) and so under the light of the full August moon Olaf asked two trolls to raise the rocks which covered the treasure hoard, a task which even they found required all their combined strength. At last the stone markers were lifted away to reveal a large pot covered with a flat stone. Olaf asked Knut to lift this away to reveal what was underneath. The trolls crowded round in excited anticipation but shrank away in horror and dismay as the first object they saw was an ornate Christian Cross, gold it clearly was but not something any troll would wish to touch, and certainly not possess. Knut put it in his pocket while Olaf indicated to the nearest troll that he should lift the pot out of its recess. This done Olaf had some difficulty in restraining the excitable trolls who rushed to get their hands on the rest of the treasure.

Olaf's threatening sword again restored order and eventually he persuaded the trolls to accept that the contents of the treasure pot must be set out in an orderly manner for all to see but this was not the time or place to do it. He could tell them that, according to what his ancestors had told him, that it contained a large number of gold and silver coins, many gold rings, brooches and bracelets, several necklaces and torques, enough gold and silver to satisfy them all. He hoped they would now keep their promise of good behaviour toward the valley folk at home. He could well understand their wish to celebrate a successful end to their long journey but he repeated his warning about the danger of alarming the castle guard patrols. There were also bands of desperate Scots who roamed the district plundering and pillaging after their defeat at the recent Battle of the Standard fought just a few miles away. They were probably more to be feared than the castle guards.

In their excitable stupidity the nine trolls ignored Olaf's warnings and they romped in high spirits over the swampy ground and on to the dry moorland plateau a short distance away where they formed a circle with the treasure pot in the centre and performed a ritual pagan dance, noisily roaring unearthly bellows, unlike anything Olaf and Knut had ever seen or heard before, but now they could only stand and watch. They also knew that trolls could not tolerate sunlight and dawn could not be far away. What would happen at sunrise?

Soon afterwards the light of a new day began to fill the sky, and across the moor Olaf glimpsed a movement in the distance which, as the light strengthened, he identified as a group of perhaps half-a-dozen men carrying battle-axes and apparently heading in their direction. How was he to calm the trolls and hide the treasure? He had experienced many desperate situations on Viking expeditions and he was not slow to act. He turned to Knut and said "Go over to the trolls and blow on your horn: that should alarm them and stop their racket and we can then warn them of the danger, but I expect they'll just keep on dancing. I'll take the pot of gold and hide it where we found it under the stones." He knew that the sound of the horn would also attract the castle guards but he guessed that they would be more concerned with the Scots raiders than with a rabble of crazy giants dancing on the moor in the cold light of dawn.

He was soon proved right. He had just managed to replace the treasure pot in its hiding place when a patrol squad of armed soldiers climbed on to the plateau, pausing a few moments to gaze in wonder at the improbably hideous and obviously harmless figures cavorting around in some ungainly dance. Their more urgent concern was with the dishevelled but clearly armed and aggressive gang rapidly approaching across the moor. A flight of arrows aimed at the patrol signalled their hostile intentions and was met with a more accurately aimed response from the soldiers which felled one of the Scots and provoked the rest to launch into an axe-wielding charge. In the fierce hand-to-hand fighting which followed injuries were inflicted on both sides but eventually the greater experience and training of the soldiers gained the upper hand and the Scots were put to flight leaving two of their fellows fatally wounded on the moor.

The trolls, meanwhile, had become so absorbed, at first in their revelry and then in the entertaining battle taking place nearby that they were taken by surprise when the soldiers, having disposed of one group of intruders on their territory, turned their attention on to the other. The trolls were ordered to form a single line and suddenly found themselves facing a threatening rank of steel-pointed spears no more than an arrow's length from their chests. The captain in charge demanded an explanation of their presence on their lord's domain, and Olaf, sensing that this could reveal the location of the treasure, signalled to Knut to blow on his horn, thus diverting the soldiers' attention. Then with wild, dramatic gestures he pointed over to the eastern horizon where the first rays of the rising sun were about to streak across the moor directly on to the nine trolls who suddenly realised their danger. But it was all too late for, as they attempted a futile escape from the sun, the soldiers thrust forward with their spears – only to find that their steel was met by hard rock.

As Olaf and Knut well knew, exposure to the sun's rays immediately turned trolls into pillars of stone and the astonished guards were faced with five tall and four smaller lifeless monoliths, not created by Nature as bed-rock but once living, if not-quite-human, flesh and bone. Time and the weather would gradually crumble the stone pillars into the piles of rock boulders or cairns, known to history as the Nine Standards, a Pennine monument and a mystery to all succeeding generations.

Olaf and his grandson returned with the pot of Viking treasure to their farmstead in the valley beneath the mountains. The golden Cross, looted more than two hundred years earlier from a Saxon monastery in Northumbria, was presented to the nuns of the Priory where Ingrid, the vanished childhood friend of Knut's mother, had been re-baptised as a Christian and restored to her human dignity. A few years later Knut inherited much of the treasure and at his wedding to his princess, Solveig, he blew loudly on his horn as a reminder of that fateful sunset meeting by the shieling high above the lake in the heart of the mountains of Jotunheim.

37

The Dissolution of monastic foundations in Cumbria, 1536-1540

In the 1530s King Henry VIII's long dispute with the Pope ended in failure to achieve the result he desired and he decided to break England's relationship with the Papacy and make himself the Supreme Head of the Church in his kingdom. To consolidate the Crown's control of this new and controversial situation it was necessary to acquire the vast estates and resources owned by the many monastic foundations. There were almost 900 religious houses in England at the time, about two-thirds of which were quite small foundations with only a few inhabitants and limited wealth, but the remaining 200-300 controlled upwards of one-quarter of the land and economic resources of the kingdom. To transfer all this to the Crown and subsequently into the hands of the rising class of gentry would ensure their loyalty to the Crown and to the new English Church. Between 1536 and 1540 almost all these mostly ancient foundations were

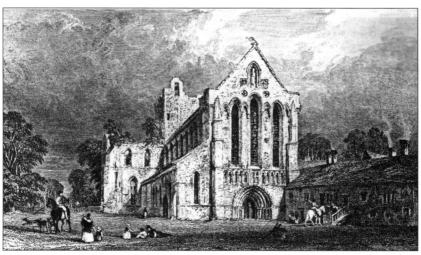

Lanercost Priory, 1835, by T. Allom courtesy of Cumbria Library Service.

surrendered to the Crown, their inhabitants dispersed, most of their buildings destroyed beyond future use, and their properties transferred to new secular owners.

At that time the counties of Cumberland, Westmorland and Lancashire North of the Sands (now Cumbria) had a number of religious houses, some quite small with few inhabitants and little property but others well-populated and prosperous and Furness Abbey was the second most wealthy and economically powerful in the country. All were dissolved between 1536 and 1541. There were five Abbeys – Furness, Calder, Holme Cultram, Dacre and Shap; (the Yorkshire Abbey of Fountains also held extensive properties in Borrowdale); seven Priories – Cartmel, Conishead, Seaton, St Bees, Lanercost, Carlisle, and Wetheral; two Friaries – Appleby and Penrith; and a Nunnery at Armathwaite.

During the years following the dissolution the estates of most of these foundations passed into the hands of the land-hungry class of country gentry most of whom were to be steadfast supporters of the Tudor monarchy and the new religious and political order.

The Court of Augmentations of the Revenue of the King's Crown was established to administer these financial acquisitions. Commissioners were dispatched to visit and prepare a detailed report on every religious house in the country. They did their work with exemplary speed and efficiency and their report, the Valor Ecclesiaticus, has provided historians with a remarkably detailed account of almost every aspect of the properties, resources, possessions and conditions in every monastic foundation. Their report is an invaluable source of information but due allowance has to be made for a marked political bias in their approach to their task: there was a case to be made to justify the act of dissolution.

This emphasis inevitably precluded any significant reference to details of the actual surrender of a religious house, the final hours of often many centuries of a monastic foundation's history, the physical expulsion of the monks and nuns, and the anguish endured by so many. The story of the past should attempt a re-creation of the effects of great historical events on the victims as well as the victors. Detailed and reliable documentation for this aspect of history may often be sparse and not always readily accessible but, certainly as far as the more important abbeys are concerned, enough trustworthy information may be gleaned for an authentic account to be created of life in a medieval monastery and of the fate of some of the inmates following the dissolution.

The following story of the dissolution of a fictional Cumbrian abbey is an attempt to portray the events which might have taken place in almost any monastic foundation at that time.

Furness Abbey, 1846, courtesy of J. C. Armytage and Cumbria Library Service.

Dissolution: The last hours of a fictional Cumbrian Abbey

It was late September in the year 1537 and the stone walls of Meredale Abbey glowed in the warm rays of the afternoon sun. Abbot Thomas Redwood sat in the north-east corner of the cloister garth, the golden light full upon him, his ample frame comfortably settled for a short rest after his long and arduous journey from London and his stressful meeting with the King's chief minister, Thomas Cromwell. He had grave news to tell the 22 Brethren who still remained in the Abbey; but, for the moment, it was good to be home again and he smiled to himself as he recalled how the whole community had gathered to welcome him on his return and had knelt to receive his Blessing. It was good, too, to see everyone busy at their various tasks about the Abbey and its grounds and to hear the Novices chanting their lessons in the Abbey Church.

He had travelled far and he had met with much kindness and generous hospitality but now he was tired. He closed his eyes and the sun placed a fleeting finger on his strong round face and gently coaxed him into unintentional but well-deserved sleep. The book he had brought to read – Suetonius's *Life of Julius Caesar* – slipped slowly from his lap, the sound of chanting faded and the murmuring of bees and doves was stilled. A golden eagle glided over the scene in slow and silent reconnaissance, surveyed the cliffs of the Abbey walls, took note of the rabbits scuttling among the orchard trees, and turned nonchalantly away.

Meredale Abbey was almost 350 years old. Founded by William de Lunesdale in the reign of Henry II, it lay in a secluded valley watered by a fast-flowing river with a small lake well-stocked with trout and char just a short distance away. Steeply-rising fell provided shelter from winter storms, and fertile fields grew good crops of barley, rye and oats. Woodlands provided timber for farm and domestic use as well as a valuable harvest of herbs and berries for cooking and for medicines; in autumn the orchard trees were laden with crab-apples and pippins and, more recently, a few rare, sweet pears; the valley pastures and the surrounding fell-sides supported a flock of sheep whose wool was sold or spun and woven into cloth for the habits of the Brethren who over the years had entered this remote Cistercian abbey to follow the discipline of that monastic Order.

Every Brother had some responsibility for the efficient running of the religious and domestic life of the abbey; every hour of the day had its appointed duties. The regular Church Offices had to be observed throughout the day and night; stores of food and drink had to be checked and meals prepared; clothing, furniture, utensils, tools and implements of all kinds had to be made and maintained; buildings needed constant maintenance; thousands of candles were required through the year; books, manuscripts, quills, inks, parchments and seals had to be provided for the library and for the scribes in their cells; the Novices had to be taught and trained; the sick had to be cared for and herbal medicines prepared; tending the bees was a sacred duty; work on the Abbey farms and in the woods, orchards, corn mills, fish-ponds, brew-house and dairies was an unceasing labour; accounts and records had to be kept, rents collected, complaint and daily difficulties attended to, and legal issues determined. The Abbey also owned extensive properties in the surrounding countryside with valuable mining, woodland, woollen and agricultural interests which involved much expert and constant administration.

The Abbot was at the head of this complex organisation and bore a great responsibility. He relied for many of the practical problems on the Prior, a man of wide experience and considerable management skills who took a personal interest in every department of the Abbey's life. He would listen patiently to the concerns of others, whether it was a young home-sick Novice or an elderly monk ending his days in the Infirmary. On this mellow autumn afternoon he took the opportunity to tour the Abbey grounds and to have a few words with the Brothers busy with their various tasks – he called at the brew-house where the first of the new season's ale was being prepared and he visited the library where an elaborate illumi-nated manuscript was being designed.

He climbed the scaffolding to inspect the progress of the masons work-ing on the stone gargoyles on the great tower. From there he crossed the river to enquire about the stock of trout in the fish-ponds and to visit the orchard to see the new crop of apples and to learn from the bee-keeper that the yield of honey was likely to be the best for some years. In the herb garden he was given some advice by Brother Matthew for the stomach ailment which had been troubling him recently and as he made his way back he had a word with Brother Mark who was cleaning out the dovecot. He returned content with his tour for he could now report to Abbot Thomas that life at the Abbey was proceeding as it had done for the past three cen-turies and would doubtless do so for many centuries more.

Prior John glanced at the sun and realised that it would soon be time for Vespers and he had not seen the Abbot all afternoon. Where could he be? He answered his own question and smiled to himself as he set off at a brisk pace to the cloister garth where in his sunny corner the Abbot slept peacefully on. His book lay on the ground and a group of hungry chaffinches waited hopefully nearby. It seemed a pity to wake him but there was duty to be done so the Prior picked up the book and, gently rous-ing the Abbot from his slumbers, said 'It is almost time for Vespers, my Lord. I hope you have rested well.' 'Yes, thank you, Prior John, I did not intend to sleep but I feel all the better for it. Have we any food to give those birds?'

The sun had left this corner of the garth by now and Abbot Thomas gave a slight shiver as the first cool breeze of the evening swept down from the high fells. A shadow fell across his face as he recalled the sad news he must first discuss with Prior John and then convey to the assembled community in the Chapter House in the morning. He eased his portly body out of his chair and together they walked across the cloister garth, pausing to admire the glossy foliage and bright red berries on the ancient yew tree: 'I believe this tree is said to be about 500 years old', the Abbot remarked. 'That would be long before our Abbey was founded. There is a tradition that Abbot Aelred held firmly to the belief that the yew tree would protect men against the plague and, when the Black Death struck in the reign of Edward III, he set up a *prie-dieu* and a small desk to hold a Bible and a Book of Hours inside the great hollow trunk and he spent most of his time there in his devotions and studies, securely guarded, as he believed, from the ravages of the plague. He actually died after eating some of the yew berries, apparently unaware that the seeds within them are highly poisonous.'

'But how could he get inside the hollow trunk?' said Prior John, 'There is only a narrow gap and our smallest Novice might hesitate before venturing through that!'

'It is possible, I suppose, that over all those years, the tree has slowly grown to close the gap and, as far as I am aware, no-one has actually entered Aelred's sanctuary since he died. His *prie-dieu* may still be there. But we must hurry; Vespers is about to begin.;

After Vespers Abbot Thomas presided at the evening meal in the Refectory and, at the end of the Reading and the traditional Grace, he asked Prior John to accompany him directly to the Abbot's Parlour. His tone of voice suggested a command rather than an invitation but Prior John still hoped that he might be offered a cup of the sweet wine which he knew the Abbot had brought from London. But there was no wine: Abbot Thomas was evidently in very serious mood.

When they were seated there was a moment of silence broken only when the Abbot said, 'I have the worst of tidings to tell you, Prior, and we have very little time to decide what we must do.'

'I am truly sorry, my Lord,' said the Prior, 'we had no idea that your illness would have so sad and sudden an outcome. We have all prayed that the physicians in London would...'

'No! No!' interrupted Abbot Thomas. 'This has nothing to do with my aches and pains from which, I am glad to say, I am now well-released. No, Prior, we are not concerned with the prospect of my early demise but with the certain and imminent extinction of all the religious houses in the kingdom. We have to accept, however painful it might be, that Meredale Abbey – and, indeed, all the monastic foundations in this country – will very soon cease to exist.'

Prior John gasped as if he had been struck by an unexpected blow. His face became taut and pale as he struggled to find words to respond, but Abbot Thomas pressed on: 'The King and Cromwell are fully determined to carry out the total dissolution and destruction of the monastic houses throughout the realm. Commissioners have already been appointed to conduct a Visitation to religious houses and to demand their surrender to the Crown. Within a short time there will be few, if any, abbeys such as ours remaining. We must inform the members of our community and all of us must make provision for the future.'

Prior John's distress finally burst forth in a torrent of anguished words: 'Who would have thought that the King's personal troubles would have led to this? We patiently endured his bitter quarrel with the Holy See and were silent at his unworthy treatment of Queen Catherine; we bowed before the Act of Parliament in the matter of the Royal Supremacy, thereby putting our very souls in danger; are so many years of dedication to the service of God to be sacrificed to the brute passions of an unhappy King and the political ambitions of his heretical henchman? Are the…'

Abbot Thomas raised his hand to halt the Prior's bitter outburst: 'I understand and share your feelings, Prior, but we must now face the harsh reality that in the very near future we shall be compelled by the law of the land to surrender this Abbey and all it possesses to the King's men. We shall all be forced to abandon the life of our Order and leave these buildings for ever. Everything will be seized into the hands of the Court of Augmentations set up to administer and dispose of monastic properties and possessions. Those who choose to defy the King will be charged with treason and almost certainly put to death.'

There was silence for a while in the gathering darkness. At last the Prior's voice whispered sadly: 'Perhaps one day, under a more Christian King, we may be able to return. It is already rumoured that King Henry is a sick man.'

Abbot Thomas rose from his seat and stood for a moment by the window, his tired face lit by the last rays of the fading day. He turned at last and in a gentle but decisive voice replied: 'There will be no return, Prior John. Not in our lifetime, not in the lifetime of our youngest Novice, perhaps not for many generations, and, most probably, never. For it has been ordered that the Abbey itself shall be destroyed and rendered uninhabitable; not even the Abbey Church will be spared the destruction. Everything will be seized, sold or burned. Nothing will be left except a roofless ruin, an empty shell.

'Furthermore, we can be sure that the men who gain possession of our estates will not be willing to part with them; they will support the Crown which enriched them. There can be no return.'

Prior John began to speak of the prophecies then being whispered in certain quarters that the Tudor rose would soon be driven from the kingdom... But the Abbot dismissed this with a wave of his hand and walked over to an oak cupboard in the corner of his parlour saying, 'I think a cup of wine and a few raisins might be in order before we take our discussion further. My visit to London was not entirely without reward.'

The wine had been praised and its country of origin briefly debated when the Abbot surprised Prior John by saying, 'Now we must decide how best we can ensure our own futures. Our Faith will survive – I have no doubt about that – but we must help it to do so. Let us discuss how we might negotiate with the King's Commissioners. Thomas Legh and Richard Layton are both gifted men with outstanding professional competence and dedicated to the service of the King; their eagle eyes will miss nothing in their work of dissolution but they can surely be persuaded, with a little pragmatic diplomacy, that men of experience, such as ourselves, could render valuable service to the King's new Church. Let us pray for God's guidance and meet here in the morning after Chapter. Goodnight Prior. Sleep well.'

At nine o'clock the following morning the bell tolled and the Brothers took their places in the Chapter House for the daily meeting. They stood for the Abbot's Blessing: 'May the Lord Almighty regulate our days and acts according to His Peace' – and listened in silence as the names of the Saints of the Day were read. This September day promised to be as uneventful as so many autumn days had been before. The Abbot rose to announce the business of the day with the familiar words: *Loquamur de Ordine nostro* – 'Let us discuss the affairs of our Order'.

Routine matters were dealt with quickly and, after the customary prayer for the souls of departed benefactors, the Brothers prepared to leave for their daily duties, but Abbot Thomas indicated that he had more to say. And to a shocked and silent Chapter he told them of the fate that would soon descend upon their Abbey and on their lives. He emphasised that there was no prospect of reprieve and that resistance would be futile and would only invite the severest punishment. All those who obeyed the King's command would be given a small pension to assist in what, for many, might be a painful adjustment to a new life. There would be a great need for priests in the new Church, for teachers in the schools, for learned clerks in the Law Courts and Offices of State; towns and villages would welcome skilled craftsmen; the houses of gentry would need chaplains, doctors and clerks able to read and write. He appealed to them not to succumb to despair in the face of this great misfortune but to trust in their Faith in God's mercy to support them in the midst of the social and religious upheaval about to take place.

In the silence which followed the Abbot hurried to sound the *tabula sonatila* and to pronounce the word *Benedicite*, the signals that the monks could talk freely – and they now had much to discuss. As he shook the three wooden tablets Abbot Thomas reflected that he would soon be doing this for the last time.

Abbot Thomas had clearly given much thought to the new political situation and Prior John could only ask for a few details to clarify the plans the Abbot had in mind. He could only express his grateful approval of the Abbot's proposals concerning their future life once their monastic responsibilities came to an end. Abbot Thomas had learned of two vacancies in the hierarchy of the new Church and if Prior John was agreeable he proposed to open negotiations with the Commissioners with a view to securing these offices for the Prior and himself.

Prior John's inner thoughts were to join the movement of outright opposition to the King's actions against the religious houses which had already organised a rebellion in some northern parts of the kingdom, but he had a deep admiration for Abbot Thomas and he left their meeting reconciled to an anxious wait to see what emerged when the King's Commissioners arrived.

Throughout the autumn the daily routine of the Abbey followed its accustomed course. Midnight Matins and early morning Lauds, Prime, Vespers and Compline continued uninterrupted and work elsewhere went on as before. Rye and barley were harvested, apples and other fruits were gathered from the orchards, honey was collected from the bee-hives, heady aromas rose from the brew-house, herbs were hung up to dry or prepared for medicine, sheep and goats were brought in for the winter. On All Saints' Day everyone welcomed the first fire in the Warming House and the first candle-light in the Refectory. Advent arrived and all was as it had always been but by the time of the Feast of the Nativity the shadow of impending doom was already cast over the celebrations. Travellers brought tales of the ruthless proceedings of the Dissolution Commissioners elsewhere in the country. The Abbots of Fountains Abbey, Kirkstead, Whalley and Jervaulx had all been hanged for resisting the Commissioners.

In the weeks following these events several Brothers had slipped away from Meredale leaving their habits hidden in the Abbey walls or in the woods. Abbot Thomas retained the loyalty of those remaining by adopting for his Cistercian Order the Pope's interpretation of the Rule of St Benedict who had forbidden members of his Order to eat the meat of any four-legged animal. Pope Benedict noted that the actual wording said that meat may not be eaten in the refectory and so permission was now given for meat to be eaten in a separate dining area known as the *misericord* (the place of mercy). Here, when Advent had passed, the now much diminished community enjoyed feasting on meat and offal of all kinds and continued their religious and other duties as if oblivious to the fate that was inescapably bearing down upon them.

On 12 January, two days after the Feast of the Epiphany, the twelve remaining Brothers were seated in their accustomed places in the Abbey Church waiting for the Abbot to arrive for High Mass. Time passed, the bell tolled on, and still the Abbot did not come. Questioning glances were exchanged and habits were wrapped more closely round shivering bodies. Where was Abbot Thomas? He was never late for High Mass. Had he been taken ill?

But Abbot Thomas was in the best of health and he had been on his way to take High Mass when the gate-keeper had come running up to him and breathlessly said that there were men at the gate demanding to enter in the name of the King. Their business was urgent and they demanded to see the Abbot without delay. 'Thank you,' the Abbot replied calmly, 'show them into the guest house and grant them hospitality in the usual way. Say that I will come to meet them when Mass is concluded.' He then continued on his way to the Church. The great bell fell silent and Abbot Thomas entered his Church for what he knew would be the last time.

The Abbot walked slowly to his stall and the ceremony of the Mass began as it had begun every day for the past 350 years but only a few minutes had passed before the doors were flung open and five or six armed men rushed in, roughly thrusting aside two of the Brothers who attempted to halt their progress and crushing underfoot a silver sprinkler which was knocked to the ground in the scuffle.

The figure of Richard Layton then appeared loudly demanding that the Mass should cease and that the Abbot should come to meet him immediately. Abbot Thomas stepped forward bearing his crozier and confronted Layton to protest at his desecration of the House of God. Layton responded that this was no longer God's House but the King's and he ordered the soldiers to escort the Abbot and the Prior out of the Church to the Abbot's Parlour and place them under guard. The Brothers were then dragged out of their seats and hustled to the cloister garth where they were subjected to abuse and mockery and were ordered to strip off their monkish habits and put on a coarse woollen garment and a pair of heavy, ill-fitting shoes, such as were worn by country folk at that time. They were allowed to collect any personal possessions and then they were escorted to the Abbey gate and thrust into the road with threats of dire punishment if they tried to return or even lingered in the neighbourhood.

Terrified and shocked the forlorn, downcast group made their way past a small crowd of local people who had gathered to gape at the events unfolding at the Abbey. Many wept and asked for a final Blessing but others jeered and shouted vulgar taunts. Only Brother Matthew showed no fear and held his head high. He glared defiantly at those who shouted insults and warned them that any desecration of the Abbey would be a sin against God and would be avenged. He brandished his Crucifix in their faces and put fear into their superstitious minds by swearing that after his death his spirit would return to haunt and terrify all those who dared to disturb its sanctity and peace. The taunts were silenced and he went quietly on his way.

Meanwhile, Abbot Thomas and Richard Layton were discussing the Deed of Surrender by which the Abbey and all its estates and possessions would become the property of the Crown. The Abbey itself was soon silent and deserted. Candles continued to burn in the empty Church; the dormitories were cold and bare; in the library manuscripts lay abandoned; in the cloisters a couple of red squirrels waited in vain for their daily charity from human hands; only in the refectory was there unaccustomed noise as the soldiers who had accompanied Legh and Layton were feasting and drinking after they had plundered the cellars and food stores. Their revelry suddenly ceased when a messenger came to inform them that the Commissioners had completed their discussions and would soon be ready to see the Abbot and Prior escorted from the premises.

When the terms had been agreed, first Abbot Thomas and then Prior John signed the Deed of Surrender, seals were affixed, the keys handed over and the long history of Meredale Abbey came to an end. Shortly afterwards the gates opened and the former Abbot and the former Prior rode out for the last time but now they had new titles as the Bishop of Lanchester and the Dean of Wychford in the Church of King Henry VIII.

Richard Layton sat in the Abbot's Parlour penning his report to Thomas Cromwell ending with a literary flourish which he knew would give pleasure in the right quarters at the King's Court: 'The papistical denne of idle and utterly unlearned beasts at Meredale is broken up and dispersed.'

In the following day the destruction began. Everything of real value – gold and silver plate, censers, patens, and other religious ornaments, candle-holders, books, manuscripts – were packed and made ready to be taken to the King's Treasury. The lead was stripped from the roofs and gutters; the brass bells were dismantled, all to be melted down on the spot in fires fuelled by the Abbey's roof timbers and choir stalls, eventually to reappear as cannon for the king's wars against France.

Then came the great auction when everything that could be removed was to be sold. Most of the local population and some from further afield gathered to join in the bidding. The High Altar was bought for a gold sovereign, a table from the refectory for seven shillings; farmers bought carts which they loaded with ploughs, scythes, flails, and hay from the barns; housewives bid keenly for pots and pans, linen and kitchen utensils; well-dressed strangers carried off stained glass from the windows, furniture and some books and manuscripts; sad matrons clutched small crucifixes, rosaries, night-boots, and articles of all kinds from the larders and the dairy; aspiring gentry bought stone from the Abbey walls for their new manor houses, as well as tiles, timber, fire-grates, and carved woodwork; even iron hooks, bolts, and latches and locks from the doors were removed and sold. In the years that followed the Abbey walls continued to be plundered for building stone and soon all that was left was open to the ravages of storm, frost and rain. Within a few generations the crumbling ruins were inhabited only by birds which made their nests high in the broken walls and lowly creatures burrowing in the piles of rubble below.

Brother Matthew was seen from time to time wandering sadly among the ruins and when he died folk recalled his threat to haunt the Abbey and terrify all who despoiled it. Soon there were tales of his ghost being seen in the ruined Church and on a seat in the remains of the Chapter House where he had frightened the Lady of the Manor as she was making a sketch of the ruins. Only the children were not afraid, and the cloister garth became their playground. When they tired of their games or when it rained they crept into the hollow in the trunk of the old yew tree to a den they had made round Abbot Aelred's prayer desk.

38

Two Legends of Lakeland: A Ghost Story and a Love Story

The tragic ghost of Martindale

Deep in the quiet Lakeland valley of Martindale, half a mile south of the old chapel of St Martin and just a few yards from the Howe Grain Beck, stands the farmstead cottage of Henhow, for many years an abandoned crumbling ruin but recently restored and made habitable once more.

A local legend would suggest that Henhow, a typical dales sheep-farm of the time, was abandoned and gradually fell into ruin as no-one wished to live there. The shepherd and his wife who lived at Henhow in the early years of the nineteenth century were troubled by strange, unexplained noises in the cottage which disturbed their quiet life. It was a lonely, isolated spot in those days and the shepherd's wife was often left alone when her husband was away on the fells tending his sheep and their lambs. He frequently had to leave home in the eerie half-light before dawn and on one day (in 1834 according to the legend) he and his dog were making their way along the lane when the dog sensed the presence of another person nearby and growled an anxious warning. The shepherd looked round and saw a young woman following him on the other side of the lane. She was carrying a baby and appeared to be in some distress. Surprised and more than a little perturbed to see her at such an hour, alone and in so isolated a place, he approached her and asked if she was in trouble.

The young woman told the shepherd her story. Many years ago she had lived a happy life at Henhow but she had been seduced by a local man and soon discovered that she was pregnant with his child. He came from a higher social class than she did and held a prominent position in the community and he provided her with some 'medicine' which, he said, would cause an abortion or miscarriage and so save both their reputations. In her youthful innocence she took the medicine and it killed both her and the child she was carrying. Her guilt condemned her spirit to haunt the cottage where she had been so happy and to wander the lanes of Martindale carrying her dead baby in her arms for a hundred years. This she had now done for forty lonely years.

The story of the shepherd's ghostly meeting soon became the talk of the valley and many of those who were young forty years ago recalled the tale of the seduction and murder of the young girl from Henhow. The guilty man, they confidently claimed, was the local priest who, of course, was never held to account for his misdeeds. A brief comment by James Clarke in his contemporary *Survey of the Lakes* (1787) may indicate the type of cleric who might have been a priest in Martindale in those years: 'on account of the smallness of the stipend', Clarke explains, there was no-one willing to accept the office and so 'anyone who could read performed the services.' Even someone, it seems, inclined to seduce a young girl and subsequently murder her and the child she conceived.

The ghost of Henhow has long ago completed her hundred years of wandering; and the restoration of her cottage from a century of ruinous neglect may perhaps signify that mother and baby now rest in peace.

Martindale Chapel courtesy of.the Reverend C. H. Barrand.

Love and Loss at Aira Force

Aira Force is the most popular of the many waterfalls in the Lake District. Thousands of visitors each year come to see the Aira Beck plunge some 70 feet (21.3m) under a rainbow spray in a peaceful woodland setting. The National Trust now cares for the property and has done much to restore the features of the Victorian parkland created by the Dukes of Norfolk two hundred years ago. The short walk from the car park to the waterfall passes through an arboretum, woodland glades bright with wild flowers in the spring, and some of the hundreds of conifer trees (cedars, firs, pines and spruce) planted in the mid-nineteenth century, an impressive pinetum frequented by playful red squirrels. The pathways are well-maintained and easy to walk along. At about the half-way point is a stunning view of Ullswater. In the days when this was private parkland there were no stone bridges across the torrent at the top and bottom of the waterfall: these convenient and protective structures were built in the early twentieth century.

The walk to Aira Force would have been the perfect, quiet, secluded setting for romantic love to flourish. And, according to the legend, so it was for Lady Emma and Sir Eglamore, long, long ago in those days of medieval chivalry when all heroines were young and beautiful and all heroes were brave knights in armour forever seeking glory in battle or rescuing damsels in distress.

In the thirteenth century Lady Emma was the beautiful daughter of the lord of the land by Ullswater whose fortified manor house stood by the lake where Lyulph's Tower now stands. Although she had many suitors, she had fallen deeply in love with Sir Eglamore, a knight of the Crusades:

> *But one she prized, and only one,*
> *Sir Eglamore was he.*

Their favourite trysting place was by Aira Force and here they spent many happy hours until one day Sir Eglamore told his love that he had to go to join the crusade in the Holy Land. At their sad parting Emma promised that she would always wait for him and Sir Eglamore promised to return to her as soon as he could.

At first Emma was brave in her loneliness and took heart whenever 'she heard her champion's deeds recounted', but as the weeks and months went by she lapsed into physical and mental decline and eventually began to wander in her sleep:

> *Month falls on month with heavier weight;*
> *Day sickens round her, and the night*
> *Is empty of repose.*

In her sleep she always made her way to Aira Force. For many dreary months her lover did not return but finally and without warning he arrived one night at the manor only to be told of Emma's sleep-walking wanderings. He knew at once where she might be and hurried to Aira Force. There he saw her in her white night robes standing fast asleep at the top of the waterfall. He was uncertain whether this was, in truth, his beloved Emma or merely her apparition. He gently touched her; her sleep was broken and, startled by her sudden awakening, she slipped and fell down into the roaring torrent.

Wordsworth's poem *The Somnabulist* which relates the entire legend, best tells the rest of their story:

> *Soul-shattered the knight, nor knew*
> *If Emma's ghost it were*
> *Or boding shade, or if the maid*
> *He touched her; what follows who shall tell?*
> *The soft touch snapped the thread*
> *Of slumber... shrieking back she fell,*
> *And the stream whirled her down the dell*
> *Along its foaming bed.*
>
> *Sir Eglamore leapt down the ravine to rescue his love:*
> *and when on firm ground*
> *The rescued maiden lay,*
> *Her eye grew bright with blissful light,*
> *Confusion passed away;*
> *She heard, – ere to the throne of grace*
> *Her faithful spirit flew, –*
> *His voice, beheld his speaking face,*
> *And, dying, in his own embrace,*
> *She felt that he was true.*

Utterly heart-broken at the loss of his love, Sir Eglamore vowed to spend the rest of his life by Aira Force where she had died. Henceforth he lived the life of a hermit in a cave close by the waterfall. As Wordsworth's poem put it:

> *Within the dell he built a cell,*
> *And there was Sorrow's guest;*
> *In hermit's weeds repose he found,*
> *From vain temptations free*
> *Beside the torrent dwelling – bound*
> *By one deep heart-controlling sound,*
> *And awed to piety.*

The modern folk song by Kate Rusby, *Sir Eglamore and the Dragon*, has no direct connection with this story from Aira Force but it illustrates well the nature of the adventures which a knight errant in the age of chivalry might be expected to meet. The final stanza points to the general respect and admiration shown for a knight's conduct and character in these encounters:

> *Now God preserve our King and Queen*
> *That all round England may be seen*
> *As many knights – and many more*
> *As brave and good as Sir Eglamore.*

About the Author

Robert Gambles was born and grew up in Derbyshire. He was a Scholar of St John's College, Oxford, where he took an Honours degree in Modern History and a post-graduate Diploma in Education. He also has a Licentiate Diploma in Music. His professional career was spent in Education, mainly in Ely and Liverpool.

He acquired a love of the Lake District early in life and he has lived in Cumbria in his years of retirement during which he has explored the whole district and written a number of books and many articles on various aspects of its history.

The author has also pursued his interest in a wider national history and a critical study of some of the well-known stories from British history was published in 2013 under the title *Great Tales from British History*, and was described by *The Guardian* as 'hugely enjoyable'.

Through his Norwegian wife he acquired a special interest in the life and history of Norway: Hayloft recently published his acclaimed *Espen Ash Lad* a collection of Folk Tales from Norway.

A keen but pragmatic interest in conservation and the protection of the natural environment has always featured in his philosophy of life and he was for many years a Trustee and member of the Executive Committee of the Friends of the Lake District. He has also worked as a volunteer for the National Trust.